ROUTLEDGE LIBRARY EDITIONS:
BUSINESS AND ECONOMICS IN ASIA

Volume 33

TRADE STRATEGY AND THE ASIAN-PACIFIC REGION

TRADE STRATEGY AND THE ASIAN-PACIFIC REGION

Edited by
HUGH CORBET

Routledge
Taylor & Francis Group

LONDON AND NEW YORK

First published in 1970 by George Allen & Unwin Ltd

This edition first published in 2019
by Routledge
2 Park Square, Milton Park, Abingdon, Oxon OX14 4RN

and by Routledge
52 Vanderbilt Avenue, New York, NY 10017

Routledge is an imprint of the Taylor & Francis Group, an informa business

British Library Cataloguing in Publication Data
A catalogue record for this book is available from the British Library

ISBN: 978-1-138-48274-6 (Set)
ISBN: 978-0-429-42825-8 (Set) (ebk)
ISBN: 978-1-138-61836-7 (Volume 33) (hbk)
ISBN: 978-0-429-46125-5 (Volume 33) (ebk)

Publisher's Note
The publisher has gone to great lengths to ensure the quality of this reprint but points out that some imperfections in the original copies may be apparent.

Disclaimer
The publisher has made every effort to trace copyright holders and would welcome correspondence from those they have been unable to trace.

Trade Strategy
and the
Asian-Pacific Region

EDITED BY

HUGH CORBET

London

GEORGE ALLEN AND UNWIN LTD

RUSKIN HOUSE · MUSEUM STREET

FIRST PUBLISHED IN 1970

IBN 0 04 382011 5

PRINTED IN GREAT BRITAIN
in 10 on 12 point Baskerville
by Ditchling Press Limited
Ditchling, Hassocks, Sussex

THE ATLANTIC TRADE STUDY PROGRAMME

The Atlantic Trade Study, registered as an educational trust, was formed in December, 1966, by a private group in London to sponsor a programme of policy research on the implications for Britain of participating in a broadly based free trade association as possibly the next phase in the liberalisation of international trade.

It is under the chairmanship of Sir Michael Wright, formerly Permanent Head of the British Delegation to the Geneva Disarmament Conference, while the Director of Studies is Professor Harry G. Johnson, of the London School of Economics and Political Science and the University of Chicago. The programme is now being administered by the recently established Trade Policy Research Centre, the Director of which is Mr. Hugh Corbet, previously of *The Times*. Set out below is the committee responsible for the programme:

As a basis on which to proceed with research, the proposed free trade association was defined as initially embracing the United States, Canada, Britain and other member countries of the European Free Trade Association; open to the European Communities and to Japan, Australia and New Zealand, as well as other industrially advanced nations; and affording less developed countries greater access to their markets.

Several proposals along these lines had already been receiving serious attention at academic, business and official levels in North America. The ATS was in fact a British response to a new trade strategy proposed in May, 1966, by the Canadian-American Committee, a non-official group sponsored by the Private Planning Association of Canada and the National Planning Association in the United States.

With the expiry on June 30, 1967, of President Johnson's authority under the Trade Expansion Act of 1962 to negotiate trade agreements with other countries, and the completion of the so-called Kennedy Round of multi-lateral tariff negotiations, made possible by the Act and conducted under the auspices of the General Agreement on Tariffs and Trade, the United

States Administration and Congress was expected to embark upon a thorough reappraisal of trade policies and practices with a view to formulating a fresh negotiating authority. The proposal for a multilateral free trade association initiated by North Atlantic countries has been one of the policy options to have subsequently come under consideration.

Meanwhile, the British Government had made a second application for United Kingdom membership of the European Communities. But whether Britain gained admission or not, the concept of a potentially world-wide free trade association was deemed, in either eventuality, as likely to prove of large significance. For in the event of membership being negotiated it was considered that the United Kingdom would then require an informed policy for the development of closer commercial and political relations between Western Europe and North America. If on the other hand the European Communities rejected Britain again, even if only temporarily, it would be important to have examined beforehand whether there exists a viable alternative.

PREFACE

This volume contains a further three studies carried out under the Atlantic Trade Study Programme on the proposal for a free trade treaty as the framework within which might be pursued the next phase in the liberalisation of world trade. The three monographs have been revised to take into account developments that have occurred since they were first published in 1968 and 1969. They deal mainly with Britain's extra-European relations and more particularly with economic and politico-strategic issues involving the countries of the Asian-Pacific region.

The book will be appearing at a time of more than ordinary uncertainty over the disposition of Western military forces in the Asian-Pacific region. On both sides of the Pacific, as on both sides of the Atlantic, all aspects of established policy are nowadays being reassessed. The studies published here are a contribution to that effort and have been designed for the general reader as well as the specialist.

An earlier volume, *New Trade Strategy for the World Economy*, published in 1969 and edited by Professor Harry G. Johnson, of the London School of Economics and University of Chicago, contained four studies under the same research programme. These dealt with the general considerations relating to the proposal for a multilateral free trade association. In the introductory part to the present volume, I have drawn on the contributions to the earlier volume, especially the paper, "Options After the Kennedy Round", by Professor Gérard Curzon and Mrs. Victoria Curzon, and much is also owed to the writings of Professor Johnson, the research director of the Atlantic Trade Study Programme.

The other three parts of this volume first appeared as pamphlets. Professor G. C. Allen's paper appeared under its present title and reflects a long acquaintance with the Japanese industrial scene about which he has written extensively since his first academic appointment at the Higher Commercial College at Nagoya in Japan. Sir Robert Scott's paper, first published as *Major Theatre of Conflict*, also draws on a long and very close association with the Asian-Pacific region. He is one of the leading British experts on East Asia and played a key part in many of the major events in the area during the post-war period. The paper by Mr. Leonard Beaton, first published as *Commonwealth in a New Era*, follows a long-standing interest in the Commonwealth and crystallises the observations of one of the most authoritative commentators in Britain on politico-strategic affairs.

Early in 1969 a shortened version of Professor Allen's paper was published in Japanese by the Ministry of Foreign Affairs in Tokyo. It was published by the ministry as a contribution to public discussion in Japan.

As this volume went to print there was in the United Kingdom a change of government. Mr. Edward Heath's Government may revise, or "rephase", the withdrawal of Britain's military presence in the Persian Gulf and South-East Asia which Mr. Harold Wilson's Government had planned to complete by the end of 1971. The position of the new government on the enlargement of the European Communities may differ from that of the old government. On these and other issues it has been too early, at the time of writing, to form a clear view of the policies which are to guide Britain towards the 1980s. But the issues discussed in the following pages remain the same and it is hoped that the treatment of them will contribute to the formation of wider perspectives on the problems involved.

While the Atlantic Trade Study Programme has provided the opportunity to contribute to the discussion of the free trade treaty proposal, the views expressed in this volume are the responsibility of the various authors. The present writer has been grateful for the assistance of Miss Haruko Fukuda and Mrs. Margaret Dobson in the editing and preparation of the manuscripts.

HUGH CORBET

London,
Summer, 1970

CONTENTS

Part I

TRADE STRATEGY FOR AN OPEN WORLD

by

HUGH CORBET

Director, Trade Policy Research Centre, London; previously a specialist writer on The Times; *joint editor of* Europe's Free Trade Area Experiment (*1970*).

Part II

JAPAN'S PLACE IN TRADE STRATEGY

by

G. C. ALLEN

Emeritus Professor of Political Economy in the University of London; author of Monopoly and Restrictive Practices (*1968*), The Structure of Industry in Britain (*1961 and 1966*) *and* A Short Economic History of Modern Japan (*1949 and 1962*).

Part III

ASIAN-PACIFIC ARENA
OF CONFLICT

by

SIR ROBERT SCOTT

Permanent Secretary, British Ministry of Defence, 1961-63; formerly Commandant, Imperial Defence College, London; previously Commissioner-General for the United Kingdom in South-East Asia; earlier Assistant Under-Secretary of State, British Foreign Office; and served in the British Consular Service in China, 1927-50.

Part IV

PIONEERS OF AN
OPEN WORLD

by

LEONARD BEATON

Columnist in The Times; *onetime Editor,* The Round Table; *formerly Director of Studies, Institute for Strategic Studies, London; previously Defence Correspondent of* The Guardian; *author of* Must the Bomb Spread? *and* The Struggle for Peace (*both 1966*).

Part I

TRADE STRATEGY FOR AN OPEN WORLD

by

Hugh Corbet

1 PERIOD OF REAPPRAISAL IN COMMERCIAL DIPLOMACY

Leading a lot of little Englanders into a mini-Europe has apparently not been Mr. Edward Heath's purpose in working for a wider European unity. Such was the comment of the then Leader of the Opposition at Westminster on the British Government's decision early in 1968 to withdraw Britain's military presence from the Indo-Pacific theatre (the Hongkong garrison excepted) by 1971.[1] Over successive applications for United Kingdom membership of the European Communities, on the first of which the London negotiators were led by Mr. Heath, there has been though a very considerable reluctance on the part of British political leaders to make clear what the purpose has been, much less how it aligns with other goals of foreign policy. Public discussion in Britain of the whole European issue has suffered from a lack of rational analysis.[2]

While just getting negotiations going on Britain's second application to join the EEC was requiring so much single-minded effort, there may have appeared little point in questioning the vague generalities which somehow justified the whole business. But after that second effort was also vetoed by France, there were indications that a more critical view was being taken in Britain of what the new Europe is all about. Alternatives to *full* membership of the EEC began to enjoy serious consideration. In the earlier years of the 1960s that had hardly been the case among London's political élite. Nor had Washington's been any wiser. Both capitals preferred to believe the only course open to the UK was to sign the Treaty of Rome. That, however, was easier said than done.

Free Trade Treaty Proposal

Towards the end of the 1960s a less enchanted view of the new Europe also began to develop in the United States. Measures

[1]*Parliamentary Debates (Hansard)*, House of Commons, London, Vol. 760, No. 74, March 5, 1968, c. 240.

[2]This chapter is based on an article by the writer, "The Multilateral Free Trade Area Proposal", *The Bankers' Magazine*, London, August, 1968, and on a paper, "The Status in Britain of the Free Trade Treaty Option", given at a conference arranged by the Atlantic Council of Canada, Toronto, November 3 and 4, 1969.

deemed necessary by the Six for building a European union, which Americans had long championed, were not being accepted very gracefully on Washington's Capitol Hill. For the wave of proposals for import quotas mooted in the autumn of 1967, following the agreement finally struck in the Kennedy Round of tariff-cutting negotiations, were partly motivated by a conviction (not necessarily well founded) that foreign governments were gradually intensifying non-tariff barriers to trade.

Revived protectionist activities aroused liberal trade forces across America and the Johnson Administration mounted a strong and courageous resistance campaign. But the quotas battle was only one aspect of a slowly growing debate over the future of US commercial policy which has been continued into the first years of the Nixon Administration. This debate (discussed in Pages 13-27 below and later) will largely determine the outcome of international discussions, tentatively begun almost as soon as the Kennedy Round negotiations finished, on the next major steps to be taken towards freer world trade. These discussions could converge on the course which may be open to Britain should membership of the EEC be indefinitely postponed. On the other hand, should she at last succeed in her Common Market endeavours, the course in question could help to minimise the consequent dislocation of her trading patterns.

What is this course that would appear to offer the British people a way out of the predicament in which they found themselves during the 1960s? It is the proposal for a free trade treaty under Article 24 of the General Agreement on Tariffs and Trade (GATT), open to all developed countries, affording less developed countries greater access to world markets and providing, too, for the harmonisation of the agricultural support policies of the signatory countries.

The basic proposition was put forward in May, 1966, by the Canadian-American Committee, an influential group of business, trade union and university leaders that is sponsored by the National Planning Association, in the USA, and by the Private Planning Association of Canada.[3] It was put forward as a fresh approach to the further liberalisation of world trade at a time when there were grave doubts about the outcome of the Kennedy Round of GATT negotiations. Considerable interest in the proposal has developed

[3] *A New Trade Strategy for Canada and the United States* (Canadian-American Committee, Washington D.C. and Montreal, May, 1966).

4

among those concerned with trade policy in the USA, Canada and Japan. In Britain a substantial body of parliamentary interest has been aroused.[4] The kind of business interest that has developed may have been reflected at the 1969 congress of the International Chamber of Commerce which called for a liberalisation programme involving the across-the-board elimination by the industrialised countries of virtually all industrial tariffs over a ten-year timetable.[5]

Because the Kennedy Round negotiations were such a tough experience there emerged a general acceptance that perhaps the time was arriving for a fresh approach to the achievement of an open world economy. Indeed, well before the Kennedy Round agreement was finalised, Sir Eric Wyndham White suggested in a key speech at Bad Godesburg, when he was still Director-General of the GATT, that future trade negotiations would have to be of a different kind.[6] Whether a new approach is adopted depends very much though on the attitude of America as the leading power in the Western world. On this the signs have been hopeful. President Richard Nixon recognised in his first message to Congress on foreign trade that the commercial problems of the 1970s will differ significantly from those of the past. "New developments in a rapidly evolving world economy will require new responses and new initiatives," he said.[7]

After the Kennedy Round ended, however, there was good cause for concern about the longer term outlook for international trade. First, a strong resurgence of protectionist activity quickly took place on both sides of the Atlantic, but most alarmingly in the USA where a general reversion to economic nationalism, even if not on the scale of the 1930s, could have a momentous effect on world trade. The effect of lesser sized economies adopting negative policies

[4]See the "early day motion" 171 tabled in the House of Commons, London, in February, 1969, which indicated that over 120 members, covering most sections of opinion in the three main parties, supported exploration of the proposal by the British Government.

[5]See Jean Royer, *The Liberalisation of International Trade* (International Chamber of Commerce, Paris, 1969). This report by Mr. Royer, the international trade policy adviser to the ICC and formerly Deputy Secretary-General of the GATT, was the basis for discussion at the congress, held at Istanbul, May 31 to June 6, 1969.

[6]Sir Eric Wyndham White, "International Trade Policy: the Kennedy Round and Beyond", Address to the Deutsche Gesellschaft für Auswartige Politik, Bad Godesberg, October 27, 1966.

[7]*Congressional Record*, House of Representatives, Washington D.C., Vol. 115, No. 190, November 18, 1969, p. S 14533.

could be nothing like as great. This is not to suggest that smaller countries cannot exert considerable influence in international economic affairs. Because of the world's growing economic interdependence they can do more in this field than they can, for instance, in affairs relating to international security.

Secondly, there appeared to take hold in the late 1960s a dangerous apathy towards trade policy issues, sufficient to cause M. Olivier Long, the Director-General of the GATT, to sound a note of warning. Speaking two and a half years after the Kennedy Round concluded, he observed that "governments, preoccupied with their domestic or regional difficulties, and frequently confronted with important problems in the economic and monetary fields, seem little disposed to seek constructive solutions or take any real initiatives in the international trade field. The result is the risk of a weakening in international co-operation and the creation of an atmosphere detrimental to trade expansion and to an active international commercial policy. It could leave the GATT, and all those concerned with these problems, operating in a political vacuum.

"Following the conclusion of the Kennedy Round," he continued, "it was fully expected that governments, industry and traders would need time to digest and evaluate the potential effects of the Kennedy Round agreement. We all knew that there would be a pause before the movement forward could be resumed. The question that one must now ask," said M. Long, "is this: How long can a pause reasonably last in a field as dynamic as world trade before it becomes damaging and before it undermines what has been built up with such difficulty over the past twenty years? In many quarters around the world there is developing a real sense of unease on this point."[8]

Little Europe or an Open World

If governments are seriously interested in the pursuit of trade liberalisation, the Canadian-American Committee's proposal needs to be discussed in this context and in relation to the various other options. Broadly, three positive options have survived public discussion: (a) another round of GATT negotiations conducted on a basis of reciprocity and non-discrimination, (b) a sector-by-sector approach to free trade, and (c) the free trade treaty option. These

[8]Olivier Long, "International Trade: the Present Challenge", Address to the National Foreign Trade Convention, New York, November 19, 1969.

6

are briefly discussed in Chapter 2. They are only mentioned at this point because the free trade treaty option has been reacted against by some who, through inattention or maybe sheer perversity, have managed somehow to miss the point, which is to do with the achievement on an open world economy. The idea has not been propounded as a trading block. Much less has it been propounded as a political power block.

What the free trade treaty proposal amounts to is the formation of a multilateral free trade association that would have to be initiated by North Atlantic countries, but would extend, hopefully, from Europe to the Antipodes. For the sake of convenience and simplicity the concept has often been described as a North Atlantic free trade association, or NAFTA for short. Critics of the idea have frequently allowed themselves to be misled by this description which implies a regional exclusivism that America, with her vast global responsibilities, has not to date been prepared to practise herself, although it is true she has encouraged the practice in others.

In the first stages of its exposure to public discussion, the free trade treaty option was subjected in Britain to much captious criticism from some sections of the national press and, too, from some sections of political life. "Wishful thinking" was the usual reaction, very often from quarters with wishful thoughts of their own to purvey. Plenty have airily, sometimes angrily, declared the idea either "moonshine", "a mirage" or "just not on". But in the early 1950s, it might be remembered, the EEC was similarly dismissed in London as impractical and unlikely to succeed.

In the 1960s the European issue became Britain's chief preoccupation in foreign affairs. It diverted attention away from other important issues. In the view of many, the question of British membership of the Common Market got completely out of perspective. The then Prime Minister, Mr. Harold Wilson, may have been reflecting this view when, as preparations were being made for a third attempt to join the EEC, he declared that "if entry into the Common Market were withheld once more, Britain could be increasingly confident of her ability to stand on her own feet outside the EEC".[9]

In order therefore to recall attention to the wider issues of international trade and economic organisation, the proponents in Britain

[9]Address to the International Chamber of Commerce, London, October 23, 1969.

of an open world economy made the most of the dichotomy which exists in the country between what are called the Atlanticist and Europeanist schools of opinion. For while there may be widespread support, as opinion polls have shown, for closer relations between Britain and other West European countries, only a narrow section of British opinion would happily support membership of the Common Market at the expense of Britain's close relations with other Commonwealth countries and with the USA.

As noted at the outset, even Mr. Heath, whose political reputation has rested on his advocacy of the Europeanist cause, reacted against the withdrawal into Europe that accompanied the Wilson Government's attempts to open negotiations with the Common Market. On numerous earlier occasions, Mr. Reginald Maudling, as Deputy Leader of the Opposition, had warned that if Britain were to join a narrow and inward-looking Europe, and withdraw her forces from East of Suez, there would be a real danger of a European isolationism. "This," he had written, "would provoke similar reactions in the USA, which would then turn westwards and, with Australia and Japan, concentrate on affairs in Asia."[10]

The development of isolationist tendencies in certain contemporary British attitudes had much to do with the studies launched in Britain on the implications for the UK of taking part in a multilateral free trade association. The response to the Canadian-American Committee's proposal was certainly occasioned to a large extent by a need to be more realistic about the country's Common Market chances. But the Atlantic Trade Study Programme was also a British response to Third Force aspirations in Europe of the kind espoused by Herr Franz-Josef Strauss when he was still West Germany's Finance Minister.[11]

The position was explained by Sir Michael Wright, Britain's former disarmamant negotiator, when he wrote in 1967 that "in either eventuality, whether the UK gains admission [to the Common Market] or not, the concept of an open-ended but initially a North Atlantic free trade association could prove of large significance. If EEC membership is negotiated, the British people,

[10]Reginald Maudling, "The Real Threat to the West", *The Sunday Times*, London, July 2, 1967. Mr. Maudling developed the same theme in an address to a conference on a "New Trade Strategy for Britain" arranged by the Trade Policy Research Centre, London, October 14, 1968.

[11]See, for example, Franz-Josef Strauss, "Karten auf den Tisch, Herr Brandt", *Bayernkurier*, Munich, September 13, 1969.

parliament and government will require an informed policy for the future development of the Atlantic community; that is, for the development of closer commercial and political relations between North America and Western Europe." Sir Michael suggested that "in an historic sense it is in the interests of Britain and of the West as a whole that ties with the USA—and, too, with Commonwealth countries—should be protected and strengthened, not neglected and weakened".[12]

It is the dichotomy, then, between those who advocate an essentially Eurocentric role for Britain and others who maintain an Atlantic or a global view, even while supporting British membership of the EEC, which largely explains why the free trade treaty option acquired in the UK context an Atlantic label. This dilemma, and the Atlantic label, may in turn explain why the concept has attracted a higher degree of interest in Britain than it has in either the USA or Canada where it might be said the idea began.

European Interest in Free Trade

Although the contemporary version of the free trade treaty proposal originated in North America, it is worth recalling that in the 1940s the British Government sought American support for Professor James Meade's plan for an across-the-board reduction of tariffs according to a pre-arranged formula. In the early 1950s France and other continental European countries sought British and American endorsement of much the same idea. But the US Administration rejected the first initiative and both the American and British governments rejected the second.[13] If the latter, at least, had been accepted the problem today of reconciling American, British and other trading interests with those of the EEC would either not exist or would be more manageable.

The six countries which had formed the European Coal and Steel Community had already begun, in the early 1950s, to exhibit a common front in GATT negotiations along with Sweden, Norway, Denmark and Austria. The comparative unwillingness of the USA and Britain to proceed with tariff reductions forced the major continental European countries to move to a regional free trade

[12]Foreword to Maxwell Stamp Associates, *The Free Trade Area Option* (The Atlantic Trade Study [Trade Policy Research Centre], London, 1967).

[13]For an account of these initiatives see Richard N. Gardner, *Sterling-Dollar Diplomacy: the Origins and the Prospects of our International Economic Order* (McGraw-Hill, New York, 1969), first published in 1956.

arrangement as the only course open to them under GATT rules. But, because of the political goals which the Six harboured, they were unable to carry with them in their enterprise either Austria or the Scandinavian countries.[14]

In the report of an official committee headed by M. Paul-Henri Spaak, then Belgium's Foreign Minister, and submitted to the foreign ministers of the Six in April, 1956, it was suggested that the customs union to be established under the Treaty of Rome might be accompanied by a free trade arrangement with other European countries.

Britain had stood aloof from the Treaty of Rome negotiations largely because of the importance she attached to her political and commercial ties with other Commonwealth countries and with the USA. When it became clear though that the Common Market was going to be instituted, the British Government did a *volte face*, partly influenced by two articles in *The Manchester Guardian* by Professor Meade.[15] From being a laggard on the matter of free trade, Britain suddenly became, or so it appeared, a champion of European-wide free trade. She took up the proposals contained in the Spaak Report.

The subsequent negotiations among the member countries of the Organisation for European Economic Co-operation (OEEC), which were conducted at the ministerial level under the chairmanship of Mr. Reginald Maudling, then British Paymaster-General, came very close to success. But in the end the inner Six could not compromise their interests in a European-wide free trade association. After eighteen months the talks were called off. The outer Seven accordingly formed the smaller European Free Trade Association (EFTA) and were later joined, in an associate capacity, by Finland and Iceland has since become a full member.[16]

EFTA's objectives are set out in the preamble and Article 2 of the Stockholm Convention. In brief, they are to seek the establishment of a single market in Western Europe and, too, "to contribute

[14]Gérard and Victoria Curzon, "Options After the Kennedy Round", in Harry G. Johnson (ed.), *New Trade Strategy for the World Economy* (Allen and Unwin, London, 1969; and University of Toronto Press, Toronto, 1969), p. 31.

[15]*The Manchester Guardian*, Manchester, March 14 and 15, 1956.

[16]For an account of these developments see Haruko Fukuda, "First Decade of EFTA'S Realisation", in Hugh Corbet and David Robertson (eds.), *Europe's Free Trade Area Experiment: EFTA and Economic Integration* (Pergamon, Oxford, 1970).

to the harmonious development and expansion of world trade and to the progressive removal of barriers to it". No political objectives are to be found in the articles of the association. For there was not then, at the end of the 1950s, and there was not at the end of the 1960s any appreciable interests in the EFTA countries in the cause of European political union (which they tend to distinguish from European economic integration). Opinion polls carried out in Britain on the subject have consisted of questions couched in very broad terms. All they can be said to have demonstrated is that the British people are interested in forgetting about Hitler's war and doing something about building closer relations with the other countries of Western Europe.

After several attempts at "bridge-building" between EFTA and the EEC, all initiated by the former, Mr. Harold Macmillan's Government decided in 1961 that the UK should apply to join the EEC. The negotiations failed. France exercised her right of veto. Before the negotiations broke down, however, much of British articulate opinion had convinced itself that Britain's destiny lay in Europe.

At that time, the case for British membership of the EEC was based on economic grounds, although the country's leading specialists in international economics—such as Professor Meade, Sir Donald MacDougall, Sir Roy Harrod, Lord Kahn and Dr. Nicholas Kaldor—were inclined to doubt, even then, whether the balance of payments effects would be favourable. But as Sir Roy Harrod remarked very early in the debate: "There [was] too much of the band-wagon about British attitudes towards the Common Market and too little precise reasoning. When a cause becomes fashionable, arguments become nebulous."[17]

In that article Sir Roy suggested that "a right-minded Europe should wish Britain, as an integral part of Europe, to go on buying more, not less, from overseas countries. If European thinking has a temporary fixation on the particular terms of the Treaty of Rome, then it is perfectly possible for us to wait until a broader view prevails there." He went on: "It has been said that we are in danger of 'missing the bus'. This strikes me as an empty phrase. If we

[17]Sir Roy Harrod, "Britain, Free World and the Six", *The Times*, London, January 12, 1962.

For a critical discussion of the debate in Britain at that time see Edward Mishan, "The Six, the British Debate and the Economist", *The Bankers' Magazine*, August, 1962.

judge that views now prevalent in Europe are too narrow, then arrangements for a greater freedom of trade within Europe can be made later."

Following the failure in 1967 of the second attempt to join the European Communities, the Wilson Government began preparing for a third attempt in the spring of 1969, after President de Gaulle's decision to retire from the French political scene. At the subsequent EEC "summit" meeting, proposed by the new President of France, M. Georges Pompidou, and held in the Hague in December of that year, the Six agreed that, "insofar as the applicant states accept the treaties [of Rome and Paris] and their political finality", by which was meant their political implications, they would be prepared to open negotiations on full membership with Britain, Denmark, Norway and the Republic of Ireland.[18]

New Economic Order in Europe?

Whatever the *dénouement*, whether the EEC is enlarged or special commercial arrangements are negotiated between the EEC and the EFTA countries, the European scheme of things seems destined, at the time of writing, to assume a new shape in the 1970s. For if the Common Market is enlarged to ten full members, and associate arrangements are made for the neutral countries—Sweden, Finland, Switzerland and Austria—the resultant economic order in Western Europe might not be very different from what would result from commercial arrangements negotiated along the lines proposed in the Brandt and Debré plans of 1968. If the latter occurred then the countries of Western Europe would be discussing just the kind of "arrangements for greater freedom of trade" that Sir Roy Harrod and others were alluding to in the early 1960s. Even the former circumstances might be viewed in much the same light.

It is difficult to imagine such a state of affairs being welcomed in Washington.[19] During the latter half of the 1960s the attitude of the USA towards the EEC has been changing as gradually it has

[18]See paragraph 13 of the *communiqué* issued after the Hague meeting and published in *European Community*, European Communities Press and Information Office, London, December, 1969.

[19]Indeed, the Johnson Administration reacted strongly against the Brandt and Debré plans of 1968. See *European Community*, January, 1969. For a discussion of the proposals put forward by Herr Willy Brandt, as Foreign Minister of West Germany, and by M. Michel Debré, as Foreign Minister of France, see Nils Lundgren, "Nordic View of Temporary Arrangements", in Corbet and Robertson (eds.), *op. cit.*

become plain that Americans have been paying a heavy economic price for a political bargain that is not being fulfilled. As European prosperity and self-confidence have been restored, the degree of interest at the level of public opinion in the idea of political union would seem to have waned, although the enthusiasts are as active as ever. In place of the dream of a United States of Europe, there is appearing the nightmare, from an American point of view, of a discriminatory trading block. Unless the European drive towards political union is dramatically revived, the USA is therefore unlikely to refrain much more from advancing American interests at the expense of the Common Market.

In the pattern of post-war trade liberalisation, which has been carried forward as fresh predicaments have had to be overcome, the USA might respond to an unwanted European development by launching a major trade initiative just as the Trade Expansion Act of 1962 was, in many respects, a response to the prospect of an enlarged Common Market in Western Europe. President Nixon stated, when sending his first trade bill to Congress in November, 1969, that a "more ambitious" trade initiative would be needed later.

What form that initiative will take could be shaped by the Commission on International Trade and Investment Policy which President Nixon also announced in his 1969 foreign trade message. The commission, he said, was to examine the entire range of the USA's commercial policies, to analyse the problems likely to be faced in the 1970s and to prepare recommendations on what should be done about them. He stressed how greater international competition, new and expanding markets, changes in cost-levels and technological advances in both agriculture and manufacturing, together with large-scale capital movements, are having profound and con-tinuing effects on international production and trading patterns. "We can no longer afford to think of our trade policies in the old and simple terms of liberalism versus protectionism. Rather we must learn to treat investment, production, employment and trade as interrelated and interdependent," he said.

"Our goal is an open world," President Nixon concluded. "Trade is one of the doors to that open world. Its continued expansion requires that others move with us and that we achieve reciprocity in fact as well as in spirit. Armed with the recommendations and analyses of the new Commission on [International Trade and Investment Policy], we will work toward broad new policies for the 1970s which will encourage that reciprocity and lead us, in growing and shared prosperity, toward a world both open and just."[20]

During the post-war period it has been the normal practice for American trade policy statements to stress the principles of non-discrimination and reciprocity. Both have been cornerstones of the GATT. But faith in the former has been eroded by the proliferation of discriminatory trading blocks that followed the formation of the EEC. Their existence has made multilateral tariff-cutting negotiations more difficult. Internal considerations have tended to be put before the wider good. In addition US business has become seriously concerned about the achievement of fair competition. The emphasis placed on the principle of reciprocity in the 1969 foreign trade message to Congress may therefore represent a significant shift in American policy.

[20]*Congressional Record, op. cit.*, p. S 14535.

2 OPTIONS FOR A LIBERAL COMMERCIAL POLICY

The integration of the world economy has reached the stage when free trade can be considered an attainable as well as a desirable objective for the governments of developed countries. By the time the Kennedy Round agreement has been implemented in 1972, tariffs will have been reduced to an average level of 11.2 per cent for the USA compared with 10.2 per cent for Britain, 9.2 per cent for Japan and 7.6 per cent for the EEC.[21]

Although considerably reduced, the tariffs that will remain will not be by any means insignificant. In many cases they will represent the "hard core" of protection for the industries concerned. What also needs to be remembered is that effective rates of protection on value added are inclined to be higher than nominal rates of duty. Extant tariffs will therefore still represent in the 1970s a nuisance tax on firms which are otherwise prepared to adjust production patterns to achieve a greater degree of specialisation in their international operations. This point is a growing concern of multi-national corporations.

After the years of depression and hostilities, order was on the whole restored during the 1950s and 1960s to the international trading system. But the system still discriminates against the interests of developing countries. Either as an automatic consequence of the bargaining process, or through the exclusion of sensitive items from negotiations, the tariff reductions agreed in successive GATT rounds have mainly been of interest to the developed world. Tariffs on goods of export interest to developing countries continue to be comparatively high. Moreover, where agricultural products are concerned there is considerable disorder in international trade and it bears heavily on the interests of developing countries, but more especially on the interests of a

[21]Maxwell Stamp and Harry Cowie, "Britain and the Free Trade Area Option", in Johnson (ed.), *op. cit.*, p. 205. The projection for Britain overstates the degree of protection she will still exercise because of the preferential access that is enjoyed by other Commonwealth countries. Duty paid by Commonwealth products entering Britain will average 1.2 per cent.

15

number of developed countries that are traditional exporters of temperate-zone foodstuffs. Trade in farm products has been accorded a "special status" in GATT negotiations which has meant their exclusion, too, from the bargaining process. As a result no appreciable impact has been made in the post-war period on the growing protection that has been given to farmers in industrialised countries. The price and income-support programmes that have been implemented for their benefit constitute the most serious problem in the field of non-tariff distortions of competition. Non-tariff barriers, as they are more popularly (but less accurately) termed, have been increasingly exposed as tariff barriers have been lowered. GATT negotiators have not yet come to grips with them, but research and experience have shown that they are not a general problem; instead, they are a series of specific problems relating to trades in specific products between specific countries.

It is thus possible to identify certain criteria by which will be judged the various negotiating techniques that could be adopted as the basis of the next major trade initiative. For a fresh approach to the further liberalisation of international trade to carry conviction it will need to contain effective means for dealing with (a) extant tariff barriers, (b) non-tariff distortions of competition, (c) agricultural protectionism and (d) the exports of developing countries.[22]

Dealing with Extant Tariffs

In dealing with outstanding tariffs it might be expected that another round of GATT negotiations based on reciprocal bargaining and most-favoured-nation (MFN) treatment could build on the success of the Kennedy Round. It would carry forward the evolution of GATT negotiations and involve no radical departure from estab-

[22]The discussion in this chapter draws heavily on Curzon and Curzon, *op. cit.*, and Johnson, "Trade Challenges Confronting Commonwealth Countries", *International Journal*, Canadian Institute of International Affairs, Toronto, Winter, 1969–70.

The last is based on a paper by Professor Johnson, "Trade Challenges to Commonwealth Countries", prepared for a conference at Marlborough House in London on May 27 to 29, 1969, jointly sponsored by the Institute of Commonwealth Studies, Oxford University, and the Trade Policy Research Centre. Along with other papers it appears in Paul Streeten and Corbet (eds.), *Commonwealth Policy in a Global Context* (Cass, London, 1971).

Also see Johnson and Corbet, "Pacific Trade in an Open World", *The Pacific Community*, Tokyo, April 1970.

lished bargaining techniques. But "hard core" tariffs are unlikely to yield to conventional approaches towards liberalising trade. Stronger resistance can be expected from the vested interests protected by them. A seventh MFN round would have to aim high. It would not be enough, after the Kennedy Round agreement has been implemented, to aim at another 50 per cent reduction. The goal would need to be the elimination of tariffs. But it is doubtful whether all the major industrial nations could be got to agree at the same time on such an objective. If they could be got to so agree the negotiations might well be so shot through with "exceptions", the products of industries which are politically sensitive, that the will to reach agreement could be seriously undermined.

Sector-by-sector negotiations towards free trade would mean that bargaining could be confined to the main countries engaged in a particular trade. The approach has the merit of affording governments considerable leeway in that protectionist forces could be divided and genuinely sensitive industries could be put to one side. But it is difficult to isolate clearly defined industries to which free trade is applicable. The problems of the sectoral approach have been summed up by Professor Edward English, of Carleton University, Ottawa: "If the sector is narrowly defined, as, for example, aluminium and its products, then there is a limited possibility that the main trading partners will be satisfied with the degree of reciprocity which can be achieved. If more broadly [defined], such as non-ferrous metals, there may be real difficulty in deciding which metals should be included. More fundamentally, free trade in one sector gives rise to important distortions in the allocation of resources. If the sector is one involving many finished goods, while important intermediate inputs to industries operating in the liberated sector remain protected, then negative effective protection can result."[23] Difficulties over achieving reciprocity might be reduced by combining the sectoral approach with traditional item-by-item negotiations or other techniques, but the problem would still be substantial.

Under a free trade treaty it would not be necessary for all the major trading nations to agree simultaneously on the desirability of moving to free trade. The pace of negotiations would thus be determined by the most eager and not by the most reluctant. Those

[23]H. E. English, "Tariffs and Trade", in *Canadian Tax Foundation 1968 Conference Report* (Canadian Tax Foundation, Toronto, 1969).

willing to reduce tariffs would not be obliged to give a "free ride" to those unwilling to reciprocate. The commitment to remove all tariffs across-the-board on an agreed time schedule would also mean that protectionist strongholds could not be excluded (although, as happened in EFTA, it would be possible to permit special arrangements in certain instances).

Non-tariff Distortions of Competition

The protectionist pressures which developed in the USA not long after the conclusion of the Kennedy Round were partly provoked, as mentioned earlier, by "unfair trade practices", including techniques by which foreign governments were thought to enhance the ability of their products to penetrate the American market by indirect subsidies, either for their manufacture or for their export. Irate attention has centred, in particular, on the discriminatory effects created in border tax adjustments associated with the new EEC system of value-added taxes which benefit exports while penalising imports. Altogether governments have notified the GATT of some 800 non-tariff measures, of concern to them, that are applied by other countries.[24] The list has been consolidated into an inventory which forms the basis of the work which will have to be done on these problems in the 1970s.

How non-tariff barriers to trade might be coped with under the traditional MFN approach has been the cause for some concern in GATT circles. Since there is no clear-cut way of assessing the distorting effect of particular non-tariff barriers it has been agreed that negotiations over them cannot expect to proceed on a basis of reciprocal bargaining. What is most likely is that each specific non-tariff problem will be dealt with on an *ad hoc* basis. In some cases rules of competition might be devised. In others it may be possible to negotiate the elimination of certain practices. With still others an elaboration of existing rules might be sufficient.

One of the main advantages of the sector-by-sector approach is that it would permit both tariff and non-tariff barriers to be negotiated upon at the same time. And it is non-tariff measures which are the main obstacles to trade in the categories of products where this technique might be most applicable. These categories break down

[24]Long, "International Trade in the 1970s: Some Immediate Problems", Address to the Bundesverband der Deutschen Industrie, Bonn, January 26, 1970.

into (a) products which have a high technological content, (b) products which are already internationally made and traded, and (c) semi-manufactured and investment products which are themselves the inputs of other industries.

By providing a treaty commitment, a multilateral free trade association could probably provide a more effective means of harmonising non-tariff distortions of competition than have the *ad hoc* proceedures of GATT experience.[25] In view of the brief but somewhat mixed record of EFTA on policy harmonisation one cannot be certain that a free trade treaty will always prove to be an efficient instrument for tackling non-tariff barriers and other harmonisation issues. EFTA has certainly been more successful than the GATT in this very difficult field.[26] "Included in the proposed free trade treaty there would be, as there is in the Stockholm Convention, an agreement to consult and negotiate on those policies and practices which have the effect of frustrating the benefits expected from free trade. Like the EFTA constitution, it would require adherence to rules of competition covering such contentious issues as restrictive business practices, rights of establishment (a serious bone of contention with Japan), public procurement policies, anti-dumping measures and government aids to industry."[27]

Agricultural Protectionism

The expansion of commercial markets for temperate-zone agricultural products can be expected to be a prime objective of the next major American trade initiative. Indeed, it appears that the USA is not prepared any more to humour the EEC, now the most highly protected agricultural market in the world with a level of protection which tripled during the 1960s. American farm exports to the EEC fell by 20 per cent in the last four years of the decade. Those subject to the EEC's variable levy dropped by 40 per cent. As if that was not bad enough, the Common Market has been raising its own level of farm protection, the resultant surpluses

[25]Theodore Geiger and Sperry Lea, "The Free Trade Area Concept as Applied to the United States", in *Issues and Objectives of US Foreign Trade Policy* (US Government Printing Office, for the Joint Economic Committee, US Congress, Washington D.C., 1967). Also see Lea, "Will Nixon Adopt Free Trade?" *The Round Table*, London, July, 1969.

[26]See Hans Liesner, *Atlantic Harmonisation* (The Atlantic Trade Study, Trade Policy Research Centre, London, 1968), p. 60.

[27]Johnson and Corbet, *op. cit.*

being unloaded on world markets at heavily subsidised prices.[28]

Besides its seriousness for the USA's trade balance, the agricultural problem could have a deleterious effect on the overall nature of American commercial policy, although one would not want to emphasise this point too much. So far the farm lobby in Washington has been a pillar of the resistance to the resurgence of protectionist activity that followed the Kennedy Round agreement. The only other major interests which can be mobilised to oppose the hue and cry for import controls have been the multinational corporations. (No longer are the trade unions strong upholders of liberal trade policies now that they regard overseas investment by multinational corporations as the "export of jobs".) Thus in order to sustain an outward-looking commercial policy it is apparent that the Nixon Administration is obliged to do something about the problems of trade in temperate-zone agricultural products.

These problems will be worsened if Britain finally succeeds in joining the EEC. The possible consequences were forcibly summarised by Dr. Harald Malmgren in the autumn of 1969, shortly after he resigned as Assistant Special Representative for Trade Negotiations in the US Administration: "The probable result of Britain's entry will be the adoption of the variable levy system and an alignment of high support close to or at present levels. This will raise the level of protection on agricultural imports into the UK, encourage home production of cereals and meat, encourage the purchase of French and German wheat and feed, as substitute for imported grains from the USA and other countries, and thus further increase exporter competition in remaining markets. In addition, the costly accumulation of surpluses within the EEC could be greatly relieved by this opening of the British market, especially for grains, dairy products and sugar. With a reduction of the pressures on the member countries of the Common Market resulting from costly stockpiling, there is less chance of a fundamental change in the internal policies of the EEC."[29]

[28]Harald B. Malmgren and D. L. Schlechty, "Technology and Neo-mercantilism in International Agricultural Trade", *American Journal of Agricultural Economics*, American Agricultural Economics Association, New York, December, 1969. Also see, for example, the despatch from Bonn: Joseph Sterne, "US Officials Worried by Common Market Threat to Food Exports", *The Sun*, Baltimore, November 17, 1969.

[29]Malmgren, "Troubles Ahead for World Farm Trade", Address to the National Soybean Processors Association, Denver, August 25, 1969.

From past experience of GATT negotiations the established exporters of farm output—the USA, Canada, Australia, New Zealand, Argentina and Denmark—have little cause for optimism. Along with many developing countries, for whom agriculture also constitutes a vital source of foreign exchange earnings, the traditional exporters have been pressing continually for the situation of growing protectionism to be remedied. Instead, as stressed already, it has been worsening and is likely to worsen still further as new grains and new production techniques, the so-called Green Revolution, convert more developing countries into net exporters of agricultural products.

Industrial countries have an interest in finding common solutions to the difficulties which confront them in the agricultural sector. Many are trying to find ways out of their present dilemma. Action under the GATT has been foreshadowed in two main directions. In the short term, it will deal with particularly urgent problems in limited sectors, such as dairy products and poultry. In the longer term, it will take up fundamental problems: support prices and policies; the establishment of appropriate conditions of access to the principal markets; evaluation of the effects of export subsidies, and acceptable compromises in regard to competition.[30]

In all major industrial countries the farming community pose difficult political and social problems. Resolving them is going to require considerable patience and goodwill. There is a general consensus among the experts that what is required is continuous discussion and negotiation over the fundamental causes of agricultural protection in order to reach an accommodation between the apparent desirability of retaining some price supports and the advantages of maintaining and expanding trade in farm products.[31]

Although governments have emphasised their national problems in international negotiations over farm trade, they have not yet demonstrated any perceptible interest in reforming their national policies. (In Britain, both sides of the House of Commons have

[30]See *The Activities of the GATT: 1967–68* (GATT Secretariat, Geneva, 1969), p. 11.

[31]For a discussion of the maze of laws and regulations aimed and raising the level of farm prices and farm incomes, and the prospects for expanding commercial markets for farm products, see David L. MacFarlane and Lewis A. Fischer, "Prospects for Trade Liberalisation in Agriculture", in Gerald I. Trant, MacFarlane and Fischer, *Trade Liberalisation and Canadian Agriculture* (University of Toronto Press, for the Private Planning Association of Canada, Montreal, 1968).

been more interested, instead, in achieving greater self-sufficiency through import-substitution.) Without any substantial interest in taking national action to correct at least part of the international disarray, the discussions under the GATT stand little chance of making significant progress.[32]

In this connection, the Roth Report on trade policy, submitted to President Johnson in January, 1969, argued that to negotiate changes in the agricultural policies of other countries, the USA must be prepared to consider changes in its own policies. Earlier the report suggested that the USA should "attempt to obtain acceptance of the principle that price regulation should be aimed at price stabilisation alone and that import charges, other than moderate tariffs, should be limited in their application to off-setting subsidisation and other measures that artificially interfere with world market prices".[33]

When the difficulties in the way of expanding farm trade are so great, the virtues of any particular negotiating technique over other techniques cannot be strongly asserted. But if the sector-by-sector approach were to be adopted, agriculture should be an early candidate for negotiation, but as in the traditional approach the first goal would need to be the harmonisation of domestic support policies rather than free trade. There would be a temptation to have such negotiations aimed at reaching international commodity agreements designed to raise and stabilise prices. Professor Harry G. Johnson, of the London School of Economics, has argued that this temptation should be resisted. Concentration by the United Nations Conference on Trade and Development (UNCTAD) "on generalising the benefits of agricultural protection in developed countries through the intractable medium of international commodity agreements, rather than on attacking the economic inefficiency and social immorality of protecting agriculture in the advanced countries at the expense of the incomes of competing producers in poor countries,

[32]John O. Coppock, *Atlantic Agricultural Unity: Is it Possible?* (McGraw-Hill, for the Council on Foreign Relations, New York, 1966), pp. 17 and 57.

[33]Special Representative for Trade Negotiations, *Future United States Foreign Trade Policy* (US Government Printing Office, Washington D.C., 1969), hereafter cited as the Roth Report, p. 37.

In an earlier report to President Johnson, the Advisory Commission on Food and Fiber, *Food and Fibre for the Future* (US Government Printing Office, Washington D.C., 1967) also recommended a more liberal policy towards agricultural imports into the USA.

has resulted in virtually no progress being made in the field of primary commodity trade".[34]

Again with the limited objective, at first, of gradually changing the direction of policies affecting agricultural trade, a free trade treaty could provide the sense of commitment and the institutional framework for consultation and negotiation on a programme of policy harmonisation. By advancing towards a liberal trade regime on a broad front, rather than on various narrow fronts as in the sectoral approach, the free trade treaty option contains considerable room for "give and take". The commitment to free trade in industrial products may contain the *quid pro quo* required for progress towards freer trade in agricultural products.[35]

Exports of Developing Countries

Since the first UNCTAD, held in Geneva in 1964, the developed countries have been conscious of the need to expand the export opportunites for developing countries. Attention has focused on a generalised scheme of tariff preferences for the manufactured and semi-manufactured exports of developing countries to the markets of the industrialised world. Agreement in principle was reached on such a scheme at the second UNCTAD, held in Delhi in 1968, but its implementation could not be so easily agreed. Efforts to finalise an arrangement which will encourage developing countries to make the most of the opportunities in world trade, rather than engage in often wasteful import-substitution, were greatly hampered by disagreements between the groups of developed countries with which they are most closely associated.

There are already numerous instances of discriminatory trade arrangements between one, or more, developed country and one, or more, developing country. The Commonwealth preference system is one. Another is the EEC arrangement with associated overseas territories. Alarm has been caused by the active consideration that has been given to new such arrangements. In the USA more is being heard of American responsibility to provide greater trading opportunities for the developing countries of the Western Hemisphere. The EEC has offended the spirit, if not the

[34]Johnson, "Trade Challenges Confronting Commonwealth Countries", *op. cit.*
[35]This theme is discussed, largely from an Australasian point of view, in Brian Fernon, *Issues in World Farm Trade* (The Atlantic Trade Study, Trade Policy Research Centre, London, 1970) with an introduction by Sir John Crawford.

letter, of the GATT through preferential trading agreements that have been struck with one Mediterranean country after another.

If the world was allowed to be divided into preferential trading zones, linking developed and developing countries, the long-run consequences for the international trading system could be extremely serious. "Apart from the adverse effects on the efficient use of economic resources," the Director-General of the GATT has said, "a division of the world into regional zones of influence would bring about a clash of trade and economic interests, which in turn could generate political tensions."[36] As the developing countries assessed the benefits for them of an UNCTAD scheme of preferences a number of them concluded that they were better off with the preferences they enjoyed on a narrower basis, whether under the Yaoundé Convention (the EEC arrangement) or in the Commonwealth or elsewhere.

Developing countries have not been conspicuous beneficiaries from previous GATT negotiations which have been conducted for the purpose of liberalising trade between developed countries and have therefore been institutionally biased in that direction. It is largely because of this common grievance that the developing countries were able to present a united front in the first UNCTAD when pressing for a generalised scheme of preferences. Another MFN round of negotiations could not be expected to command strong support from Third World countries.

Nor would a sector-by-sector approach attract the particular interest of developing countries although they would benefit under the MFN clause from the tariff reductions negotiated between developed countries. The point here is that the sectoral approach is most appropriate in trades (categorised on Page 19 above) which are of overwhelming interest to highly industrialised countries.

A free trade treaty under Article 24 of the GATT could develop into "a rich man's club", but all proposals along these lines have stipulated that this approach to trade liberalisation should be accompanied by a commitment to grant developing countries greater access to industrial markets.[37]

[36]Long, "International Trade in the 1970s: Some Immediate Problems", *op. cit.*

[37]This possibility is thoroughly explored in David Wall, *The Third World Challenge* (The Atlantic Trade Study, Trade Policy Research Centre, London, 1968).

Tariff preferences for developing countries would be much more acceptable politically, and of greater value economically, if incorporated in a multilateral free trade association among developed countries. By contrast the UNCTAD scheme offers industrial nations no short-term benefits and will be hedged by protectionist safeguards. Although a preference system would offer much to developing countries, it would also call for great concessions from developed countries. Structural changes would be needed in the industries of the latter in order for them to withstand market disruption from lower-cost competition. But if a preference system was established concurrently with a free trade regime between developed countries the need to reorganise structurally would already exist. If developed countries could agree on the objective of free trade, they would also be more likely to agree on how to assist developing countries. Whether it is to be by trade or aid, or a combination or both, an international solution to the problem of the poor depends upon agreement among the rich.

Protectionist Pressures

There is one other criterion by which the various optional negotiating techniques should be assessed and that relates to how they might counter the protectionist pressures which tend to develop when the pressures for liberalisation are relaxed.

The Director-General of the GATT has been among those to warn against allowing the momentum of trade liberalisation to run down. "In commercial policy matters," two other seasoned observers of the trade negotiating scene have observed, "the world does not stand still. We are either in a period of progression or one of regression. At the moment we are moving forward and this has been realised by protectionist forces in all the industrial countries. Voices are to be heard in the USA and EEC," they wrote in 1969, "that we should do nothing for the time being and should wait for the results of the Kennedy Round to be digested. Yet in the absence of any positive move forward, it is highly likely that back-sliding will take place, given the *perpetuum mobile* of human affairs. And the back-sliding, once started, might be all the greater because of the impressive degree of trade liberalisation that has been achieved in the past two decades."[38]

If the momentum of trade liberalisation is to be maintained, a

[38]Curzon and Curzon, *op. cit.*, p. 69.

bold and imaginative initiative is required as an effective counter to the protectionist pressures which have developed since the Kennedy Round agreement was reached. From this point of view a seventh MFN negotiation would be too "humdrum".[39] The Roth Report called for legislative authority for the President of the USA to negotiate on non-tariff barriers, generalised preferences for developing countries and agreements on border taxes and farm trade. As such it was chiefly interested in consolidating past gains from trade liberalisation. In commenting on the report Professor Raymond Mikesell, of the University of Ohio, wrote that "it may be argued that, without a really dramatic programme presented by the Administration and an all-out effort to put such a programme through the US Congress and to persuade other countries to support it, the forces of protection will soon destroy the gains of the past".[40]

In a liberal climate of opinion, the flexibility of the sector-by-sector approach might be deemed an advantage, but that very flexibility would be a considerable disadvantage when protectionist forces were instead gaining and not losing ground. For in the latter circumstances more industries would be by-passed as "sensitive" areas. Under the guise of a liberal trade measure this negotiating technique would thus provide only a partial solution to the problem of protectionism. In any case such a negotiation would be very slow and subject to default on the part of a major trading partner.

One of the main attractions of the free trade treaty option is that it would provide a dramatic and effective counter to protectionism. The point has been recognised by the Committee for a National Trade Policy, one of the major liberal trade lobbies in Washington, whose executive director has urged the US Administration "to invite other industrialised countries to join with us in charting the rest of the way to free trade in accordance with a realistic timetable incorporating meaningful codes of fair competition".[41] With the lobbyist's aversion to politically provocative phrases, the term "free trade treaty" is not used in the committee's proposals, but a free

[39]*Ibid.*, p. 71.
[40]Raymond F. Mikesell, "Changing World Trade Patterns and America's Leadership Role", *The Annals*, American Academy of Political and Social Science, Philadelphia, July, 1969.
[41]Recorded in *Trade Talk*, Committee for a National Trade Policy, Washington D.C., Summer, 1969.

trade programme is what is meant.[42] A free trade treaty, however, would be more than a counter to protectionist pressures. It would provide a framework within which to deal constructively with the problems that have provoked protectionist demands. For this reason there has been an inclination in American public discussion to put the emphasis on rules of conduct in international trade with a view to correcting distortions of competition.[43]

[42]In a paper, David J. Steinberg, "Our Foreign Trade Policy is Bankrupt", *Congressional Record*, Vol. 348, No. 493, April 16, 1969, the committee's chief economist was more explicit about the need for "a free trade charter".

[43]In this connection see *Constructive Alternatives to Proposals for US Import Quotas* (Canadian-American Committee, Washington D.C. and Montreal, 1968) where it is suggested "that the time is ripe for all industrialised nations to work together toward some international 'code of competition'. To some extent EFTA may offer a useful precedent," the statement continues, "its own 'rules of competition' having established a modest beachhead, but one that is operational and growing". This proposal is discussed in Lea, *op. cit.*

3 INSTITUTIONAL FLEXIBILITY AND GLOBAL SECURITY

In the immediate post-war period "the developed world" and "the North Atlantic region" were virtually synonymous terms. In Western Europe and North America were concentrated the nations whose wealth and power gave them special responsibility for world order and prosperity. At the onset of the 1970s this is still largely true. But during the 1960s the geopolitical boundaries of the 1950s began to blur as new powers began to make an impact on international relations. No longer was it appropriate for international institutions to be confined to Atlantic countries. Japan joined the Group of Ten and also the Organisation for Economic Co-operation and Development (OECD) where Australia, too, participates in certain activities. In addition, greater account now has to be taken of Mexico, New Zealand and South Africa and the countries of the Third World are also figuring larger in world affairs.

Above all, the Japanese have come to occupy a conspicuous place in the world economy. Their enterprises have been expanding in developed and developing countries on an ever greater scale and, indeed, the growing importance of the Pacific region as a trading community is largely attributable to Japan's economic expansion. It is doubtful, though, whether those in the Western world concerned with future arrangements for international trade have accommodated their thinking to the significance of Japan's emergence as the third largest industrial power in the world or, for that matter, to the increasing significance of the Pacific trading community.

With the growing integration and interdependence of the world economy it is necessary in the 1970s to think in global terms. Political integration in Western Europe has been promoted on a functional basis. But technological advances in transport and communications, together with the liberalisation of trade and international capital movements, have resulted in functional integration taking place on a world-wide scale. The integration of the world economy may still assist political union in the European region. It will not do so, however, if political endeavours are bent towards staying functional integration with the rest of the world. Such energies would be spent more constructively on resolving the political problems accompanying economic interdependence. Institutionally this may require more attention to functional, and less attention to regional, organisations.[44]

Inter-regional integration has gone too far for the world to be compartmentalised into regions pursuing their exclusive integration. On the other hand disparities between regions are too great for integration to be pursued on a unified global front. "The end of functionalism," it has been argued, "is not a world of continental governments, but a world in which communities are held together by a mass of inter-locking, over-lapping and cross-cutting loyalties."[45] For these to develop institutional arrangements need to be as flexible as possible.

When considering the economic organisation of developed countries, with a view to promoting closer integration, free trade associations have the virtue of allowing members to exercise full national sovereignty in their trade relations with third countries. They are therefore far less exacting than customs unions; in fact, they do not imply a political commitment in the way that customs unions do. For this reason the USA could participate in a multilateral free trade association without upsetting the political balance of the developed world. And Britain could also adhere to one without dislocating her traditional extra-European trading and political ties and without forgoing efforts to develop new ones across the Channel. It would be a positive step, as Mr. Lionel Gelber has written, "to espouse a world-wide venture that would create new unities without destroying old ones". Mr. Gelber goes on to argue, in his paper under the Atlantic Trade Study Programme, that "beyond Europe lies most of what is alive and dynamic in the West. It is with all that is energetic in the world overseas that Britain must align herself if, as she revives flagging energies, she is to reassert a political identity of her own."[46] In this respect the position of Japan cannot for long be overlooked.

[44]This theme is developed in John Holmes, "The Fearful Symmetry: Dilemmas of Consultation and Co-ordination in the North Atlantic Treaty Organization", *International Organization*, World Peace Foundation, Boston, No. 4, 1968.

[45]Murray Forsyth, "The Political Objectives of European Integration", *International Affairs*, Royal Institute of International Affairs, London, July, 1967.

[46]Lionel Gelber, "World Politics and Trade Strategy", in Johnson (ed.), *op. cit.* p. 80.

Japanese Interest in Trade Proposals

The Japanese have become well aware of the positive benefits that participation in a free trade programme would confer on their country. They are aware as well of the dangers to their prosperity and security that such an initiative might avert. The establishment of the EEC and EFTA, and the effects these groupings have had on the trade of other countries, have induced Japan's political and business élites to speculate about a similar grouping in the Pacific region. Professor G. C. Allen discusses in Part II below the proposals along these lines that have been put forward by Professor Kiyoshi Kojima, of Hitotsubashi University, and Mr. Takeo Miki, the former Foreign Minister, and relates them to the free trade treaty option as envisaged in Britain, the USA and Canada.

In the latter half of the 1960s the concept of an Asian-Pacific sphere of co-operation evoked very considerable interest in Japan. Professor Allen contends that an association "with common interests in the stability of South-East Asia would reinforce Japan's own efforts at a moment when, for the first time since World War II, she is being called upon to undertake heavy responsibilities for the political security and economic development of the region".[47] If these aims are to be achieved it is necessary to ensure above all a continuing American commitment to the region. This is one of the chief merits, from a Japanese point of view, of a free trade association embracing developed Pacific countries and Atlantic ones as well.

Stability in South-East Asia cannot be ensured if the nations there remain impoverished. Japan has accepted that she must be more generous with her assistance to developing countries and since 1966 has been to the fore in encouraging closer collaboration in South-East Asia. Because she "regards herself as too weak financially to carry the main burden of providing aid and investment, the possibility of associating the developed countries of both the Pacific and the Atlantic with plans for South-East Asian development makes a strong appeal to her".[48] Such has been the appeal to Japan of the Asian Development Bank and the establishment, too, of the Private Investment Corporation for Asia (PICA). "If the developing countries are left to fend for themselves," Mr. Yoshizane Iwasa, the Chairman of the Fuji Bank, has said, "they will undoubtedly

[47] G. C. Allen, "Japan's Place in Trade Strategy", Part II below, Page 102 *et seq.*
[48] *Ibid.*, Pages 102–3.

generate political unrest and become a serious obstacle to the world's economic progress. The advanced countries cannot expect prosperity if the economies of the less developed countries are left in a rudimentary state."[49]

As far as Japan herself is concerned, a multilateral free trade association, having the widest possible membership, would meet the interests of the most rapidly growing economy in the world. The country's progress is likely to become increasingly dependent on expanding opportunities for her foreign trade. Many of Japan's problems could be eased, moreover, if she subscribed to a free trade programme along with other industrial countries. For instance, the difficulties arising out of trade imbalance with particular countries, Professor Allen mentions, would be alleviated if all formed part of a broad free trade association. The strains of structural change brought about by industrial development in the Pacific region could be dealt with more easily by common policies or plans than if they were left to actions by individual countries.

Professor Allen examines, and puts in perspective, the three main obstacles to Japan's adherence to a free trade treaty. First, she would have to expose her manufacturing industries, many of which continue to enjoy various forms of protection, to outside competition. Secondly, Japan would have to abandon to a large extent her policy of supporting the peasantry. Thirdly, she would have to withdraw the outstanding restrictions on capital investment by foreign interests in her own industries.[50] The paper finds though that there are already forces at work which are moving policy in these directions. In addition, Japanese leaders are well aware of the adjustments that have to be made and are acting accordingly.

British Interest in Global Stability

Like Japan, Britain also has a substantial interest in promoting stability in South-East Asia. No other West European country has as big a stake there. The direct and immediate motive of British policy is therefore economic self-interest. But Britain shares with

[49]Yoshizane Iwasa, "Japan's Foreign Economic Policy", Address to the Foreign Affairs Club, London, June 10, 1969, and published in the *Anglo-Japanese Economic Institute Quarterly Review*, London, July, 1969. Mr. Iwasa has been one of the driving forces behind PICA, which was established in 1968 on the initiative of the Pacific Economic Co-operation Committee, a non-governmental organisation of business leaders from Australia, Canada, Japan, New Zealand and the USA.

[50]Allen, *op. cit.*, Pages 94–101 below.

Japan a special concern for stability in the region and the creation of conditions in which social and economic change can be effected peacefully. As a great seafaring and trading nation the UK has a permanent interest in international order. Sir Robert Scott argues in Part III that it matters a great deal to Britain, as it does to other trading nations, that international order is maintained, particularly in the Indo-Pacific theatre. A stable home environment is essential. But Britain is also vulnerable to distant crises. "If external policy is to serve long-range national interests," he asserts, "it must be directed towards world stability and prosperity."[51]

It is in the Indo-Pacific theatre that the world power balance may be decided. East Asia cannot in any case be divorced from the world power situation. Since the area, like the Middle East and Southern Africa, is not within the clear sphere of influence of either of the super-powers, there is an inclination, the paper suggests, for the Soviet Union and the USA to seek advantages over one another there that are foreclosed upon in Europe, the main theatre of direct Russo-American confrontation.

The situation is further complicated by the "emergence of China from a period of humiliation" and her assertion of "world status as the leader of radicalism and revolution", although external policies, says Sir Robert, are subordinate to internal affairs. The fall of Indonesia's President Sukarno, breaking the Peking-Djarkarta axis, has been an incentive to an even more thrusting and politically aggressive policy elsewhere. The most important factor in world strategy today, it might be added, is that Chinese policy has again become unpredictable at a moment in history when China, on the way to becoming a nuclear power, is herself in ferment, when fighting continues in Vietnam and when Korea and the Middle East are simmering with trouble.[52] The analysis contains a comprehensive survey of the South-East Asian scene.

Besides Russo-American rivalry in the Asian-Pacific region, and the tension between China and the USA, the Sino-Soviet dispute over ideology and power has resulted, on the one hand, in increased Peking support for Communist subversive and insurgency activities in the countries bordering China and, on the other, in increased Russian activity of a more orthodox character on the side of "govern-

[51]Sir Robert Scott, "Asian-Pacific Arena of Conflict", Part III below, Page 169.
[52]*Ibid.*, Pages 115–22 below *et seq.* Also see Scott, "China, Russia and the United States", *Foreign Affairs*, Council on Foreign Relations, New York, January, 1970.

ments of the day" in the area. The Russians have cautiously set about establishing diplomatic, trade and cultural ties with the local powers and have proposed a collective security system for South-East Asia, which Peking has predictably condemned as an anti-China device.

In the end these Soviet initiatives might not amount to very much. South-East Asia is handicapped by a wide variety of divisive elements. Yet, as the Secretary-General of the South-East Asia Treaty Organisation has pointed out, the Russian overtures coincide with renewed Chinese designs on a number of South-East Asian nations. In the light of Britain's reduced military role in the theatre the interest of the USSR may be considered useful in resisting such increased Chinese pressures. There have been doubts, moreover, about the continued American ground presence in the area, although there is little likelihood of a reduction in the US commitments to assist South-East Asian countries against externally-inspired insurgencies. As the governments that succeeded colonial rulers have achieved greater self-confidence, they have been able to pay more attention to external relations and, in consequence, are appreciating more the benefits, economic and political, of regional co-operation. Russian activities have in any case been scrupulously confined to the normal exchanges that take place between friendly countries and have eschewed anything which might suggest that they wish to promote their own view of communism. Finally, there is a spreading opinion in South-East Asia that "a cautious dialogue with the Communist powers must be achieved in some way if regional security is to be attained".[53]

While there may be short-term gains, perhaps in the form of economic assistance, from closer relations with the Soviet Union, the countries of South-East Asia will have to set these against longer-term risks: further threats to stability through countervailing measures on the part of Communist China; the possibility of political subservience to Communist Russia; and, thirdly, the consequences at some distant date of the Sino-Soviet dispute being resolved, perhaps with the passing of Chairman Mao Tse-tung.[54] But whatever store is set by these, the strategic mobility of Soviet

[53]Secretary-General of the South-East Asia Treaty Organisation (Lt.-Gen, Jesus M. Vargas), *Report of SEATO: 1968-69* (SEATO Secretariat, Bangkok. 1969), p. 6.
[54]*Ibid.*, pp. 7 and 8.

naval strength could transform the world scene for the West as a whole. Such has been the expansion of Russian sea-power that the West "will now have to be more alert than ever from the Baltic to the Western Mediterranean to the waters of the Middle East and the Indo-Pacific theatre".[55]

While the first task of British defence policy is security of the homeland, a second task—the product of the UK's dependence on world trade and sea communications—is to contribute to international stability and the protection of merchant shipping. The two tasks pose a dilemma for a country obliged to limit defence spending. For they call for different organisation, different logistic and telecommunications support, different degrees of mobility and different training and equipment. Britain must therefore rely on the help of others. She must demonstrate, too, that she can effectively contribute to common purposes.

Mr. Wilson's Government announced the withdrawal by the end of 1971 of Britain's military presence in South-East Asia, but declared that a continuing political interest in the area would be maintained. Ministers also sought to encourage the development of British economic interests there. But British political influence in any given situation depends on the extent to which Britain is sharing responsibility. Her military withdrawal would thus seriously weaken her ability to influence American policy in the Indo-Pacific theatre. The point needs appreciating in any revision of British policy by Mr. Heath's Government.

If Britain is serious about continuing a political interest in South-East Asia then it will be necessary to maintain strong diplomatic missions in the area. And if she wants to share in the decision-making she must be prepared to share military responsibility for the maintenance of political stability. The issue for defence policy in Britain is not whether to withdraw or continue a military presence East of Suez. Instead it should relate, Sir Robert Scott argues, to the minimum size and shape of forces needed to support policy.[56]

Need to Control Foreign Policy

If the countries in and around the area are anxious for Britain to contribute to peace-keeping in the Indo-Pacific theatre, they should

---

[55]Gelber, *op. cit.*, p. 137. This study discussed the development of Soviet sea-power and the implications for the West. See pp. 133–46.

[56]Scott, "Asian-Pacific Arena of Conflict", *op. cit.* Page 166 below.

be prepared to enter into new security arrangements. There is no question of Britain continuing a dominant military role. What is being urged is a British contribution to a joint effort that has nothing to do with imperial illusions. The paper accordingly relates the East-of-Suez issue to Britain's role in Europe in terms of control of foreign policy.

"If Britain is to make an effective political contribution to East Asian stability," Sir Robert writes, "she must retain—within the limitations of an increasingly interdependent world—an independent political status and power for independent initiative. Neither is compatible with subservience to the USA or with absorption in a European union."[57] The importance of Britain's capacity to sustain an individual role in world affairs has been thoroughly explored in the paper, referred to earlier, by Mr. Gelber whose analysis necessarily begins with a close examination of what might be entailed, in politico-strategic terms, if the UK was to become a member of the EEC. Some of the basic points raised in that analysis are worth re-stating here.

Europeanists expect the new Europe in the long run to play a part in world affairs comparable to that of Russia and America. "But the EEC cannot play that part until it has been unified to a similar extent. Political aims have been enunciated for the new Europe that only a single overall statehood could accomplish." There may be delays along the path to union, and perhaps the goal of Europeanists could be frustrated altogether, but the EEC has set in train a criss-cross of economic forces which will eventually have to be regulated by federalising measures if an economic union is to work. "If participants are to gain from the dynamic effects of economic integration, policies must be harmonised in both the fiscal and monetary spheres," Mr. Gelber points out. "Involved here are important political implications. For the determination and supervision of common economic policies pre-supposes the existence of a supranational decision-taking authority."[58]

The principal motive for British membership of the EEC is said to be political. Those who say it assume though that Britain "could always pick and choose between the political consequences of Europeanisation. . . . As long as Britain retains control of defence and foreign policy she may retain an individual role in world

[57]*Ibid.* Page 163 below.
[58]Gelber, *op. cit.*, pp. 85-91.

politics." But the members of the EEC will in the end have to abandon so cardinal a feature of sovereignty if a political union is to work. There is no way in which Britain, as an integral part of a European union, could expect to retain separate and special ties with outside countries. In a multilateral free trade association, however, which would not have the political implications of the EEC, Sir Robert Scott and Mr. Gelber agree that Britain would be able "to play the kind of global role which best suits her global interests and capacities. With Pacific countries also participating, such a framework would offer the flexibility and scope that is still, as in the past, essential to overseas policy."[59]

Effects of British Withdrawal

An exclusively Eurocentric defence policy, based on a continentalist strategy, could not adequately safeguard the UK's worldwide political and economic interests. Whatever her military status is to be, Britain will remain a world trading nation. Beyond Europe she will retain a very substantial interest in the protection of investments, raw material sources and access to markets, not to mention an interest in the continued strength and viability of trading partners. Important as these tangible considerations are, however, there are certain intangible considerations that are of greater moment. For Britain also has a very substantial interest in the maintenance of British institutions of law and government, along with other political and economic links, in as many countries as possible where they have been established. She thus has a very substantial interest in the maintenance of the international security system, not only because (as mentioned earlier) British fortunes can be affected by distant crises, but to ensure that weak countries can be reasonably secure.

Britain's post-war contribution to peace-keeping around the world, which in the period 1950-66 entailed eighty-five operations of one kind or another, twenty-two being of major proportions,[60] produced a military apparatus and level of experience that could be used to develop the international security system, given the co-operation of other countries. In this respect the British contribution to the system has an advantage over the American contribution. The latter is based on a doctrine of containment of Communism

[59]Scott, "Asian-Pacific Arena of Conflict", *op. cit.* Page 164 below.
[60]Geoffrey Williams, *Natural Alliance for the West* (The Atlantic Trade Study, Trade Policy Research Centre, 1969), p. 25.

which means that it can be put in doubt by changes in the Communist threat. On the other hand, the British contribution derives from historical associations, the UK reinforcement of Malaysia in 1963-66 requiring no such identification with anti-Communism.

In more than one sense, then, the international security system was dealt a serious blow when the Wilson Government announced early in 1968, following the devaluation of sterling, the accelerated and more complete withdrawal of Britain's military presence from the Indo-Pacific theatre. Apart from diminishing the confidence of lesser powers in the UK's readiness to assist in the maintenance of security and stability in the Persian Gulf and South-East Asia (for which provision was made through the retention of "a general capability", based in Europe, to air-lift troops), there was the likelihood as well that Britain's capacity to influence greater powers would be much impaired. British influence in world affairs has been sustained in the past by the UK's maritime tradition and overseas commitments and, more recently, by her modest nuclear capability. The kind of influence that results from global affinities might not be that easily replaced by greater involvement in European affairs where, with the exception of a small nuclear force, the UK will have little to offer militarily that is not already well provided for.

One of the dangers associated with a complete dismantling of Britain's military apparatus in the Indo-Pacific theatre has been the adverse affect it might have on American involvement in Western Europe's defence. Left on her own as the only major Western power prepared to underpin East Asian security, America may be faced in the 1970s by increasing internal pressure to run down her physical commitments in Western Europe. As the Heath Government, which took office in mid-1970, was preparing to revise British policy East of Suez, the USA decided to extend the range and area of responsibility of the American Seventh Fleet beyond the central Indian Ocean to the East African coast, in response to the challenge of increased Russian naval activity in the area.[61] British involvement in a Commonwealth security arrangement in South-East Asia (which is what the Heath Government had in mind on taking office) might help to keep the USA strongly committed to European defence. Britain's peace-keeping role outside Europe should be seen, as it has been in the past, as an important European asset, demonstrating that the USA has not

[61] *The Sunday Times*, London, July 26, 1970.

been underpinning the international security system on its own.

Britain's capacity to influence the USA has been directly related to the importance to the USA, at a particular time, of the areas of British interest. The preoccupation of the USA with East Asia has therefore been particularly favourable to Britain.[62] If Western Europe was to become overwhelmingly important, as at the time of the Berlin crisis in 1961, or if Latin America was to become an area of major apprehension, as during the Cuban missile crisis in 1962, the value of Britain's military efforts outside Europe in maintaining America's efforts inside Europe would be somewhat lessened. But this was not the way these things were being viewed in Britain at the end of the 1960s.

During the 1960s the UK became increasingly preoccupied with the achievement of British membership of the EEC. Attention was diverted from numerous other important issues in foreign policy. If the EEC was anything more than a system for co-ordinating certain economic policies there may have been good grounds for viewing with equanimity the further contribution Britain's announced withdrawal into Europe made towards the increasingly critical American attitude towards European isolationism. But the prospects for a new super-power emerging in Western Europe able to take care of West European security have been very dim indeed. For the foreseeable future the security of Western Europe will remain dependent on the USA and especially on the American nuclear capability.

Commonwealth in a New Era

The areas beyond Europe that are of British interest are largely associated with the Commonwealth, many of whose members are part of the Indo-Pacific theatre, in its broadest sense. The Commonwealth aspects of the UK position are discussed in Part IV by Mr. Leonard Beaton in the light of three objectives of overseas policy: (1) Britain's security, (2) her prosperity and (3) the achievement of the most acceptable character in the world as a whole.

"The Commonwealth association has played a major part in shaping British trade policy and political commitments over the years," Mr. Beaton says. But it has fallen into disfavour as a result of the British Government's conduct of overseas negotiations in the

[62]Leonard Beaton, "Some Political and Strategic Aspects of British Foreign Policy", Paper for a seminar on British defence and commercial policies in the 1970s at the University of Southampton, March, 15 and 16, 1969.

1960s. The sense of over-commitment that developed in Britain made itself felt most sharply over the European issue. Yet prior to the 1961-63 negotiations the Macmillan Government committed itself not to take Britain into the EEC, the Beaton paper points out, unless reasonable arrangements were made for the rest of the Commonwealth, the other EFTA countries and British agriculture. But Britain was forced to agree to the near complete dismantling of Commonwealth trade arrangements for "artificial and mistaken negotiating reasons".

Mr. Beaton reasons that "had the EEC been designed to include Britain, or were it to expand willingly for the purpose, Commonwealth trade would be dealt with rationally and constructively". Instead, Commonwealth trade has been regarded as a liability, rather than an asset. Nearly all the other Commonwealth countries have come to consider British membership of the EEC as injurious to their interests, he points out, and the UK "has become obsessed with the alternatives of Commonwealth or Common Market".[63]

The debate has been balanced by the knowledge that America no longer stands "as automatically as she herself thought on the European side of the argument". The USA has come to appreciate more than before the British contribution to security in the Asian-Pacific region. Washington has jibbed at "the Eurocentric destiny that once seemed so obvious for Britain". Second-thoughts in Washington on the political aspects of European integration have been accompanied, as mentioned above (see Pages 4 and 13), by second-thoughts about the economic aspects of the EEC's formation and development.[64] As new policies are devised in the 1970s to satisfy these second-thoughts, and to take into account the need for greater flexibility in international political and economic arrangements, the possibilities for developing Commonwealth relationships are likely to be enlarged. Broadly the Commonwealth has been interested all along in a liberal world economy. As members of an inter-regional association the countries of the Commonwealth have contributed, each in their own way, to the achievement of an open world and world-wide outlooks such as these need to be carefully nurtured.

[63]Beaton, "Pioneers of an Open World", Part IV below, Pages 180-86.
[64]On this point see the speech by Mr. Robert Schaetzel, US Ambassador to the EEC, to the German Foreign Policy Association, Bonn, February 12, 1970, and reported in *The International Herald Tribune*, Paris, February 14, 1970.

Part II

JAPAN'S PLACE IN TRADE STRATEGY

by

G. C. Allen

1 JAPAN'S INTERNATIONAL TRADE

Plans for the creation of a multilateral free trade association among the advanced nations, as a means of maintaining the momentum of trade liberalisation, must obviously show regard for the attitude of Japan towards participation.[1] She is now the world's third greatest industrial power and the third most populous of the developed countries. Her annual average rate of growth during the last fifteen years has amounted to about 10 per cent and, as it is confidently expected that that rate will be maintained until 1975, her relative importance in the world economy will probably continue to rise. Although Japan's income per head is still much lower than that of Western Europe, her exceptionally high rate of economic growth is likely to remove this disparity within a generation.[2] To any Pacific trading bloc her presence would be vital, for she is the only highly developed industrial country in Asia and her value, both as a supplier and as a customer, to all countries trading in the Pacific is likely to be enhanced during the next decade. Japan herself might be expected, *a priori*, to welcome any movement towards the elimination of trading restrictions, for, as an aggressive competitor for world markets, her interests seem to lie in the greatest possible freedom for international transactions.

Yet, to ignore for the moment the attitudes of her trading partners, Japan's participation in any wide trading community is confronted on her side by a number of obstacles which are, in some respects, different from those which qualify the enthusiasm of other countries for membership. Although the country has become a leader in modern industry and rivals West European countries in technology,

[1]See, in particular, *A New Trade Strategy for Canada and the United States* (Canadian-American Committee, Washington D.C., and Montreal, May, 1966). For a discussion of other proposals, both before and since, see David Robertson, "Scope for New Trade Strategy", in Harry G. Johnson (ed.), *New Trade Strategy for the World Economy* (Allen and Unwin, London, 1969), pp. 270-81.

[2]Cf. Saburo Okita and F. Murobuse, "Japan's Economy in 1985", in *The World in 2000* (Japan Economic Research Centre, Tokyo, December, 1967) p. 270, where it is estimated that in 1985 national income per head will be $4,300 in the USA, $2,800 in West Germany, $2,200 in Japan, $2,000 in France and $1,900 in Britain. Today these forecasts seem reasonable enough, but time doubtless has some surprises in store!

it cannot be regarded simply as an offshoot of the Western world. On the other hand, Japan is not now predominantly Asian in sympathy or outlook. This is not only because her economic success has raised her material conditions far above the squalor of her fellow Continentals, but also because her historical experience has cut her off from them culturally. She does not fall easily into either a Western or an Eastern group of nations. Japan can claim to match others for her contributions to some of the finest expressions of the human spirit as well as for practical capacity. At the same time she takes pride in her uniqueness among the nations, even to the extent of exaggerating it. Events and policies among her nearest neighbours have encouraged this tendency towards isolation. The roots of her civilisation are in China. But the changes of the last century and the establishment of Communist rule in 1949 have left her estranged from the people to whom she was in the past most akin.

In any examination of the possibility of Japan's participation in a wide economic group, her uniqueness—or her own idea of her uniqueness—must be kept in mind. Economic advantage, of which she takes a clear-sighted and unemotional view, and other national purposes may sometimes be found in conflict and some of these other purposes she may be reluctant to surrender even to gain substantial economic benefits. This does not mean that she will not admit compromises among conflicting ends or that she will not ultimately yield to the persuasion of economic interest. These questions will be returned to when, towards the end, this paper comes to speculate about the willingness of Japan to participate in a free trade association initiated by North Atlantic countries (and hence NAFTA), but extending hopefully to cover the whole developed world and providing less developed countries with expanded opportunities in world markets.

1. *Japan's Dependence on Foreign Trade*

It is commonly asserted that Japan's economic progress has been (and remains) closely dependent upon her foreign trade. Before assent can be given to this proposition, the meaning in this context of "dependence" needs to be considered. If it is to be measured simply by the ratio of imports to the national income, then Japan's dependence is at present low by international standards and, compared with pre-war times, it has steeply declined. Thus, in 1934-36 the ratio of the retained commodity imports to the gross national product (GNP) was 23 per cent, whereas by 1955 it was only 11 per cent, a ratio roughly the same as in the middle 1960s. For exports the corresponding ratios were 23 per cent, 9 per cent and 10 per cent. The post-war ratios are much lower than those for the United Kingdom and for most West European countries.[3]

These figures are consistent with the changes that have taken place in Japan's share of world exports. For most of the post-war period this share was far less than before the war. It was not until 1965, when the proportion reached 5.1 per cent, that the pre-war level was exceeded. For manufactured goods, however, Japan's share has for some time been greater than it was before the war, when a high proportion of her exports consisted of primary products and of semi-manufactured goods, such as raw silk. It was of course the relative advance in manufactures that was responsible for the impression in Western countries that Japan was achieving outstanding success as an exporter some years before this opinion was justified. So far this examination suggests that Japan's dependence on foreign trade is quite moderate.

Even if one is concerned primarily with the dynamic aspect of trade, and if one judges the degree of dependence by the contribution of the export demand to the growth in the national income in the post-war period, the answer to the question is much the same. There can be little doubt that, whatever the importance of exports to economic recovery during the 1930s, during the last 20 years the main stimulus to the development of the economy has been given by domestic investment and that the role of exports has been secondary. But this conclusion must be qualified in two respects. First throughout the period and especially in the early and middle 19 American special procurement expenditure[4] in Japan contributed substantially to the growth of demand. Goods sold to the Americans under this head should properly be regarded as a form of export, even though most of them were not shown in the trade returns. Secondly, the sharp rise in exports at the time of the trade recessions of 1958, 1962 and 1965 did much to offset the decline in domestic orders. In other words, the increased demand from abroad served to sustain demand in a period when investment had contracted.

[3]Except for France, where the ratio is only slightly above Japan's.

[4]This covered the purchase of equipment for American forces in the Far East, the employment of Japanese by the US Army in Japan, the consumption of American soldiers and civilians and also some off-shore contracts.

Further, the buoyancy of exports in these periods had a favourable effect on the balance of payments and so permitted the monetary authorities to embark on a reflationary policy at an early stage. One can conclude that, although exports have been subordinate to domestic investment as an instrument of growth in the post-war period, recovery from recent recessions has been, in part, export-led.

Finally, if one measures dependence in physical terms, by the extent to which the country is self-sufficient in food and raw materials, then it is clear that Japan is highly dependent upon her foreign trade. This applies less to food than to raw material imports. Before the war Japan obtained about a quarter of her staple food (rice) from her colonies (Korea and Formosa), and in the years of low agricultural production just after the war, the towns-people were fed to a considerable extent by imports from the United States. Since the early 1950s, however, the growth in the domestic rice production, together with the fall in consumption a head, has reduced the ratio of rice imports to total consumption, despite the increase in population. The same is true of wheat and soya beans. On the other hand, the changes in the people's diet and in the structure of agricultural production have required very heavy imports of animal feeding-stuffs and during the last few years food imports as a whole have moved up steeply. As will be seen later, this trend is likely to be accentuated during the next decade.

As to raw materials, nearly all Japan's manufacturing industries rely on foreign sources of supply for the bulk of their needs. For most of these industries the volume of imported raw materials which they use is much greater than the volume embodied in their exports. Similarly, for the primary sources of fuel and power Japan is closely dependent upon foreign countries. Her domestic coal industry and her hydro-electric stations supply a steadily declining share of her power requirements and practically all her mineral oil and much of the coal she needs are bought from abroad. It is expected that by 1975 four-fifths of Japan's energy requirements will be met by imports.

In this last sense, therefore, Japan is closely dependent upon imports for her economic growth. Such a conclusion is quite consistent with the decline that has taken place during the last three decades in the ratio of imports to GNP. That decline can be attributed largely to structural changes in industry, notably the fall in the importance of textiles (especially those using natural fibres) and the disproportionately large increase in the output of products with a small import content—such as machinery, chemicals and goods made of synthetic materials—as well as to the relative advance in services in the economy. Nor should import dependence be considered solely in terms of food and raw materials. In recent years an increasing share of the imports has consisted of manufactured goods, chiefly capital equipment. Like other advanced industrial Japan relies for many types of instrumental goods on foreign suppliers pre-eminent in their manufacture. For the progress of her science-based industries such imports are as indispensable as raw materials. Import dependence in the immediate future will probably increase. To sustain a rate of growth of about 8 per cent a year between 1967 and 1971, it was estimated that a growth of imports at an annual rate of over 9 per cent would be necessary.

Two questions at once arise. First, will the imports required be available to Japan on good terms? Secondly, what are the prospects of her finding means to meet the bill not only for the commodity imports but also for the consistently large deficit on account of services, a deficit attributable mainly to heavy overseas payments for shipping services and patent royalties? These questions will be approached by an examination of the country's exports.

In the early post-war years, before new markets had been found to replace those lost through the political and technical changes of the war period, Japan faced a chronic deficiency in her balance of payments which only American aid and, later, special procurement expenditure enabled her to meet. Throughout most of the 1950s the contrast between the steep rise in industrial production and in the GNP and the laggardliness of the export trade was constantly emphasised by observers. It was not until 1959 that the pre-war volume of exports was exceeded. The Industrial Bank of Japan, in its *Economic Study of Japan's Exports*, published in 1967, called attention to the fact that from 1950 onwards Japan's exports grew more than twice as fast as world exports. The significance of the rapid growth in the early years of this period is, of course, qualified by the low level from which the rise began. It is, however, remarkable that after the recovery had been achieved the elasticity of Japan's exports in relation to world exports still exceeded 2 (2.045 between 1960 and 1965). A performance of this order was shown to be necessary in order to achieve the 8 per cent annual growth rate postulated in the 1967-71 plan. Indeed, the planners considered that an annual rate of export growth of 10.5 per cent (at constant prices) was required for the period 1967-71.[5] Japan is, therefore, much concerned both that international trade shall remain buoyant and also that her own opportunities in foreign markets shall be enlarged.

2. *Imports and Sources of Supply*

The changing pattern of Japan's import trade during the last fifteen years is shown in Table 1 where the broad commodity structure of the trade at different dates is set out. It will be observed that the volume of imports increased 2½ times between 1960 and 1967 and by five times between 1954 and 1967. Within this general trend marked changes occurred in the relative importance of the main classes of imports. Since 1960 raw materials have consistently declined in importance, while mineral fuel and manufactured goods

TABLE 1
THE STRUCTURE OF THE IMPORT TRADE
(percentage of total value)

	1954	1960	1966	1967
Food	27.2	12.2	17.6	15.5
Raw Materials	48.0	49.2	40.7	38.5
Mineral Fuel	11.1	16.5	18.9	19.2
Manufactured Goods	13.7	22.1	22.8	26.8
Quantum (1960 = 100)	48.6	100.0	208.2	259.6

have increased. With food the trend has been upwards, although there have been variations from year to year according to the size of the local harvest. Among the raw materials, the structural changes in industry have brought about a steep decline in the proportion of textile fibres in the total and a rise in the share of ores. In recent years textile fibres have accounted for 20-25 per cent of the total raw materials; ores, scrap and concentrates, for 34-36 per cent. The next most important raw material import consists of timber and timber products, including pulp; this is, in fact, the most rapidly growing of all the imports. Of the fuel imports, four-

[5]These were the estimates of the Government's Economic Planning Agency in its "Economic and Social Plan for 1967-71". So far they have all proved to be too low.

fifths now consist of oil and oil products; the rest, coal. The manufactured goods have included a wide variety of capital and intermediate products, such as machinery, transport equipment, chemicals and metals. The import of finished consumer goods until recently has been very small, but it has lately started to rise quite steeply. Many of them are luxuries and include high-grade woollen and worsted goods and branded specialities.

If the pace of Japan's industrial expansion is maintained, it is probable that the structural trends of the last decade will be carried further; that is to say, the labour-intensive industries will continue to recede in importance, while the capital-intensive, science-based industries will take an increasingly dominant position. The chief class of goods in the first category (textiles) has a much higher import content than those produced by the engineering and chemical industries and others in the second category. It is therefore probable that the rise in raw-material imports will occur at a slower pace than that of the import trade as a whole. Nevertheless, Japan will need access to substantially greater supplies of ores, both ferrous and non-ferrous, pulp and chemical raw materials. Until the time comes when atomic energy can supply a large part of her power requirements, she will continue to rely on oil, which is likely to make up a growing share of her total imports.

It is more difficult to estimate the future of food imports, since these depend to a considerable extent on her policy towards domestic agriculture. This uncertainty applies particularly to rice and other grains. For foodstuffs which have only recently become important in her diet the prospects are easier to judge. Because of the shortage of grazing land it is improbable that she can greatly increase her output of beef, mutton and dairy products. To the extent that she is able to expand her production, she will have to buy greater quantities of animal feeding-stuffs. It has been estimated that by 1975 she will have to import 171,000 tons of beef and veal (compared with 5,000 tons in 1960-3) and 76,000 tons of mutton (compared with 32,000 tons in 1960-3).[6] Even if agricultural protection is maintained, therefore, her foodstuffs imports are likely to grow at least as fast as her imports as a whole. As to imports of manufactured

[6] This was an estimate of the United Nations Food and Agricultural Organisation. Recent experience suggests that it was a serious under-estimate. See L. V. Castle, "New Zealand Trade and Aid Policies in Relation to the Pacific and Asian Region", in Kiyoshi Kojima (ed.), *Pacific Trade and Development*, Vol. I (Japan Economic Research Centre, Toyko, February, 1968), p. 98.

goods, the experience of other industrial countries is that these increase in importance as the economy expands and there is no reason to suppose that Japan will be an exception. Finished consumer goods from abroad may well find a substantial market as Japan becomes more affluent and as her tastes approximate to those of other advanced countries.

One of her chief preoccupations will be that of ensuring that she can obtain not only the raw materials and fuel but also the essential equipment that she needs on good terms. In recent years, with this purpose in mind, she has much extended the range of her suppliers. The changes in the relative importance of the different countries are shown in Table 2.

TABLE 2
SOURCES OF IMPORTS
(percentage of total value)

	1954	1960	1966	1967
Asia	*30.6*	*30.4*	*33.2*	*30.7*
China (Mainland)	1.7	0.5	3.2	2.3
South Korea and Formosa	2.7	1.8	2.3	2.0
Malaysia and Singapore	2.6	4.6	3.5	3.2
India, Pakistan and Burma	6.3	3.2	2.6	2.6
Indonesia	2.6	1.6	1.8	1.7
Philippines	2.8	3.5	3.4	3.2
Thailand	2.9	1.6	1.6	1.4
Iran, Saudi Arabia and Kuwait	6.0	7.5	9.4	9.1
Europe	*8.2*	*10.9*	*12.8*	*15.1*
EEC	4.5	4.7	4.7	5.6
EFTA	2.7	3.5	3.9	4.0
USSR	—	1.9	3.2	3.9
*North America**	*46.0*	*42.8*	*36.1*	*35.8*
USA	35.3	34.3	27.9	27.5
Canada	5.1	4.5	4.7	5.4
South America	*7.4*	*3.2*	*4.7*	*4.5*
Oceania	*5.7*	*9.0*	*8.7*	*8.2*
Australia	4.9	7.7	7.1	6.8
Africa	*2.1*	*3.7*	*4.4*	*5.7*
South Africa	.4	1.9	1.4	2.3

*Includes Mexico, El Salvador, Panama, Cuba.

This table shows that Japan now draws her imports from all over the world, in striking contrast with pre-war days when four countries (China, Korea, Formosa and the USA) supplied three-fifths of them. At the present time well over three-fifths of the imports come from countries bordering the Pacific Ocean, two-fifths of them from North and South America. If one classifies the suppliers into three groups of countries, developed, under-developed and Communist, the proportion of imports which each supplied in 1966 was 51.5 per cent, 41.3 per cent and 7.2 per cent respectively. During the last decade the developed countries and the Communist bloc increased their share at the expense of the under-developed countries.

This trend deserves examination. The growth in the Communist bloc's importance as suppliers can be attributed partly to some relaxation of political restraints on trade with China and partly to Japan's more cordial relations with Russia. As seen above, Japan has been anxious to extend the sources of her food, raw material and fuel supplies and these countries have been able to provide her with oil, timber, metals and ores, soya beans and maize. The imports from the under-developed countries have also consisted, as might be expected, of industrial raw materials and it is significant that each of these supplying countries specialises on a rather narrow range of goods. For example, imports from Malaya have consisted mainly of iron ore and rubber, and those from the Philippines of copper, iron ore and timber. Formosa has sent mainly sugar and other foods; India and Pakistan, cotton, jute and iron ore; Latin America, cotton; Thailand, maize and rubber; Indonesia, oil; and West Asia, oil. All these commodities are essential to Japan's industrial production, but by no means all these suppliers have an assured future in Japan's market. The oil-producing countries of West Asia are an exception. Their exports to Japan have increased enormously during the last few years and their prospects for many years to come are very favourable. In most other classes of raw materials, however, the Asian countries are meeting with serious competition from the developed countries. For example, Australia has moved to the front as a supplier not only of wool, but also of ferrous and non-ferrous ores, coal and wheat. Canada is one of the most important sources of wheat, timber, pulp and ore. South Africa also has been supplying increasing quantities of ore. The USA, by far the most important single source of supply of Japan's imports as a whole, has sent a wide variety of raw materials as well as fuel and food. Indeed, over three-fifths of the imports from the USA have lately consisted of these primary products. Thus, the under-developed countries, most of which specialise on a narrow range of exports, have lately found their opportunities in Japan for the sale of primary products constrained by the successful competition of the advanced countries, the products of which are usually more reliable than theirs in quality and delivery.

The changes in the industrial structure and in habits of consumption already referred to have strengthened this tendency. For instance, the comparative stagnation in Japan's cotton industry, and its concentration on high-quality products, have reduced the demand for Indian cotton in favour of supplies from North and South America. Again, dietetic changes have helped to destroy the market for South Asian rice, while stimulating the demand for Australian and New Zealand meat and dairy products and for Canadian and Australian wheat. The continuing strength of these countries in Japan's markets has been assured by the long-term contracts which Japan has placed with them for raw materials. These contracts are the result of her desire to safeguard her future supplies. She has made long contracts, for example, with Australian and Canadian producers of ores and fuel. Even before the war she had established enterprises overseas, including several mining undertakings in South-East Asia. In recent years she has gone further afield and has participated in joint enterprises in Canada, Australia, Central Africa, South America and the Persian Gulf.

In consequence of the increasing importance both of the developed and the Communist countries as suppliers of raw materials and food, East and South-East Asian countries have lost ground. The figures for Asia as a whole disguise this change. It will be seen from Table 2 that over the last decade that Continent has just about retained its importance as a supplier, but this is simply because of the steep proportionate increase in imports from the oil producers of West Asia and because of the growth in trade with Communist China.

For imports of manufactured goods Japan for a long time past has depended mainly upon the USA. Since 1960, however, Western Europe has grown in importance as a source of machinery and equipment, and its share of Japan's imports has consequently increased. Here again Japan in her anxiety to secure improved terms of trade welcomes the competition of European firms with the once overwhelmingly predominant Americans. These are some of the outstanding facts of the import trade. Their significance will be discussed further after an examination of the country's exports.

3. *Exports and Markets*

The structure of the export trade and the chief markets are shown in Tables 3 and 4. Japan's exports, in volume, have increased by seven times in the last 13 years and they have also become far more diversified in regard to both commodities and markets. The growth has taken place in the face of keen competition from other countries, for whereas imports have consisted predominantly of goods that were

TABLE 3
THE STRUCTURE OF THE EXPORT TRADE
(percentage of total value)

	1954	1960	1966	1967
Food	8.3	6.6	3.9	3.6
Textiles and Clothing	40.3	30.2	18.0	16.3
Chemicals	4.8	4.2	6.9	6.5
Non-metallic Mineral Manufactures	4.3	3.6	2.9	2.8
Metals and Metal Manufactures	15.3	13.9	18.2	17.1
Machinery and Transport Equipment	12.4	23.0	38.4	42.1
Miscellaneous	14.6	18.5	11.7	11.6
Quantum (1960 = 100)	39.2	100.0	264.9	278.1

complementary to Japan's own production,[7] exports have been made up of manufactured goods of kinds produced not only by the advanced manufacturing countries but also, increasingly, by countries in early stages of industrialisation.

Up to the middle 1950s the export trade was highly specialised to textiles and other light products (for example, pottery and miscellaneous consumption goods), but it now closely resembles in structure that of the advanced industrial nations of Europe and shows a strong concentration on metals, engineering goods and chemicals. Nearly two-thirds of the exports (64 per cent in 1966 and

[7]This statement must be qualified in three respects. Imports of fuel compete with the local coal industry, but Japan has now decided to run down her coal industry and rely mainly on imported fuel. Imports of foodstuffs compete with home-grown foods to some extent and policy in regard to this matter has not yet been resolved. Imports of many types of manufactures are, of course, competitive with Japan's products.

TABLE 4
EXPORT MARKETS
(percentage of total value)

	1954	1960	1966	1967
Asia	48.9	36.0	33.6	34.1
China (Mainland)	1.2	0.1	3.2	2.8
South Korea and Formosa	8.3	5.0	6.6	7.1
Malaya and Singapore	2.9	2.9	2.4	2.4
India, Pakistan and Burma	8.9	5.8	3.2	2.0
Indonesia	7.3	2.7	1.2	1.5
Thailand	4.0	2.9	2.8	3.3
Philippines	1.9	3.8	3.0	3.5
Hong Kong	4.8	3.8	3.8	3.3
Ryukyu Islands	2.7	2.3	2.3	2.6
Iran, Saudi Arabia and Kuwait	1.9	1.8	1.7	1.9
Europe	9.0	13.2	16.1	16.0
EEC	4.0	4.3	6.1	5.3
EFTA	4.1	5.7	5.4	7.0
USSR	—	1.5	1.2	1.5
*North America**	21.7	33.2	35.8	34.7
USA	17.0	26.7	30.4	28.5
Canada	1.3	2.9	2.6	2.7
South America	9.7	4.4	2.9	2.7
Oceania	2.2	4.5	4.1	4.5
Australia	1.7	3.6	3.0	3.4
Africa†	8.5	8.7	7.5	8.1
South Africa	1.9	1.4	1.6	1.5

*Includes Mexico, El Salvador, Panama and Cuba.
†Exports include sales of ships for Liberian registry.

66 per cent in 1967) now fall into these three categories which are generally referred to as "heavy industry products". In the Industrial Bank of Japan's export analysis which was mentioned above, it was shown that machinery and equipment were responsible for two-fifths of the growth in exports between 1954 and 1964, and metals and metal manufactures for nearly a quarter. On the other hand, the aggregate contribution to export growth of the once predominant exporting industries, cotton, silk and pottery, was very small, about 3 per cent. Nevertheless, despite this striking change in composition, the exports of the light industries still occupy a much more important place in Japan's trade than they do in that of other advanced

countries.[8] They constitute a special problem for Japan since many of them are produced by the small-scale sector of her industry.

Japan's markets have also changed. In 1954, 67 per cent of her exports were sent to the under-developed countries, 31 per cent to the developed countries[9] and only 2 per cent to the Communist bloc. By 1966 the proportions were 43 per cent, 51 per cent and 6 per cent respectively. Thus, sales to the developed countries have been responsible for by far the greater part of the increase in exports, although the rise in exports to the Communist bloc, which were negligible in the middle 1950s, has been quite substantial. It must be emphasised that, although the markets in the less developed countries have declined relatively, this was consistent with a large absolute increase in Japan's exports to them.

The course of the trade in recent years presents something of a paradox. Japan's sales to the developed countries are still weighted, broadly speaking, to the side of light industrial products and her sales to the under-developed countries to the side of heavy industrial products. Yet, as already shown, her markets in the developed countries have grown faster than those elsewhere, while it is the sales of the heavy industrial products that have been the most buoyant. The apparent inconsistency can easily be resolved. Japan still sends a higher proportion of her exports to the under-developed countries than do other industrial countries. Her strong position in those markets can be explained by special circumstances (for example, reparations payments effected in the delivery of capital goods), geographical proximity and the relative cheapness of her products. The disparity in the rate of growth of exports to the developed and the under-developed countries has arisen partly because incomes have grown much faster in the former than in the latter and partly because, compared with other industrial competitors, she is still a cheap supplier of labour-intensive goods. Finally, the reason why Japan's most rapidly growing exports have consisted not of these labour-intensive goods but of heavy industrial products is, first, that

[8]In 1964 the export-specialisation coefficient of Japanese exports relative to those of the five chief industrial countries was 3.16 for textiles (7.67 for cotton fabrics) and 12.0 for pottery, but only 0.81 for machinery and equipment. This last figure, however, is an average which conceals the fact that the coefficient for ships was 9.25. This was at the end of a decade in which Japan's exports of heavy industrial products had grown twice as fast as those of other industrial countries.

[9]The developed countries are those of North America and Western Europe together with Australia, New Zealand and South Africa.

the growth of world demand for the latter has been exceptionally great in recent years and, secondly, that it is in the heavy industries that her productivity has risen fastest, with the result that her costs in those industries have fallen very steeply. It should be added that the heavy industries have not been affected as much as the labour-intensive industries by two adverse factors that h ave made themselves felt since 1960. One is the marked rise in wages that is the consequence of the drying up of labour reserves. The second is the appearance of competitors in Japan's overseas markets from the newly-established light industries of the developing countries.

2 TRADING PARTNERS IN THE ASIAN-PACIFIC REGION

The trade among the Pacific region countries (excluding mainland China) amounted in 1965 to about 22 per cent of the world's trade compared with about 20 per cent in 1958. Japan's own trade with that region has amounted in recent years to nearly two-thirds of her total trade. Thus the region has a dominant position in her foreign commerce, although its importance to her has diminished slightly during the last decade with the wider extension of her trading interests. What is more, the contribution of the different parts of the region to her total trade have changed markedly. Japan's relations with the most important countries in the Pacific area will now be examined.

1. *The United States*

The USA has long been Japan's chief trading partner. This position she has continued to occupy despite far-reaching alterations in the types of goods exchanged. In the early post-war years Japan depended on her for aid-financed food and raw materials and even in 1954 well over a third of her imports came from the USA. To a considerable extent these were financed by special procurement dollars, for her direct exports were comparatively small. Since then, between 1954 and 1967, Japan's purchases from the USA have almost quadrupled, while her exports to that country have increased more than ten times.[10] In this period the *relative* importance of the USA as a supplier declined, while her relative importance as a customer substantially increased. The former change, which has still left the USA predominant, occurred because Japan succeeded in finding new sources of supply both for raw materials and fuel and for manufactured goods. This extension in the range of her suppliers has already been noted. That the USA should be the leading supplier of manufactured goods, especially machinery and equipment, is not surprising and it was to be expected that the relative importance of this part of the trade should tend to increase. But it is a matter for remark that the bulk of the American exports

[10]In value.

to Japan (nearly two-thirds of them in value) should consist of raw materials (timber, pulp, raw cotton, ore, metal scrap and oil seeds), fuel and food. In 1966 no less than 23 per cent of Japan's imports from the USA were food and tobacco; purchases of wheat and animal feeding-stuffs have grown exceptionally fast. The predominance of primary products among Japan's imports from America is, of course, to some extent the result of the protection given to Japan's manufacturing industries.

Her exports to the USA once consisted mainly of the products of a few small-scale industries (notably raw silk, fish and tea). After World War II silk and tea lost all their importance and the growth in trade during the last decade was set going by an expansion in the American demand for the products of numerous light manufacturing industries, textiles, clothing, pottery, sewing machines and other consumer goods. These industries still send a high proportion of their exports to the American market. This trade has lately been supplemented by rapidly increasing sales of goods produced by the new large-scale industries, such as electrical apparatus, steel, motor cars and engineering goods in great variety. It is difficult to exaggerate the value to Japan of the US market, just as it is necessary to remember, for an understanding of American commercial policy towards her imports from Japan, that the prosperity of certain primary goods producing regions of the USA is bound up with Japan's demand for their products.

America's "special position" in Japan's foreign commerce and in her economic relations cannot be understood solely by reference to the goods exchanged. It has already been shown that, after the Korean War, US expenditure in Japan played an essential part in the rehabilitation of industry. In supplying the knowledge by which Japan was able to narrow the technical gap between herself and the Western world, American firms took the lead and by technical agreements with Japanese firms they infused fresh knowledge into a wide range of industries, old and new. In the early 1960s, when special procurement expenditure declined, the flow of capital, both long-term investment and short-term loans, furnished the resources that were to enable Japan to maintain a rapid rate of growth despite recurrent deficits in her balance of payments. Later the direct and indirect effects of American expenditure in connection with the Vietnam War gave a further stimulus to Japan's export trade; it has been estimated that about 8 per cent of her exports in

1966-7 were attributable to that cause. Furthermore, American firms have co-operated with Japanese firms in developing overseas markets for the latter's products.[11] This co-operation did much to hasten the recovery and expansion of the export trade during the 1950s.

In assessing Japan's attitude to participation in any Pacific trading bloc, weight must also be given to the fact that during the last 20 years the USA has profoundly affected the whole fabric of Japanese life. Japanese institutions were modified by the reforms introduced during the Occupation and, despite the reaction of the so-called "reverse course" period, the impress remains. The Land Reform, which transformed tenant farmers into peasant proprietors, allayed unrest in the countryside and caused at first an improvement in agricultural productivity. The labour laws helped to create a trade union movement well adapted to Japanese circumstances and the Fair Trade Law reinforced the hotly competitive conditions in industry. The "purges" of the old, conservative leaders in government and industry brought the young and enterprising into the seats of power and may have contributed towards the "economic miracle".

The influence of the USA has remained very powerful. For the last 20 years Japan has played a major role in US strategy in the Far East and the Japanese Government was at first compelled, and was later persuaded by self-interest, to accommodate its policy in the commercial as well as the political sphere to American requirements. Even the insistence that Japan should renounce military and naval forces and content herself with a small defence force was acceptable. It accorded with the pacific inclinations of large sections of the population and it permitted the country to concentrate its resources on economic growth instead of dissipating them on armaments.

It is true that the American contribution to Japan's success has not been universally acclaimed. For instance, some businessmen, especially those of Western Japan, have been critical of the limitations imposed under pressure from the Americans upon trade with Communist China. They look back to the time during the late 1930s, when much of China was part of the "yen bloc" and constituted one of Japan's major trading partners. They have persuaded themselves,

[11]Cf. W. S. Hunsberger, *Japan and the United States in World Trade* (Harper and Row, New York, 1964) p. 251.

like the merchants of other nations in earlier times, that China presents immeasurable opportunities for profitable business once the political barriers are down, and their unfortunate experiences since commerce with China was resumed some ten years ago have not changed their minds. So they resent the American influence that excludes them from this El Dorado and they condemn their own Government which is by no means prepared to surrender the solid advantages of the American connection for the fairy gold of the China trade.

The tact of the Japanese Government has also been exercised in smoothing over another difficulty in relations with the USA. Since the war the Americans have been in occupation of the Ryukyus, including Okinawa, which has become one of their chief bases in the Pacific. The occupation has been resented by many Japanese whose national pride is affronted by the presence of the foreigner in this part of their territory. Changes in the strategic situation, however, have lately helped to solve the problem. The development of nuclear weapons by China has reduced the value to the Americans of their advanced bases, and the USA has agreed to restore sovereignty over Okinawa to Japan in 1972, subject to certain strategic safeguards.

The increasing burdens on the USA are at the same time giving rise to a demand that Japan should play a more important role, politically as well as economically, in the Far East. For many years she was content to play a passive part in international affairs. Now the USA is anxious that she should share the burden of safeguarding the "free world", and the Japanese themselves, some with eagerness and others with reluctance, are preparing to pursue a more active policy in the Far East. Japan may be able to take such a step without alarming her neighbours since most of the resentment left by her former aggression, both in the countries occupied by her in World War II and in Australia and New Zealand, has disappeared. With the adoption of a new positive political role, however, she would inevitably lose some of the economic advantages which have accrued to her from the single-hearted pursuit of industrial and commercial success. If she takes up the burden of her own defence and contributes to the support of her allies, she will lose the considerable benefit of concentration on industrial development. Up to recently the ratio of her defence expenditure to the national income has amounted to only 1-$1\frac{1}{2}$ per cent. To raise this substantially may be detrimental to industrial investment and it may add another factor contributory to raising total demand at a time when inflationary forces are already strong. However, she is much better fitted to carry this new burden than she was ten years ago, and in the main she may consider herself fortunate that she was for so long able to leave the task of her defence to others.

2. *South-East Asia*

The South-East Asian countries fall into a clearly defined group with many problems in common. Japan's interest in them is second only to her interest in the USA. These countries in 1966 took 27 per cent of Japan's exports and provided 17 per cent of her imports.[12] It should be observed, however, that in that year (and in 1967) the exports were swollen by demands that arose out of the Vietnam War.[13] Previously there had been a decided tendency for the relative importance of these exports to contract. This applied even more forcibly to imports from that area with the result that Japan's trade with South-East Asia had become unbalanced, with exports far in excess of imports. This unbalanced condition was particularly evident in the case of South Korea, Formosa, South Vietnam, the Ryukyus, Thailand and Burma; the Philippines and Malaya were exceptions. The explanation is easily found. The purchases of these countries from Japan have been financed to a large extent by aid and investment. Some of this has been provided by Japan herself in the form of reparations payments or loans, but most of it has come from the USA. The investment has had a notable effect in some countries, especially South Korea and Formosa, in stimulating economic development and Japan's sales to those countries have benefited accordingly. For instance, her exports to Formosa nearly doubled between 1964 and 1967, and since her commercial treaty with Korea (1965) her exports to that country have grown more than threefold.

[12] For 1967 the proportions were 28 per cent and 15 per cent. South-East Asia in the Japanese trade statistics includes Hong Kong, the Philippines, Malaya, Singapore, Vietnam, Cambodia, Laos, Indonesia, Thailand, Burma, India, Pakistan, Ceylon, Afganistan and, since 1958, South Korea and Formosa, together with several smaller states.

[13] The rise in exports attributable to this cause took place not only in Japan's trade with South Vietnam itself, but also in her trade with other countries, especially South Korea and Thailand, which have themselves provided supplies for the war.

Japan's exports to the area are in sharp contrast to those sent to North America, for they consist mainly of capital goods and chemicals, 79 per cent of the total in 1965 and 66 per cent in 1966. The composition of the exports is indicative of the extent to which they depend on investment and aid; indeed, the exports financed by reparations and long credits have by agreement consisted of capital goods. It may also reflect the increasing tendency of those countries to produce the textiles and consumer goods they need.

The relative weakness of South-East Asian countries as suppliers of the Japanese market is to be explained, as already shown, largely by the successful competition of the advanced countries in primary products. About a fifth of Japan's imports from the region consists of food and three-fifths of raw materials. Much of the benefit of her increased demand for these products has accrued to North America and Oceania, partly through changes in the Japanese diet which have altered the kind of foodstuffs purchased, and partly because the advanced countries are cheaper and more reliable sources of supply. This is true even of such raw materials as cotton and oil seed. It is significant that the countries that have an export surplus to Japan (Malaya and the Philippines) supply her with the two commodities for which her demand has grown especially fast, namely iron ore and timber.

Japan is troubled by the weakness of the countries of South-East Asia as suppliers and by the dependence of much of her export trade to them on aid or temporary factors. She is conscious that her future exports to the area will be closely affected by the rate of economic development of the region. At the same time the industrialisation of some parts of the area, particularly South Korea, Formosa and Hong Kong, is already confronting her with the necessity of making structural adjustments in her industry. It may well be that the export prospects of these countries are more favourable for light industrial goods than for primary products. Because of their low wage costs they are already proving active competitors for such products, not only in the under-developed world but also in the West. Thus trade between them and Japan may presently cease to be complementary and become competitive, at least until she has switched more of her resources to the heavy industries. The same may be true in future of Japan's trade with Communist China which is now competing in light industrial goods in the markets of the world.

3. Canada, Australia and New Zealand

Japan's trade with Canada, which has grown at about the same rate as her trade as a whole, has followed much the same course as that of the USA. But whereas the latter trade is fairly well balanced, Canada has been accustomed to sell to Japan about twice as much as she has bought from her. Most of Japan's purchases have consisted of raw materials (especially ores, timber and pulp) and food (mainly wheat). There is every probability that Canada's importance as a source of supply of these products will grow and the Japanese have invested in a number of mineral projects in order to ensure supplies. Exports to Canada comprise mainly textiles, iron and steel and metal goods. The dominance of the USA in the Canadian market, the preferences enjoyed by British producers and the protection given to Canadian industries explain the comparatively modest performance of Japan's exporters in that market.

Japan's trading relations with Oceania are the reverse of those with South-East Asia, for she buys twice as much from that region as she sells to it. The disparity was even greater before the Commercial Treaty in 1958 reduced some of the barriers to mutual trade. Since then Japan's imports from the region have grown at the same rate as the import trade as a whole while the exports have grown faster. Australia, the most important trading partner in the region, has directly benefited from Japan's industrial expansion, and her exports have responded to the changes in the industrial structure of her customer. When Japan specialised on textiles, Australia sold mainly raw wool to her. This is still the leading export, but Japan now takes in addition great quantities of coal, copper and iron ore as well as wheat and meat. In 1964, Japan became Australia's best customer and took 18 per cent of the total exports. Until recently Japan's exports to Australia consisted mainly of textiles, but their range has been extended and now includes machinery, motor cars and chemicals. The prospects for a very great increase in mutual trade are favourable, for Japan's demand for the materials that Australia can supply is likely to grow very fast. It has been estimated that by the early 1970s, two-fifths of Japan's imports of iron ore and coal are likely to come from this source.

The lack of balance in the trade, however, if it were to continue, might harm these prospects, for Japan is under pressure from countries with which she has a favourable balance to increase her imports from them. The imbalance can be attributed chiefly to the protection afforded to Australian manufacturing industry and to discrimination in favour of the UK. A leading source of the difficulty is that while Australia's exports to Japan are for the most part complementary to Japan's own production, Japan's exports to Australia compete directly with home manufactures. Although Australia now gives Japan most-favoured-nation treatment and has surrendered the right to invoke Article 35 of the General Agreement on Tariffs and Trade (GATT), Japan is still affected by quota restrictions imposed on some classes of her exports and by "voluntary" limitations on others.

New Zealand's trade with Japan was fairly evenly balanced until recently, chiefly because her export specialisation lies in foodstuffs, the import of which Japan strictly controls. Since 1964, however, the balance has moved against Japan because of her increased purchases of meat and wool. Whether the prospects for trade expansion among these countries are realised depends largely on the commercial policies pursued by their governments, a question to be considered later.

3 JAPANESE COMMERCIAL POLICY

1. *Japan's Trade Restrictions*

The weakness of Japan's international financial position obliged her throughout the 1950s to maintain stringent controls over foreign trade and foreign exchange transactions. At that time imports were subject to licensing and all foreign payments were rigidly supervised. A biannual foreign exchange budget was drawn up which covered the allocation of the total exchange available among different uses and the import licences issued to traders were governed by these limits. The controls were accommodated to the various types of international trade agreements, including barter and other bilateral arrangements, to which Japan became a party. They were also associated with devices for encouraging exports. One was the "link system" by which the grants of import licences for particular materials were given on condition that the licensee exported a specified amount of manufactured goods. This was equivalent to an export subsidy since the disparity between the foreign and domestic prices of the goods imported enabled the licensee to make a profit on the transaction thus encouraging him to subsidise the export which was the condition of his obtaining the licence. Exporters were also favoured by being allowed in some circumstances to retain part of the foreign exchange that resulted from their sales and to use it for trade promotion abroad. Firms which were parties to approved arrangements for the import of foreign technology were likewise privileged. Tax discrimination was exercised in favour of the export industries and export bills were discounted at low rates of interest through the Bank of Japan. The Export-Import Bank, an official institution, also provided both long and short term loans at low rates of interest to exporters. On the other hand, imports were discouraged by a stipulation that merchants must deposit cash at the time of their receiving an import licence.

There can be little doubt that these controls placed a powerful instrument in the hands of the authorities for the direction of the economy and it is probable that the Government was able to take risks in pressing forward with rapid economic expansion which could not have been contemplated in their absence. Much of this structure has now been dismantled. During the late 1950s Japan came under strong pressure from her fellow-members of the International Monetary Fund (IMF) and the GATT to liberalise her commerce and her international payments system—and with some reluctance she acquiesced. In 1963 she agreed to abandon exchange controls over current transactions (as required by Article 8 of the IMF) and, after acceding to the demand that she should adopt Article 11 status under the GATT, she began to dismantle her quantitative restrictions on imports and to modify her methods of encouraging exports.

By the end of 1967 the proportion of trade liberalised had risen to about 93 per cent, according to Japan's own calculations. This proportion is no doubt formally correct, but some comment on it is necessary if it is not to mislead. For one thing, an understanding of the significance of this proportion is affected by the fact that in 1959 (the reference year for the calculation) many types of manufactured goods which overseas suppliers could have sold to Japan were not imported at all because of the controls. Such goods included several types of finished consumer goods.

In the second place, most of Japan's imports, as earlier noted, consist of raw materials and fuel which Japan wants to acquire at the lowest possible prices and she has always been ready to admit these without restrictions. She has taken a very different view, however, of food imports which enter into competition with her high-cost farmers. Rice, meat, dairy products and other foodstuffs are known as highly "sensitive" parts of the import trade and these are still subject to quantitative restrictions.[14] In addition, there are a few classes of manufactured goods, including some consumer goods, heavy chemicals, electrical machinery and motor cars and components which have not yet been freed.

The quantitative restrictions on imports and the export subsidies have been replaced to some extent by other kinds of restrictions, or compensation provided for producers damaged by liberalisation. Tariffs have been raised, or tariff schedules manipulated, to protect some of the "sensitive" sectors of the economy. Japanese tariffs, however, are not high by international standards. A large part of

[14]In addition to quota restrictions, fairly high import duties are imposed on foodstuffs. For example, there is 25 per cent *ad valorem* on beef and veal, 20 per cent on wheat, 10 per cent on mutton and lamb and 45 per cent on dairy products. See I. A. McDougall, "The Prospects of the Economic Integration of Japan, Australia and New Zealand", in Kojima (ed.), *op. cit.*, Vol. I, p. 120.

the imports are duty free. Of the goods subject to tariffs about half fall in the 15 to 20 per cent range of *ad valorem* duties, although for a few classes of manufactures the protection is sufficiently high to exclude imports. Some revenue duties, which have recently been raised, fall heavily on high-priced foreign luxury products—for example, Scotch whisky. Nevertheless, it appears that Japan's import duties compare favourably with those of some of her trading partners. For instance, it is estimated that in 1964 the average nominal rate of protection was about 20 per cent for Japanese industry compared with 30 per cent for Australian industry.[15] The duties will, of course, be reduced when the decisions of the Kennedy Round are fully implemented.

Powerful external forces are now being brought to bear on Japan to accelerate the process of liberalisation. At recent conferences held between her representatives and those of the USA, it was urged that she should reduce not only import duties on motor cars but also certain domestic taxes on them, as these were said to discriminate against American imports. Pressure was also exerted with the object of securing the removal of the remaining quantitative restrictions on motor components. Resistance to these demands, it was pointed out by the Americans, would strengthen protectionist sentiment in the USA. Since Japan is now the second greatest producer of motor cars in the world, she can hardly claim that her industry needs protection because of its commercial or technical inferiority—and the Japanese Government shows signs of giving way. This is probably symptomatic of the future trend of policy.

It is very difficult to obtain evidence about the importance of other kinds of restrictions or subsidies that remain. For example, it is known that the Export-Import Bank has been increasing its financial help, by the grant of low-interest loans to producers dealing with foreign markets. It is also contended by exporters to Japan that the sales of Western motor cars have been adversely affected by restrictions imposed on the credit terms allowed by dealers in such cars. There are, however, corresponding measures of discrimination to be found in many other countries.

For many years the Japanese Government has encouraged firms engaged in the export trade to form associations for the purpose of

[15]McDougall, *op. cit.*, p. 118. Cf. Bela Balassa, "Trade Protection in Industrial Countries: An Evaluation", *Journal of Political Economy*, University of Chicago Press, Chicago, December, 1965.

encouraging or regulating the quantity or quality of the export goods. During the middle 1950s the associations set up under the Export-Import Trading Act of 1953 engaged in projects for dumping goods abroad. Some of them raised levies on the sales of their members in the home market in order to provide the means for subsidising exports and recent examples of this practice can be found in the synthetic fibre industry. Of late years, however, the associations have been largely occupied not so much with dumping as with carrying out arrangements for "voluntary" export restrictions (in order to forestall import restrictions by customer-countries). They have also been concerned with the maintenance of export prices. Private cartels, however, have a precarious existence in the fiercely competitive environment of Japanese industry. They are numerous, but loyalty to price maintenance arrangements can seldom be preserved for long. This has been evident in the steel industry.

There can be no doubt that Japan has gone a long way towards the liberalisation of her trade. But it is also true that some serious obstacles still remain. Whether these are greater than those imposed by other nations which have lately paid obeisance to free trade is by no means certain. The Japanese, especially the manufacturers and the government department most concerned with their interests (the Ministry of International Trade and Industry [MITI]), have been somewhat reluctant converts to liberalisation, partly because they are still doubtful about the capacity of some industries to hold their own in conditions of free competition, and partly because of some doubts about the balance of payments. The barriers are not all official and legal. The strong national spirit of the Japanese which causes them to take pride in their own products does not exclude a love of the novel and the exotic and certain foreign products enjoy a considerable prestige among consumers. On the other hand, the highly integrated character of much of Japan's economy may sometimes lead to discrimination against outside suppliers—including overseas suppliers—to the home market. It is, however, easy to exaggerate the extent to which a firm in a particular group—such as Mitsui, Sumitomo or Mitsubishi—is given privileges by the other members. At the level of economic policy, the Government does not wear a seamless robe. The Foreign Office, with its anxiety to improve foreign relations, takes a more liberal view than MITI with its intimate and continuous contacts with the industries to whose interests it is devoted.

Foreigners who have had commercial dealings with Japan are inclined to retain suspicions that ill-defined hindrances to competition continue to exist even when the formal and official barriers have been cast down. Some of these suspicions are no doubt justified, but the obstacles which the foreign competitor encounters often spring out of differences in business conventions or contrasts between the economic environment of the Japanese and that of his own people. The extent to which trade liberalisation opens up opportunities for free competition rests in part on the existence of a community of trade practice. In Western countries there is usually sufficient mutual knowledge of the non-official impediments to the freedom of trade that a would-be competitor is likely to encounter in the various markets to enable him to judge of the progress to freedom actually achieved. But Western firms in general have little understanding of Japanese social and business conventions and where they are ignorant they are suspicious. The Japanese who trade in Western countries find similar difficulties and share similar suspicions, although when abroad they are cautious about expressing them.

There is one type of restriction which both government and industry are exceedingly loth to relax and that is the restriction on foreign investment in Japan, especially on the acquisition of shares in Japanese firms by foreigners. This fear is based chiefly on a suspicion that if freedom were allowed a considerable part of Japanese industry might pass under foreign control. Up to 1960 the acquisition of shares by foreigners in a Japanese firm (without the approval of the Foreign Investment Council) was limited to 8 per cent of the issued shares, or only 5 per cent in the case of such industries as public utilities, banking and mining. Further, the repatriation of foreign capital was then subject to onerous restrictions. The freeing of current exchange transactions from control prepared the way for some mitigation of the restrictions on capital movements. Gradually these controls were also relaxed, especially in connection with joint ventures between Japanese and foreign firms. Yet the validation of investment proposals was readily given only when the foreign firm was introducing new technology and even then it was usually limited to a 49 per cent share in the capital of the joint venture. It was seldom granted at all for consumer goods industries.

Japan has been under strong pressure from other countries to ease these restrictions. This pressure increased when in 1964 Japan joined the Organisation for Economic Co-operation and Development (OECD). In 1967 a major step forward was taken. The Government then adopted the policy of carrying out a progressive liberalisation during the next five years. The cumulative ratio of share ownership by foreign investors in existing Japanese concerns was immediately raised to 20 per cent, except in certain industries, such as banking and public utilities, where it was fixed at 15 per cent. For joint ventures between foreign and Japanese concerns industries were classified into three groups. Where the technical efficiency in Japan was believed to have reached the foreign level, foreigners were to receive automatic approval for their investments up to 100 per cent of the company's capitalisation. For industries considered to fall somewhat below that technical level, the ratio was fixed at 50 per cent, and for a group of "sensitive" industries where, because of technical backwardness, there was a possibility of their falling under foreign control, individual screening remained necessary.

If this rule is followed, an important sector of Japanese industry will still remain closed to foreign enterprise. It is in the still highly restricted group that foreign firms are likely to see their most ample opportunities and where, of course, Japan stands most to gain by the infusion of superior technique and management. One may suppose, however, that the chief concern of the Government in framing this policy is still that of safeguarding Japanese industry against the danger of foreign control and not with stimulating the introduction of improved foreign methods. A recent example may be of interest. In the autumn of 1967, Phillips Petroleum Company of the USA gave up a plan to join in the management of the Tsurusaki Petro-Chemical Company, and to provide 35 per cent of the capital, because of objections from MITI. The grounds for the refusal were that the Japanese petro-chemical industry is still technically inferior to the foreign industry and therefore needs protection against foreign attempts to take it over. The fact that the infusion of foreign management and knowledge might be presumed to improve the technical level of the Japanese undertaking was not of over-riding importance.

The new policy, however, marks an important stage in progress towards ultimate liberalisation. Further concessions to foreign investors were made at the beginning of 1969 and it is supposed that the process of liberalisation will be formally completed in the early 1970s. But the Japanese industries themselves are still able to fight a powerful rearguard action if they feel so inclined. Industries which feel the greatest anxiety about foreign control can find their own means to frustrate it by making regulations, for instance, to stabilise share ownership or by restricting the part that foreign directors can play in management. Thus, in February, 1968, the Toyota Motor Company barred foreign directors from participating in its management and in this policy it was supported by MITI.

2. *Trade Discrimination against Japan*

The restrictions are not all on one side, for Japan has long suffered from discrimination by other nations. This discrimination can be traced back to the 1930s when Japan's textiles and miscellaneous consumption goods were ousting Western products from many markets. The discrimination was carried over to the post-war period. Even after Japan was admitted to full membership of the GATT in 1955, fourteen countries still invoked Article 35 which enabled them to withhold from her some of the privileges of membership. The discrimination practised by these nations, among which were some important customers, usually took the form of quota restrictions. Even countries which did not invoke Article 35 often protested with effect at any sudden growth of imports from Japan. Sometimes they brought pressure on the Japanese Government to limit sales of certain classes of goods by means of "voluntary" export quotas. For instance, from 1956 exports of cotton fabrics to the USA were controlled by this type of restriction and later other types of goods were covered in the same way. The "voluntary" export quotas were administered by MITI in conjunction with the Japanese Cotton Textiles Export Association. In 1961-2, a multilateral agreement was negotiated under the auspices of the GATT. This settled quotas for various textile exporting countries and a bilateral agreement between Japan and the USA gave effect to the policy so far as Japan was concerned. Efforts to extend this arrangement, however, have lately broken down. In May, 1969, the Japanese refused to join in further multilateral negotiations on textile exports which were expected to lead to the extension of the "voluntary" quotas on her textile exports to the USA, and in June, 1970, a further attempt to reach agreement on the quotas again failed.

Similar types of quota were applied to a few exports of manufactures to the UK even after the Trade Agreement of 1963 between the two countries and pressure was put on Japan to maintain "voluntary" restrictions on certain classes of goods which were not covered by the formal quotas. In the same way pressure exerted by the US Administration at the beginning of 1968 persuaded Japan to agree to keep down her steel exports to the USA to 4.4 million tons for that year. In general, however, one may conclude that the importance of this discrimination has much diminished during the last few years, although MITI claims that, according to the results of a 1969 survey of theirs, Japan suffers from American non-tariff barriers to a greater extent than the USA suffers from Japanese non-tariff barriers.

3. *Organisation of Foreign Trade*

It has already been suggested that Japanese methods of doing business and the institutional structure of the economy may create difficulties for foreign competitors in the Japanese home market, even if fiscal and legal barriers are lowered. The concentration of a high proportion of industrial production, commerce and finance in the hands of a relatively small number of great business houses each with widely ramifying interests is an example of this type of obstacle. It was observed earlier that the extent to which firms discriminate in favour of others in the same group is often exaggerated by outsiders and it certainly differs among the several groups. But foreign firms intent upon doing business in Japan are unwise to ignore the integrated character of much of Japan's economy. The predominance of a few great merchant houses in both home and overseas trade and the association of these houses with large industrial groups have certainly affected the character of competition between Japanese and foreign business. So these merchant firms deserve a brief discussion.

The concentration of a high proportion of overseas trade in the hands of a very small number of merchants has long been characteristic of Japanese commerce. In recent years over two-thirds of the export trade and four-fifths of the import trade have been conducted by about 40 houses, of which four are outstanding, namely Mitsubishi Shoji, Mitsui Bussan, Marubeni-Iida and C. Itoh. The first two of these are constituents of what are known as the old *Zaibatsu* (literally, money groups).

The origin of Japan's mercantile organisation is not far to seek. In the early days of the country's modernisation the Japanese naturally resented the dominant part played by foreign merchants in the conduct of overseas trade and they were determined to establish their own system as soon as they had gained sufficient experience. The early manufacturers of export goods, moreover, for the most part lacked the knowledge and resources necessary for dealing in foreign markets in competition with the well-established Western houses. So the leading business concerns, which the government had adopted as their agents for the execution of its economic policy, set up trading companies to handle both the goods produced in their own establishments and also the products of others. Through their links with the banks belonging to the same groups the trading companies had access to ample financial resources and they were associated also with firms providing ancillary services to traders. Two of these companies, Mitsui Bussan and Mitsubishi Shoji, became what they have since remained, the greatest trading firms in Japan. Other merchant houses were set up to serve the cotton textile industry, the first branch of Japanese manufacture to develop large-scale methods. These firms were engaged both in the importing of the raw cotton and the exporting of the yarn and piece goods. After World War II some of the leading textile merchants, intent upon adjusting themselves to the changes in industrial production, merged with dealers in metal and engineering goods and turned themselves into highly diversified export and import merchants.

The predominance of the great merchants was strengthened during the period in which Japan's foreign trade was subject to stringent and complicated controls, since firms without special experience found these perplexing. Today these merchant houses remain linked financially and personally with many of the manufacturing firms whose goods they handle and frequently take part in joint ventures overseas in conjunction with Japanese manufacturing and mining companies and with foreign undertakings. In the capital goods industries, where specialised technical knowledge is needed for marketing, the manufacturers themselves are now participating to a greater extent than formerly in the handling of foreign sales. Yet in general they still prefer to associate themselves with one of the great merchant houses which usually employ technical staffs well-equipped for this type of business. A recent example is the formation of a sales company in Rotterdam by two machine tool manufacturers (Hitachi Machinery and Toyoda Machine Works) and a trading firm (Toyo Menka, in pre-war times a cotton importer and exporter) for the purpose of promoting the sales of machine tools in Europe.

The great trading companies operate a network of branch offices in the chief commercial centres of the world. Since they are on intimate terms with the relevant departments of MITI they serve as effective instruments of trade policy. They have, in addition, another important role. As they are concerned with the domestic as well as with the overseas market, foreign exporters to Japan usually find it advantageous to appoint them as agents or to become associated with them in joint selling ventures.

4 REGIONAL ECONOMIC CO-OPERATION

After World War II, Japan had to abandon her ambitious plans for expansion in Asia and the pursuit of an independent foreign policy was denied to her. The small defence force which was allowed to her by the Peace Treaty of 1951 left her without any capacity to intervene in the strategic arrangements of the area and the concentration of her resources on industrial growth seemed to be entirely congenial to the nation's mood. Even enterprise of a purely commercial character outside her own shores was for a time limited partly by the suspicions with which she was regarded by other Pacific countries and partly by her need for capital for her own development. Until her industries had been re-equipped and modernised she had few resources to spare for foreign investment. The precarious condition of her balance of payments during most of the post-war period meant that she could not contemplate doing much to assist in the development of the poorer countries; indeed, she considered that she herself fell into that category.

Yet she could never consider isolating herself from her neighbours in Asia. Her close dependence on the USA might discourage any independent initiative on her part overseas and the developed countries of the world might provide far more ample opportunities for her exporters than the under-developed countries of South-East Asia. Nevertheless, her national interests were bound up with the stability and prosperity of that region. Disorder and deepening poverty there, which might encourage the spread of Communism, would threaten her security, while the rapid economic growth of the South-East Asian countries would present her with fresh markets. So, gradually, as her economy recovered, she began to take tentative steps towards resuming the role in the world, especially in the Pacific area, that was merited by her economic power.

At first she had to proceed cautiously. The countries of East and South-East Asia which she had ravaged during the war were still hostile and, in renewing relations with her, they were at first simply concerned with exacting adequate reparations. Australia and New Zealand were still suspicious and her former colonies, especially South Korea, retained bitter memories of the past. By 1960, however, the reparations problem had been solved by a series of agreements with South-East Asian countries, and the rise of Japan as a leading customer for Australian and New Zealand raw materials and foodstuffs had dispelled the former resentment. Friendship with South Korea took longer to establish, but in 1965 a series of negotiations led to a resumption of diplomatic relations and created large opportunities for commercial intercourse. Trade with Communist China was negligible for fifteen years after the war, but the signing of the Liou-Takasaki Agreement in 1962, and the expressed willingness of China to do business through a number of so-called "friendly" firms, led to a substantial growth of business between the countries.[16] As time has gone on Japan has become increasingly active in promoting economic co-operation within the Pacific area and some of the means employed deserve a brief description.

Her participation in the development of South-East Asian countries began, as already indicated, with the reparations agreements between herself and her war-time victims. By 1963, when a supplementary agreement with Burma was made, the total amount of reparations specified reached $1,220m. (including an Indonesian trade debt which had been written off). Over half this sum has now been paid, mainly by the delivery of goods. Japan has also taken part in international activities for encouraging the development of the area. After 1954, when she participated in the Colombo Plan as a donor country, she provided technical assistance to several countries, and on becoming a member of the United Nations in 1956 she took part in the development projects of the various special agencies. After she was admitted to full membership of the GATT in 1955, and, later, to the OECD, she co-operated in measures to liberalise trade. She has been an active member of the United Nations Economic Commission for Asia and the Far East, and in 1967 she acted as the host country for the 23rd session. In 1965 she responded to the American appeal for co-operation in providing increased

[16]The Liou-Takasaki Agreement, which was in force for five years, provided for the exchange of Japanese steel, chemicals and other manufactures in return for raw materials of equivalent value at prices negotiated annually by the representatives of the Peking and Tokyo governments. The "friendly" firms were those with permission from the Chinese authorities to deal with the Chinese trade corporations. These firms have recently accounted for about three-quarters of the total trade. The Agreement was re-negotiated in March, 1968, and the trade was renamed "Memorandum Trade". The new Agreement is re-negotiated annually and the specified value of the trade has been reduced.

economic aid to South-East Asia and she took a leading part in the establishment of the Asian Development Bank, which is designed to finance enterprise in that region; the first president was Mr. Takeshi Watanabe.

Japan herself has taken the initiative in calling a number of conferences to consider programmes of economic aid. In August, 1967, a ministerial conference between herself and South Korea was held to assess Korea's requirements in foreign aid to enable her to carry out a five-year development plan. In this connection Japan agreed to provide credits for financing imports into Korea of machinery and ships. She made similar credits available for Formosa. A year earlier she had set going informal discussions on economic development with eight South-East Asian countries and in the spring of 1968 a conference of these countries (the third) was held at Singapore to examine the problems of the area. It considered such matters as the deployment of the Agricultural Development Fund (set up under the Asian Development Bank), the establishment of regional fishery development centres and regional transport problems. Proposals were made for starting multinational factories in particular countries in cases where the market in any single country within the area was too small to give access to economies of scale.

Japan has encouraged these tentative co-operative efforts, but so far she has been cautious about committing herself to actual projects that would require her to increase her aid substantially. The importance of the last conference, as of its predecessors, is to be found not in any positive achievement in economic development, but in the fact that this large group of countries now accepts the proposition that economic co-operation among them is desirable and feasible. The intention is to construct an institutional framework through which Japan, and other advanced countries, can provide the means for economic growth throughout the region.

On the other side of the Pacific a joint Japan-United States Committee on Trade and Economic Affairs has held periodical meetings for several years past. At the 1967 meeting the Committee dealt particularly with the contributions of the two countries to the Agricultural Development Fund administered by the Asian Development Bank. This meeting also brought out some of the difficulties in economic co-operation that have still to be overcome. The Japanese were given evidence of the strength of the protectionist lobby in the USA and of the extent to which it is exerting pressure on the US Administration to curb Japanese imports. At the same time, the American participants insisted on the necessity for Japan's liberalising her regulations about foreign participation in Japanese industry.

During a meeting in May, 1969, these questions were again discussed. The Americans, as previously, insisted that Japan should relax her restrictions on trade and investment without delay and, at the same time, they proposed that she should establish new "voluntary" quotas (as mentioned earlier) on her textile exports to the USA. The Japanese rejected both proposals. Thus little progress was made, and negotiations conducted in June, 1970, were equally unsuccessful. At the 1969 meeting the danger that Japan's refusal to "liberalise" would expose her trade to attack from the American protectionists was again emphasised. A recent American writer on the subject considers that "protectionist pressures offer another threat that is greater in 1969 than in 1961" and he lists the numerous proposals then before Congress for the imposition of quotas on imports from Japan.[17] It is significant that MITI, in a White Paper published in August, 1969, acknowledged that the rapid growth of Japan's export trade and the strength of her balance of payments are arguments in favour of liberalisation and accepted the principle that a more rapid advance towards freer trade was desirable.

The co-operative efforts have not been limited to governments. Business leaders of the Pacific countries have realised the importance of making personal contacts with each other, especially when they are confronted with differences in convention and outlook between men of diverse civilisations. Up to recently the business relations of the Australians were mainly with their counterparts in other English-speaking countries, while the Japanese had little first-hand acquaintance with the requirements of the Australian market for manufactures. As Japan begun to take Britain's place as the chief customer for Australian exports, and also made inroads into the markets for finished goods, the necessity for closer personal contacts among the participants in the trade asserted itself. Hence there was set up in 1963 the Japan-Australia Business Co-operation Committee.

[17]Sperry Lea, "The Future Shape of US Trade Policy: Multilateral or Free Trade Approaches", in Kojima (ed.), *Pacific Trade and Development*, Vol. II (Japan Economic Research Centre, Tokyo, April, 1969), pp. 20 and 21.

Similar bodies have been founded to foster co-operation among businessmen in other countries in the region. In 1967 the business-men of five Pacific countries (the USA, Canada, Australia, New Zealand and Japan) established the Pacific Basin Economic Co-operation Committee. At the first meeting in May, 1968, in Sydney, the representatives of various countries discussed the effects on all of them of sterling devaluation and of the measures taken to defend the dollar. They also discussed ways of collaborating in the promotion of private investment in South-East Asia and subse-quently formed the Private Investment Corporation for Asia.

The merchants and manufacturers of Asian countries also have interested themselves in joint planning schemes. For example, a conference of Asian Chambers of Commerce developed considerable interest in the proposal to set up the private investment company for Asia mentioned above. The object of the company has been described as the enlistment of private investors and technical consultants from all over the world in the promotion of industrial ventures in Asia. It was expected that the company would work in close association with the Asian Development Bank. All these conferences and schemes indicate the strong interest in the possibili-ties of co-operation among South-East Asian countries, at any rate for the purpose of enlisting financial help from abroad. They look particularly to Japan.

The amount of the aid so far given has fallen short of what international opinion considers that Japan should reasonably make available. That is to say, during the last few years it has been much lower than the 1 per cent of the national income which is now regarded as a creditable proportion. In 1965 it amounted to only 0.71 per cent; in 1966, to 0.69 per cent. In 1967 it rose to 0.73 per cent, chiefly through a large increase in government aid. In that year, when 70 per cent of the total of $669m. went to Asian countries, the distribution was as follows·

Government Aid:	$ *400m.*
Bilateral	$ 137m.
Loans	$ 219m.
Subscriptions to International Bodies	$ 44m.
Private Investment:	$ *269m.*
Direct Investment	$ 109m.
Export Credits	$ 160m.

Most of the government credits have been provided through the official Export-Import Bank and the terms have been distinctly more onerous than those recommended by the OECD for loans to under-developed countries. For instance, the loans made a few years ago to India and Pakistan carried a rate of interest of 5.7 per cent and were repayable in 18 years. More recently the loans to South Korea and Formosa carried a rate of 3.5 per cent repayable in 20 years. These terms were regarded as exceptionally favourable as judged by the previous practice of the Export-Import Bank; even the Overseas Economic Co-operation Fund, recently set up by the Japanese government to make "soft" loans, prescribed a minimum of 3.5 per cent. It will be recalled that the recommendations of the OECD for loans to under-developed countries were for a rate of 3 per cent and for a term of 25 years.

The Japanese Government has now accepted in principle the obligation to raise the proportion of its aid to 1 per cent of the GNP, but practice is likely to lag behind, for Japan is not easily persuaded to dissipate her resources in ventures which do not obviously promote her interests. There has been some hard bargaining between her representatives and potential beneficiaries. For instance, in the spring of 1968 she resisted strong pressure from Indonesia that she should increase her aid beyond the amount of $60m. already promised for that year. However, it seems likely that she will be compelled to show more generosity simply in order to meet the competition of Western countries in the South-East Asian markets for capital goods. Her political interests will probably push her in the same direction.

This is only one example of how Japan's rapid economic progress and her ambitions for the future have given rise to problems which cannot be solved simply by the tireless pursuit of an inward-looking and self-regarding policy. The arguments in favour of international economic co-operation have consequently become increasingly persuasive for Japan, for, in the absence of such co-operation, relations with many of her trading partners might become less harmonious. Her future relations with the USA, for instance, are menaced by the importunity of the American manufacturers in demanding that their government shall increase the restrictions on competing Japanese imports. The Japanese have long been aware that they must avoid actions likely to strengthen the arguments of the American protectionists, and they have every inducement to welcome schemes of international co-operation which might have the effect of reducing the pressures. The trade balance with most of the South-East Asian countries is in Japan's favour and is likely to remain so for reasons already discussed. Japan has fears that these countries may discriminate against her goods or that she may be left with an excessively heavy burden of financing—by aid or long credits—the imports which they would otherwise lack the means to purchase. International co-operation may help in the solution of this problem by enlisting the support of other countries. In her Australian trade Japan meets with the opposite difficulty. Although she has become the chief market for some of Australia's chief exports, Australia is reluctant to match these sales by purchases of Japanese manufactures. If Japan were compelled by the pressure of the countries with which she has an export surplus to divert her purchases of materials and food from the cheapest sources of supply. this would be likely to raise her costs. Trade with New Zealand presents a different problem. Its expansion is mainly handicapped by Japan's own policy of agricultural protection. While some of the obstacles to increased trade may be overcome, in part at any rate, by bilateral agreements or bargains limited in scope, it seems that a complete solution can be reached only by whole-hearted economic co-operation among all the countries concerned.

Another argument which may help to overcome resistance to such co-operation is that her own interests, as well as pressure from her trading partners, will probably oblige her to incur much heavier expenditure than in the past of a kind that does not yield quick returns. One of the reasons for her rapid growth during the 1950s and early 1960s was that an exceptionally high proportion of her investment was directed into undertakings which yielded quick returns. If she now has to raise substantially her expenditure on defence and aid, some part of the former advantage would be lost to her and the additional burdens might serve to moderate her rate of economic growth. Moreover, if the additional aid is not to be wasted, Japan must be prepared to accept products from the developing industries of the countries she assists. This will compel her to make structural adjustments in her own industry. She is, of course, much better equipped to cope with these strains than she was a decade ago, but she has every inducement to seek to share her burdens with others by forms of mutually beneficial economic co-operation.

5 JAPANESE PROPOSALS FOR A PACIFIC FREE TRADE AREA

The measures of economic co-operation discussed in the previous chapter do not carry the countries concerned very far on the road to economic integration. But they indicate the presence of a trend which, if it persists, might be expected ultimately to lead to a Pacific trading community. The creation of such a community, which was first tentatively suggested by President Kennedy, has now entered the arena of academic and political debate. In Japan it has enlisted serious support from several quarters. This support is none the less real because the presiding motives of its chief protagonists differ widely. The realisation that there are common interests among the Pacific countries which such a grouping might promote, and common dangers which it might help to avoid, gives the proposal its plausibility. At the same time events in the outside world have provided a sharp stimulus to Japanese thinking on the subject. Thus the establishment of the European Economic Community (EEC) and the European Free Trade Association (EFTA) and the effects of these bodies on the trading activities of their members, and on those of other countries, have induced Japan to speculate about the contribution that a similar grouping of Pacific countries might make to her future prosperity.

Trends in international trade within the area have also been persuasive. The steep growth of intra-regional trade in the Pacific basin during recent years has been accompanied by the diversion of the commercial interest of some countries, notably Australia, from their European to their Pacific trading partners. This shift of interest has prompted the idea that by deliberate organisation the mutual benefits of association might be increased. Yet, although the course of Japan's trade over the last decade has drawn her closer than before to the developed countries of the Pacific, she cannot afford to be negligent of the fortunes of the under-developed countries of East and South-East Asia. Her interest in forging closer links with the USA is not based solely on the outstanding importance of that country as a market and source of supply. It is essential to her well-being that the USA shall retain her concern with the Far East and that other advanced countries shall also assume responsibilities in that region. This is because the contribution that she herself can make to the security and development of Asia is still, in her view, narrowly limited.

A closer association of the advanced countries of the Pacific might, on the one hand, help to mobilise forces against the spread of Communism and, on the other hand, by providing investment and technical aid to the region might encourage stable government and economic progress with great benefit to the Japanese economy. The political and economic aspects of the problem are clearly closely related. Those whose preoccupation is primarily with the likely effects of a Pacific free trade area (PAFTA) on Japan's foreign trade and national income are aware that the economic objectives cannot be isolated from politics, while those to whom the attractions of the proposal are to be found in its contribution to the security of the area understand that international economic co-operation is essential to the realisation of their political purposes.

It is useful to examine the views of Professor Kiyoshi Kojima, of Hitotsubashi University, Tokyo, and of Mr. Takao Miki, the former Minister of Foreign Affairs, as representative of two schools of protagonists for a close association of the Pacific countries. They approach the question from different points of view and are moved by different arguments. But they seem to reach the same general practical conclusions. Professor Kojima's views have been set out in several articles, notably "A Pacific Economic Community and Asian Developing Countries" in the *Hitotsubashi Journal of Economics* for June, 1966, and "Japan's Interest in the Pacific Trade Expansion" in *Pacific Trade and Development* published by the Japan Economic Research Centre in February, 1968. Mr. Miki's opinions have been presented in speeches delivered at the Conference for the Development of South-East Asia, held at Manila in April, 1967, and at a monthly meeting of the Keizai Doyukai (Committee for Economic Development) on the subject of "Asia-Pacific Policy and Japan's Economic Co-operation".

1. *Professor Kojima's Proposals*

Professor Kojima's thesis is, broadly, that although trade among the five developed Pacific countries—the USA, Canada, Australia, New Zealand and Japan—has been growing rapidly, it has not grown as fast as intra-European trade since the formation of the

EEC and that, since the Pacific countries have at least as great a potential for economic development as Europe, close co-operation among them should be sought in order to realise that potential. If this were achieved and a PAFTA arrangement established, then the group of developed countries could (and should) associate the under-developed countries of the Pacific in the increased prosperity that mutual free trade would confer on them by according to the latter aid, investment and trading privileges. These benefits each country in isolation might be reluctant to grant on the scale required either because of its own lack of resources, or because it could not face alone the structural consequences for its own economy of the industrial development of those countries.

Professor Kojima has not neglected the alternatives to PAFTA. He has acknowledged, for instance, that the best choice for Japan would be freedom of trade with all countries of the world. This choice is dictated by her dual pattern of trade with developed and developing countries, by her own industrial capacity and by her geographical situation. But a further global tariff reduction (a second Kennedy Round) hardly seems practicable for many years to come and in any case it would be likely to stop far short of completely free trade. Yet complete freedom of trade within the group of highly developed countries would have a much more potent effect on expanding their trade than the kind of qualified freedom likely to be achieved by a global tariff reduction. Professor Kojima is firmly of the opinion that Japan cannot afford to be isolated commercially in a world which, despite the Kennedy Round, seems to be moving in the direction of trade blocs. In the circumstances likely to confront her, membership of a free trade area among the five advanced countries of the Pacific, with the under-developed countries of South-East Asia and South America associated in some way, would be the most prudent policy for her to adopt. If EFTA (and the EEC) were brought in, so much the better.

In his various articles Professor Kojima analyses the trade of the Pacific countries and speculates about the effects on each of them of the establishment of a free trade area. He shows that intra-regional trade among the Five in recent years has grown faster than their trade with the outside world and that this trend is likely to continue. Japan's trade in particular is concentrated on the group. The ratio of her regional trade (with the other four Pacific developed countries) to her total trade has risen from 29 per cent in 1958 to

37 per cent in 1965 and 38 per cent in 1967. Professor Kojima attempts to measure the likely effects of the elimination of tariffs among the five countries and he concludes that Japan would be the chief beneficiary of the policy. While the intra-area trade as a whole would grow by 28 per cent, Japan's exports to the other four members would rise by 56 per cent and her imports from them by 14.7 per cent. It follows that her balance of payments would be improved at the expense of certain of the other members. This result would occur chiefly because Japan's exports are more heavily concentrated on manufactures than are those of the other countries and, also, because the elasticity of demand is higher for manufactures than for primary goods.

There are clearly formidable obstacles to the realisation of this proposal and of these Professor Kojima is well aware. The uneven distribution of the benefits of PAFTA would almost certainly bring criticisms and objections from Japan's trading partners. This would be particularly so where free trade increased the competitive strength of Japanese exports in certain markets without providing sufficient compensating advantages to the exporters of the receiving countries. Furthermore, the existence of a free trade area among the five rich countries would probably damage the economies of the under-developed countries of Asia and South America by diverting trade from them. This is one of the reasons why it would be necessary to associate the poorer countries of the region with PAFTA so as to offset this deleterious effect. If the poorer countries were given preferences in the markets of the Five for their raw material, food and light manufactured exports, this in itself would promote their growth. It would also be necessary, however, for the Five to provide them with capital and technical assistance. Moreover, since this policy would require all the Pacific countries to make considerable adjustments in their economic structure, concerted planning among them would be desirable for the purpose of bringing this about smoothly. Even if joint plans were agreed by governments, it is very probable that there would be much resistance from the interests adversely affected. Some of Japan's light industries might lose their grip on (say) the North American market for manufactured consumer goods and even their predominance in the home market might be threatened as competitive industries developed in South-East Asian countries. Her farmers, also, would resent the opening of the ports to Australian and New Zealand foodstuffs, while the manufacturing industries of the USA, Canada, Australia and New Zealand would be affronted by more vigorous competition from Japan and other Asian countries. The American and Canadian manufacturers of motor cars and steel, as well as of light consumer goods, would almost certainly resist bitterly the dismantling of all barriers against Japanese imports.

Professor Kojima's review of these obstacles leads him to the opinion that, although PAFTA would result in a large expansion of intra-area trade, the distribution of gains between the several countries would be so unequal that agreement could scarcely be reached. Before its establishment, therefore, "concerted action of the PAFTA countries to promote export-oriented industrialisation of Canada, Australia and New Zealand would be needed".[18] This is a somewhat cryptic utterance, since if PAFTA is to have a massive effect on the incomes of its members, they must presumably be prepared to specialise, and if policy is to be directed towards off-setting the influences of trade liberalisation on the structure of the several economies, the benefits would be lost.

The attitude of the USA to the proposal is obviously of crucial importance to Japan. Most of the advantages to be derived by her from PAFTA would depend on the presence of the USA in the organisation. Without her, Japan's interest would be tepid, not only because she is the predominant trading partner, but also because unless America were associated with the ambitious development projects for South-East Asia, these could not be carried through. In fact, the whole argument emphasises the point that one of the chief motives behind the proposal is that of ensuring the continued American interest in the Far East. Moreover, the creation of PAFTA, or even a definite move in that direction, would be likely to check certain developments in American commercial policy that threaten Japan's trade prospects. Reference has already been made to the activity of the protectionist lobby in connection with Japanese imports and it has been observed that the threat from this quarter has stimulated the Japanese Government to accelerate the liberalisation both of trade and capital investment. Again, the USA has shown interest in the proposal to assist the under-developed countries by giving their exports tariff preferences in the American market. This kind of discrimination might seriously damage

[18]Kojima, "Japan's Interest in Pacific Trade Expansion", in Kojima (ed.), *op. cit.*, p. 166.

Japanese exporters of light industrial goods. If, however, the policy were introduced as part of a general reduction in trade barriers over a wide area, its adverse effects on Japan would be more than offset by the benefits that would accrue to her.

Nevertheless, the difficulties confronting any attempt to set up a fully-fledged PAFTA in the near future are so formidable that Professor Kojima thinks that the scheme must be regarded as premature. It remains, however, a desirable ultimate objective, a rational solution for Japan's future economic problems. In the meantime, steps can be taken to encourage closer co-operation among the Pacific countries. These steps are listed as:

1. An increase in the flow of financial resources from the USA to the under-developed countries, especially those bordering the Pacific;
2. The encouragement of "horizontal" trade among the five advanced countries of the Pacific in heavy manufactures and chemicals (in which Japan's future as a manufacturing country is mainly to be found), and the expansion of production and trade in raw materials and intermediate goods in the region as a whole;
3. The readjustment of production and trade in agricultural commodities among the five Pacific countries with the object of increasing the exports of the Asian and Latin-American under-developed countries;
4. The readjustment of production and of trade in light manufactures in order to provide greater access for the Asian and Latin-American under-developed countries to the markets of the advanced countries.

It is suggested also that the Five should accept a Code of Good Conduct in trade policy which would mean in effect the surrender of the right of individual countries to raise tariffs or to impose other forms of restrictions. This would be supplemented by a Code of Overseas Investment which would provide for the flow of American capital to the under-developed countries through joint ventures between American and Asian nationals, and finally the setting up of a body similar to the OECD for the Pacific together with a Pacific Bank for Investment.

Professor Kojima developed his proposals further in a paper entitled "Asian Developing Countries and PAFTA: Development, Aid and Trade Preferences" in the second volume of *Pacific Trade and Development* published in April, 1969, by the Japan Economic Research Centre. In his view, the failure of the second United Nations Conference on Trade and Development, held at New Delhi in 1968, indicates that the prospects for any immediate advance towards a global solution of the trade problem is bleak. He argues that this strengthens the case for a regional solution, even if it is considered as a step towards a global solution. In his paper he stresses the importance of structural economic adjustments within the several countries of the Asian-Pacific region. These adjustments, he considers, are essential concomitants of policies for liberalisation and development. "Structural adjustment in developed countries is an essential element if new development policies are to be successful," Professor Kojima writes. "Structural adjustment is also a key factor in the liberalisation of trade."

2. *Mr. Miki's Policy*

While Professor Kojima stresses the economic benefits to be derived from closer co-operation among the Pacific countries, Mr. Miki, as a leader in the Diet, regards the question from its political aspect. His primary aim is not the establishment of a Pacific free trade area and the economic advantages that this would confer on Japan, but rather the containment of the Communist advance into South-East Asia and the strengthening of Far Eastern security. He considers how Japan can best fulfil this task. She is fitted by her geographical position and her economic achievements to act as a bridge between the advanced countries of the Pacific and Asia, but she is not at present capable of playing any significant role in regional politics or strategy. On the other hand, the growth of her industrial power has given her the opportunity of participating in the economic development of the region and in this way of taking a share in preserving its stability. At present Asia, especially South-East Asia, comes off badly in the allocation of aid. The amount of aid per capita works out at $4.2 for Latin America, $6.2 for Africa and only $2.55 for South-East Asia.[19] Japan's international financial position is still too weak to enable her to make more than a modest contribution to the increased aid that these countries require, especially as heavy domestic investment is needed for the re-equipment of her own small-scale industry and agriculture, and also to improve the backward sectors of her infra-structure. Mr. Miki thinks that, since

[19]Figures for 1964.

Japan's contribution is likely to remain inadequate, it must be for others to provide the bulk of the aid.

It would obviously be greatly to the advantage of Japan if American, Canadian and Australian resources could be enlisted in a common task. The co-operation of these countries could most easily be obtained if they were associated in a trading bloc. PAFTA is thus regarded by Mr. Miki as a means to a political end. He does not, however, consider that the grouping need necessarily be exclusive to countries bordering on the Pacific. He recognises that European countries, especially the UK, have interests in South-East Asia and he would encourage them to maintain their presence. Whatever the membership might be, however, Mr. Miki, like Professor Kojima, regards the Pacific as the focus of the policy. In his scheme also, the USA plays a key role. In strategic terms he is worried lest, with the termination of the Vietnam War and the disillusionment with Asian ventures that is sweeping over that country, there might be a tendency for the USA to withdraw from the area and to concentrate her attention on Europe. Every effort must be made, therefore, in Japan's interest, to encourage the USA to stay. Since this is in the interests of Australia and New Zealand also, support for the scheme can reasonably be expected from them.

Mr. Miki does not propose the setting up of any formal organisation at present to bring his ideas to fruition. At this stage he prefers to rely on informal methods and conversations which he has indeed initiated. He is in favour of the international conferences among businessmen, to which reference has already been made, and the new Private Investment Corporation for Asia, founded to assist the development of Asian countries, benefited from his support. From joint projects for aid and investment it might be possible to move gradually towards PAFTA, and in this way the forces behind the security of Asian countries might be continuously strengthened. Both Mr. Miki and Professor Kojima are impressed by the argument that the increased incomes which the advanced Pacific countries would gain through the operation of PAFTA would provide them with additional resources which they could share with Asia.

3. *Australia and PAFTA Proposals*

It has been emphasised that American participation in economic integration, whatever form it may take, is a condition of Japan's own willingness to move in that direction. The US attitude to the proposals just discussed is, therefore, of crucial importance and about this it is difficult to make confident assertions. It may be thought that the USA would be more likely to welcome a trading community focussed on the Atlantic, with members also drawn from the developed countries of the Pacific, than to join a Pacific community that excluded Europe. Indeed, the Japanese politicians suspect that this may be so and fear any tendency for America to lose her interest in the Far East. The US attitude must be left to other writers and cannot be discussed further here.[20] It is, however, necessary to examine the question of the participation of Australia and New Zealand. This is of particular interest to the UK because of the effects on British trade and the British connection.

Several factors have lately converged to enlist support in Australia and New Zealand for proposals to strengthen economic co-operation among the Pacific countries. The retreat of British power from South-East Asia and the replacement of Britain by the USA as the main protector of Australia's and New Zealand's security are among the most powerful political influences. The appearance of Japan as the largest customer for Australia's exports[21] and of the USA as the largest source of her imports are economic factors which have diverted attention from Europe to the Pacific. The efforts of Britain to join the EEC have also convinced both Australians and New Zealanders that the preferences they enjoy in serving the British market are in jeopardy and that they must seek their economic future among the tribes of the rising, not of the setting, sun (*Shayozoku*).[22]

Australian prospects in the Japanese market are clearly very favourable. Japan has to ensure the continuity of raw-material supplies for her heavy industries and Australia's mineral resources are readily available to her. It has been noted that by the early 1970s she expects to obtain two-fifths of her imports of coal and ore from that country. Indeed, Australia's export of these products will be geared to Japan's rate of growth. New Zealand, like Australia, has found a valuable market in Japan for her wool, timber products

[20]See Lionel Gelber, "World Politics and Trade Strategy", in Johnson (ed.), *op. cit.*, and also Robertson, *op. cit.*

[21]Between 1950 and 1967, Japan's share of Australia's exports rose from 4 per cent to 19 per cent and her share of Australia's imports from 1 per cent to 10 per cent.

[22]"The tribe of the setting sun" was a term originally used by a Japanese writer in discussing the decline of certain social and economic groups in his own country.

and foodstuffs and with the large growth in Japanese imports of meat (and probably dairy products) that is expected to occur during the next seven or eight years, her exporters have turned their attention increasingly to that market.

At first sight is seems that Japan and Oceania possess complementary economies and that among them the traditional vertical pattern of trade has maintained its importance at a time when, in the world as a whole, the horizontal pattern is becoming more usual. This has led to speculation about the possibilities of some kind of economic integration among Japan, Australia and New Zealand. At present a spontaneous further growth of mutual trade is impeded by various kinds of protective measures in all three countries.[23] The Commonwealth preference system means that the rates of duty imposed on British exports to Australia are on an average about 14 per cent lower than the most-favoured-nation rates of duty; the discrimination is particularly great for textiles and machinery. There can be little doubt that if the three countries were part of a free trade area, trade among them would expand even faster than in the recent past and that a large volume of Australian and New Zealand purchases would be diverted from the UK to Japan. If Britain joined the EEC the diversion would be on a much greater scale, since the UK would then be under an obligation to replace Australia and New Zealand by Europe as suppliers of dairy products and other foodstuffs and this would react unfavourably on the treatment accorded to British exports to those countries. By the middle 1970s Japan might well occupy the position, both as supplier and customer, that Britain enjoyed before World War II. The Japanese might even assume the part that British firms have hitherto played in developing Australian mining and manufacturing industries. They have already established a number of joint enterprises for the exploitation of mineral resources.

There are, however, serious obstacles to any approach to economic integration among these three countries in the near future. Both Australia and New Zealand attach great importance to the expansion of their manufacturing capacity and they would be reluctant to throw open their markets to Japanese competition, especially

[23]The rapid growth of trade between Australia-New Zealand and Japan began after the commercial treaties of 1957-8 which removed much of the discrimination against Japan and permitted also an easier flow of Oceanian exports to that country. The treaties were renewed and extended in 1962-3.

in the light industrial products which are the most vulnerable. It is true that in the long run some pattern of industrial specialisation might be planned (if it were not left to be determined by the operation of market forces), but international agreement on matters of that kind is not to be reached quickly. The experience of the free trade area arrangements between Australia and New Zealand themselves is not encouraging. An agreement between them, signed in 1965, succeeded in bringing to an end an era of rather chilly commercial relations, but its approach to free trade was very tentative. It provided for a gradual reduction of duties over an eight-year period, but the goods affected were comparatively few and consisted of those in which fairly extensive trade already took place. Most manufactured goods were excluded. It may be claimed that the agreement gave recognition to a new commercial attitude on the part of both countries and provided institutional arrangements by which freer trade in the future might be attained. But this was a very modest achievement. It may be argued that the experience is not relevant to what might happen if Japan were included. Yet, although the benefits to be gained by her inclusion would certainly be far greater than those of an arrangement confined to Australia and New Zealand (which even together are too small to enable the economies of scale to be realised in many branches of modern manufacturing industry), the threat to established interests would also be more serious.

On the other hand, strong pressures are building up that may ultimately sweep away these obstacles. Japan's trade balance with Australia, and to a less extent with New Zealand, is very unfavourable, it has been noted, largely because of the protection given to Australian and New Zealand manufacturing industry. Unless she is allowed to correct this by increasing her exports of manufactured goods, she may be forced to moderate her raw material purchases from Australia and New Zealand and to divert them to countries where the trade balance is the other way, for example, the South-East Asian and African countries. The problem will be the more easily resolved the wider the free trade area. The inclusion of the USA and Canada, with South-East Asian countries brought into association with the community, would remove much of the pressure for the bilateral balancing of trade. Besides widening the sources of capital for development, it would also remove fears on the part of Australia and New Zealand of economic domination by Japan. If the membership were wider still and included Britain, or EFTA as a whole, the Japanese, whose interests as an advancing industrial power lie in the widest possible extent of free trade, would be better pleased. At the same time Australia and New Zealand, while benefiting from the growing markets of the more dynamic members of the community, would not be forced to make such violent readjustments in their pattern of trade, or indeed in their traditional political attachment. There would also be fewer opportunities for effective retaliation by those left outside.

While, therefore, bilateral negotiations for improved trade relations can yield valuable results (as the experience of Japan and Australia in such negotiations both at the official and the business level demonstrates) it is improbable that any of the three countries just considered would seriously contemplate the establishment of a free trade area among themselves alone. A wider grouping would be more generally acceptable. The same conclusion applies to the vague proposals that have been put forward for setting up a South-East Asian trading bloc. The economies of these countries are competitive not complementary and most of them are broadly in the same stage of development. It is improbable that they could agree to regulate jointly the sale of their primary products so as to give them better prices. Even if they succeeded the result would probably be a transference of business to other areas. Except as a group for exerting political pressure such an association would have little to commend it. Above all, these countries need closer links with the richer and more rapidly growing economies which can provide them with markets for their newly-established manufacturing industries as well as for their primary products and, also, with capital for development. Japan, despite her interest in South-East Asia, would have little inducement to join in a bloc with them alone. She has not, in her own opinion, the financial strength to take responsibility for their development and she is anxious to ensure that the growth of their exports of light manufactures is not achieved solely at the expense of similar industries in Japan. Finally, she is aware that unless she can enlist the support of the rich countries in financing new enterprises in South-East Asia, her trade with that area is likely to stagnate.

6 IMPEDIMENTS TO JAPAN'S ADHERENCE TO A FREE TRADE TREATY

The political and economic advantages for Japan of participation in an extensive free trade treaty have been set out. It is now necessary to consider whether Japan is likely to be ready to pay the price. Before engaging in this speculative exercise, however, a word must be said about the distinctive advantages of alternative groupings. For reasons which need not be repeated, the likelihood can be dismissed of Japan taking an interest in any group which did not include the USA. If that condition is satisfied, then the wider the extent of the free trade treaty the better from her point of view. But her enthusiasm is likely to be affected by the location of the area's centre of gravity. The NAFTA approach composed initially of the USA, Canada, EFTA and possibly Australia and New Zealand, with its attention focussed on the Atlantic area, would attract her less than PAFTA, composed initially of the five advanced Pacific countries and with East and South-East Asia brought into some kind of association. If EFTA also joined, this would be an additional merit, provided that it did not deflect the attention of the group from the problems of the Pacific. In other words, the contribution of a free trade scheme to the security and economic development of East Asia provides one of the most persuasive arguments for bringing Japan within any free trade area. A proposal which did not make any such contribution would be regarded as decidedly second best. This is not to say that participation in any group that included the USA would not be better than remaining outside and isolated.

Even if the composition of the group and its associates were such as Japan favoured, some formidable obstacles would have to be overcome before she could agree to participate. The obstacles are of three kinds which will be examined in turn. First, there is the objection from manufacturing industry to exposure to unrestricted competition in the home market from the outside world. It has been shown that liberalisation has already been carried quite far in Japan during the last decade and that the general level of industrial tariffs is not high, but that a few important industries still enjoy high protection. In the immediate future the prospects for further liberalisation in this sector of the economy are favourable and it is likely that the resistance of the manufacturers will steadily diminish. The Japanese now consider that they have attained the European level of technical accomplishment. They have proved themselves to be successful competitors in markets for even the most advanced types of manufactured goods. The rationalisation of the major industries now going on will presently enable them to enjoy economies of scale which have been previously denied to some of them. This will raise the confidence of the industrialists themselves. Easy access for their own manufactures to foreign markets will be cheaply bought at the cost of the removal of the remaining restrictions on foreign competition in industrial products in Japan herself.

This applies especially to products of the heavy industries—engineering, metals and chemicals—where Japan competes with the chief industrial countries. Pressure to complete her liberalisation of these products is being exerted by the US Administration which has hinted that, unless Japan complies, there will be great difficulty in opposing the demands of American industrialists for protection against Japanese imports. This point has been urged very strongly in connection with the motor car industry, hitherto excluded from liberalisation.

The older labour-intensive industries, especially textiles, find themselves in a different situation. Here Japan is now meeting with formidable competition from certain Asian countries, especially Hong Kong and South Korea and also from the Communist bloc. It is ironical that the very class of goods in which Japanese competition was once feared in the West is that about which the Japanese themselves now feel anxiety. So far the competition has been encountered in foreign markets, but it may invade the home market as Japan's wage costs rise with her growing shortage of labour. The small-scale section of her "dual economy" has already come under pressure for this reason. However, it is likely that her industry will become increasingly concerned, like that of other advanced industrial countries, with the technologically advanced and capital-intensive products. She is well aware that her future lies in that field. It is therefore improbable that she would strongly resist the liberalisation of imports of consumer goods manufactured by Asian countries whose development she is anxious to promote. While much has been heard in Japan of the plight of the small producers already damaged by these changes, the Government has done comparatively little to sustain them.

On coming to the objections to the liberalisation of agricultural products, however, a very different attitude is met. Agriculture is perhaps the most "sensitive" area of trade policy. In most industrial countries it claims, and receives, exceptionally favourable treatment. In Japan its special position is the more readily acknowledged because of its size and the political and social importance ascribed to it. Although the proportion of the manpower engaged in agriculture has fallen from nearly 40 per cent in the middle 1950s to about 18 per cent in 1968, it still gives full-time or part-time employment to nearly 9m. persons. The post-war fall in numbers has been accompanied by mechanisation and the introduction of other labour-saving devices, with the result that output has increased substantially in quantity and its composition diversified. Japan herself still provides over four-fifths of the food she consumes. But agriculture is now facing serious difficulties. Far from being an apparently inexhaustible source of recruits for industry, as it once seemed, it is now suffering from a labour shortage. A high proportion of the farmers are elderly; 78 per cent of the family workers are women. To overcome these difficulties a thorough reorganisation is judged to be necessary. The typical farm is very small[24] and the land is laid out in scattered strips. In order to improve efficiency, the concentration of the small holdings into large units is urged. Some movement in this direction has occurred, but for the most part the old structure remains intact. The elderly farmers cling to their land because of the security that it offers, and even their children, most of whom are engaged in full-time or part-time work outside agriculture, regard the family holding as a refuge in bad times.

The preservation of this structure in a period in which costs have been rising sharply has been achieved by various means of protection, subsidies and price support. The basic crop is still rice and the farmer's income depends to a considerable extent on the price fixed by the Government at its annual price reviews. The trend has been steadily upwards. Since 1960 the retail price of rice has risen by 80 per cent. At the time of writing the price of Japanese rice is over twice the world price, although the effect on the cost of living has not been quite as great as it would have been in pre-war times because

[24]The average size is 0.55 hectares compared with 2.51 in Italy, 4.27 in France and 6.55 in Britain.

of the changes in the nation's diet. Agriculture has been diversified. The once extreme concentration on grain has been modified by the increased production of fruit, vegetables, dairy products and meat. But the further extension of livestock farming is handicapped by the shortage of grazing land; the growth so far achieved has been made possible only by heavy imports of feeding-stuffs. The price of the secondary products, especially vegetables, has also soared in recent years.

It was noted in Chapter 1 that since 1960 the share of food in the import trade has increased. It is probable that this tendency will continue as the population grows and as food consumption per head, which is low by international standards, rises. The question that is of immediate concern in the context of the present paper is how far the Government is prepared to go in sustaining the present organisation of domestic agriculture and in restricting imports of cheap food. Many Japanese economists are of the opinion that it should employ its financial resources for reorganising agriculture instead of for preserving the small peasant farmer. A more efficient agriculture employing a far smaller number of persons would result and this, together with more liberal treatment of food imports, would check the steep rise in consumer prices. The labour released from the land could be employed more productively in industry.

This policy, which seems rational to economists, is not politically practicable. The governments that have been in office throughout the post-war period have derived much support from the rural areas. If they were to introduce measures which provoked disaffection among the peasants and other rural workers, their authority would be threatened. Furthermore, agriculture and the rural life are still held to constitute the foundation of Japanese society. They are thought of, not necessarily with realism, as the source of ancient virtue and the support of social order in a period of bewildering change. It is therefore unlikely that Japan will expose her farmers in the immediate future to unrestricted foreign competition.[25] It is more probable that the Government will acquiesce in the slow

[25]This conclusion is borne out by the results of the discussion held in December, 1968, between the Japanese and American governments on trade liberalisation. Whereas Japan offered no resistance in principle to the proposals for the liberalisation of several classes of industrial products, including electronic goods, they refused the American request to remove restrictions on the import of various agricultural products, including beef.

transformation in agricultural organisation, which is bound to come since the present generation of farmers is not being fully replaced,[26] and that it will prefer only gradually to relax its import restrictions.

The changes may, however, be accelerated by political pressure exerted by other interests. The towns-people have become increasingly critical of the persistent advance in food prices. If the cost of living of the urban workers continues to rise this is likely to affect industrial costs. As the rural population diminishes in size, its political importance will steadily decline and the interests of the towns-people will command more official attention. Furthermore, it is recognised that an unwillingness to liberalise food imports may jeopardise some of Japan's markets by providing excuses for the maintenance of foreign restrictions on her goods. One may conclude tentatively that Japan would probably require PAFTA, or NAFTA, to allow her some special dispensation for the continued protection of her farmers for some years to come, but that the agricultural problem does not constitute a permanent barrier to the attainment of free trade. In return for trade concessions by other countries she is likely to press on with the contraction and reorganisa-tion of her agriculture. But this may take a decade or more.

Restrictions on food imports are thus defended by social and political rather than by economic arguments. The same is true of the other restrictions which Japan has shown the greatest reluctance to remove under pressure from her trading partners. These are the restrictions imposed on investment by foreigners in Japanese industry. By tradition the Japanese have been reluctant to incur long-term financial obligations to foreigners, especially when these were likely to lead to some measure of control over Japanese enterprise. Before World War II, the Government borrowed abroad only in times of emergency, as during the Sino-Japanese and Russo-Japanese wars, and after the Great Earthquake of 1923. It is true that several foreign firms had been pioneers in Japanese industry: for example, in electrical engineering and pneumatic tyre manufacture. After World War II the help of foreigners was enlisted in closing the wide technical gap which then existed between Japan and the West. Many technical agreements between Japanese and

---

[26]By 1985, according to conservative estimates, the numbers engaged in agriculture will have fallen to under 5m. persons, about 9 per cent of the total occupied population.

foreign firms were made and these proved to be a factor of great importance in the expansion of the science-based industries. In the early post-war years, however, foreign investors showed little inclination to participate in Japanese manufacturing undertakings, for they were then doubtful of the country's prospects. The impressive achievements of the last ten or fifteen years have changed their attitude. Foreign firms have lately tried to insist that they should be allowed to participate more directly in the benefits of Japanese industrial development as the price of making available technical information and experience. The Japanese have allowed some of them to associate in joint ventures. One of the recent examples is the establishment of a chain of retail stores by Woolworths in co-operation with Takashimaya, one of the chief departmental stores in Japan.

Furthermore, foreign investors, both individuals and institutions, have shown considerable appetite for Japanese shares, and the flow of foreign investments, both long-term and short-term, into Japan since 1960 has been large. Yet the Japanese have an ambivalent attitude to this tendency. On the one hand, they are anxious to obtain access to the most up-to-date technical information and to acquaint themselves with the most recent advances in managerial methods. They also welcome additions to their still exiguous supply of capital. But they are exceedingly reluctant to admit foreigners to a share in the control of their industries. Even those who realise that they might have much to gain from the introduction of American management into certain manufactures are inclined to think that American control would be too high a price to pay for more rapid progress. The rigid restrictions on the acquisition of shares by foreigners in Japanese enterprise were described in Chapter 3, where it was seen that only limited progress had been made in liberalisation, and that very recently.

In part the reluctance to share control with foreigners arises from a keen sense of uniqueness, a belief that Japanese ways of conducting business affairs and personal relations differ widely from those of Western countries. This point was referred to in Chapter 1. The Japanese are probably more conscious of these differences than the foreigners with whom they come into contact, since they make greater efforts to adjust their behaviour to alien conventions than the average American or European businessman. They are well aware of the misunderstandings likely to arise between Japanese and foreign members of managerial teams. Many of them would feel uneasy if they had to sit on boards of directors on which Americans predominated. Foreign control of Japanese enterprise is feared, therefore, not only because it is offensive to the spirit of Japanese nationalism, but also because the Japanese doubt if foreign management would successfully accommodate itself to Japanese conditions. Critics of Japan's attitude in this matter have suggested that control by foreigners would be unlikely to go very far even in the absence of restrictions. But it is reasonable to reply that since the capital structure of most Japanese companies is very highly geared, takeovers by foreign firms could be easily accomplished, and the low price-earnings ratio of most Japanese industrial companies provides a strong inducement for such transactions.

Ever since she was admitted to the OECD Japan has been under strong pressure from other countries to liberalise capital movements and the Government has been compelled to yield ground despite strong opposition from industry and widespread public fears. But, as seen in Chapter 3, there is still some way to go before Japan's trading partners are satisfied. This may well be a serious obstacle to adherence to a free trade treaty, one that cannot be easily overcome because it is rooted deeply in national sentiment. But it is reasonable to suppose that the gradual relaxation will continue and that the disposition of the Japanese towards the problem will change as the peculiar features of their economic and social life lose their prominence. Moreover, if Japan is to maintain her rate of progress, she cannot insulate herself from the influences that are transforming industrial organisation in the world as a whole. An increasing part of industrial enterprise is passing into the hands of great firms which operate in many countries and draw their capital and management from all over the world. These firms are cosmopolitan in interests and outlook. The great oil companies and Unilever are examples. Such concerns have been able to develop in Japan only to a limited extent, for the Japanese business outlook has not been affected by this movement towards the internationalisation of enterprise. Even those Japanese who control firms with extensive business overseas are preoccupied with the problems of their own economy, and their outlook is usually circumscribed by their view of the national interest. Unless Japan accommodates herself to this world-wide trend, she may find herself isolated and then her economic progress might be adversely affected. The spirit of nationalism which contributed so powerfully to economic development in the past might prove to be an obstacle to progress in the future. Yet it would be uncharacteristic for the Japanese to cling for long to policies which are conspicuously at variance with their material interests.

7 SUMMARY AND CONCLUSIONS

1. *Balance of Advantages for Japan*

The concept of a free trade treaty among developed countries has attracted the attention of the Japanese for a variety of reasons. They have become well aware both of the positive benefits that participation in such a treaty might confer on their country and also of the dangers to their prosperity or security that it might avert. Politically it appears that a closely knit group of nations with common interests in the stability of South-East Asia would reinforce Japan's own efforts at a moment when, for the first time since World War II, she is being called upon to undertake heavy responsibilities for political security and economic development in that region. If these aims are to be achieved, it is necessary to ensure above all a continuing American commitment to the region and this is one of the chief merits of a free trade treaty from the Japanese point of view. It is, of course, not only a military commitment that is in question. Stability in South-East Asia cannot be ensured if the nations of that area remain impoverished. Since Japan, though now persuaded that she must be more generous than in the past, regards herself as too weak financially to carry the main burden of providing aid and investment, the possibility of associating the developed countries both of the Pacific and of the Atlantic with plans for South-East Asian development makes a strong appeal to her. An association which did not bring in South-East Asia in some way or other would be much less attractive to her.

On the economic side, a free trade treaty of the widest possible extent is recognised to accord, in principle, with the interests of the most rapidly growing economy in the world, especially as its progress in future is likely to become increasingly dependent on ample opportunities for foreign trade. Many of Japan's problems would be easier to solve if she were a member of a free trade treaty. The difficulties arising out of trade imbalance with particular countries would be alleviated if those countries all formed part of a free trade association. The strains of structural change brought about by industrial development in the Pacific region could be dealt with more easily by common policies or plans than if they were left to actions by individual countries. This applies to the problems of American, Canadian and Australian manufacturing industries in the face of Japanese competition and also to the difficulties of Japan's own light, labour-intensive industries of which the position in some markets is now being challenged by the industrialisation of the Asian developing countries.

These difficulties are particular instances of a general problem. In the next few years competition in industrial products from the developing countries is likely to extend to an increasing range of markets and vested interests threatened by the changes may call on their governments for protection. It would, however, be inconsistent for the developed countries, having provided aid, to refuse to buy the products of the new manufacturing industries which their investment has helped to establish. In association they can afford to be more rational than in isolation. This is especially so because the creation of a free trade area may be expected to raise substantially the volume of trade and the national incomes of all the participants and so to make possible generous treatment of the developing countries in the form of both financial help and trade privileges. Japan herself has naturally been much impressed with this argument since it is estimated that her exports and her balance of trade will benefit to a greater extent than those of other countries in the Pacific basin from the establishment of a free trade area, at any rate in the short run. At present Japan does not enjoy trade preferences in any market. Clearly it would be to her advantage if she were put on an equal footing with all her competitors, some of whom enjoy valuable privileges. Further, as a customer whose demands are likely to grow very fast in the next decade, Japan naturally welcomes the extension of the field of supply and the disappearance of any barriers that might prevent her from obtaining what she wants at the lowest prices. This applies not only to raw materials and fuel but also to manufactured goods. She does not wish to limit her purchases of plant and equipment to the USA and is gratified by the presence of European manufacturers among her suppliers. For this among other reasons she would be pleased if the EFTA countries, and the EEC, were included in the free trade association.

Nevertheless, there are certain obstacles to her participation in a multilateral free trade treaty among developed countries. She would have to expose her manufacturing industries, many of which still enjoy various forms of protection, to outside competition. She would have to abandon to a large extent her present policy of supporting the peasantry. And she would have to withdraw her present restrictions on capital investment by foreigners in her own industries. The first obstacle no longer appears to be very formidable. Even the weakest of her modern large-scale industries are now in process of rationalisation and re-equipment. It is unlikely that they will need support for much longer or that their claims for protection will be admitted by the Government. In the small-scale, labour-intensive industries the firms, to a large extent, are being left to adapt themselves to modern conditions by reorganisation as an alternative to going out of business. It is no part of the Japanese Government's long-term policy to maintain the "dual economy" in industry and trade.

The agricultural problem is more intractable. The permanent preservation of a rural society of small peasants is no longer regarded as practical policy, and, despite the support still given, agriculture is rapidly shrinking in size. But for political and social reasons, it is likely to be a decade or more before Japan is ready to draw a substantially increased proportion of her food from abroad and it is not to be expected that she could at once abandon her rural population to international competition. As to restrictions on capital investment, these again are defended on social and political grounds. They are being gradually relaxed, but here Japan is likely to fight a stubborn rearguard action against those who urge their abandonment.

These objections on her part to a complete surrender to the free trade principle make it improbable that Japan herself will take the initiative in pressing for the creation of a free trade area in the Pacific basin. She is, however, likely to give active support to schemes of regional economic co-operation, as described in Chapter 4, in order to promote the political and economic purposes by which she sets much store. She will, moreover, exert herself to discourage the revival of protectionist sentiment among her customers, especially the USA, and she can hardly avoid further measures of liberalisation herself in order to defeat this tendency. If a free trade treaty were launched Japan would almost certainly be anxious to join it, for she could not contemplate being isolated from a bloc which included the USA. She might find it difficult to meet fully the conditions of a free trade treaty if one were to be formed in (say) the next five years, but with a steady transformation of agriculture and the modification of traditional social attitudes, the barriers to free trade in agricultural products and to industrial investment by foreigners are likely to crumble. Under the persuasion of the political and economic advantages to which participation in a multilateral free trade association would admit her, they might crumble very fast.

2. *Britain and Japanese Participation*

In conclusion, it is necessary to consider briefly the direct effects on Anglo-Japanese trade and on British industry of the establishment of an Atlantic-based free trade area in which both Japan and Britain were participants. For much of the post-war period trade between the countries was seriously impeded on both sides by quantitative controls, but since the Commercial Treaty of April, 1963, most of these have been removed and provision has been made for a progressive relaxation of the remainder. Between 1960 and 1967 trade between the countries increased at about the same rate as Japan's foreign trade as a whole, but considerably faster than Britain's. At the close of the 1960s the trade was roughly in balance and amounted to about $2\frac{1}{2}$ per cent of Japan's total trade.[27] The abolition of all quantitative controls and tariffs would almost certainly result in a large increase in business, since the "sensitive" areas in both countries are quite heavily protected at the present time.

Which country would gain the most from the change and which of their industries would suffer most severely from the intensification of competition are highly speculative questions. In recent years Britain and Japan have exchanged a wide variety of products. British exports to Japan have consisted almost entirely of finished manufactured goods, a third of them machinery. The largest item in Japan's exports to the British market has consisted of food, especially fish. This has accounted for about a quarter of the total and the rest has included electrical machinery, textiles, metals and wood manufactures. A considerable proportion of the trade is made up of specialities which are not, strictly speaking, competitive with the products of the customer-country. This applies to such British exports

[27]British exports to Japan in 1967 amounted to £82.8m. (f.o.b.), re-exports to £4.7m. (f.o.b.), and imports from Japan were £91.2m. (c.i.f.). See *Overseas Trade Accounts* (Board of Trade, London, 1968). For 1969 the figures were £124.7m., £3.9m. and £104.5m.

as Scotch whisky and engineering components, and also to Japanese trade exports of foodstuffs and plywood. Under conditions of free Japan would probably make inroads into the British market in electronic apparatus, watches and clocks, small metal goods and perhaps motor vehicles, while Britain could reasonably expect to increase substantially her exports of non-electrical machinery, engineering components and a wide variety of luxury goods. British exports to Japan, being mainly finished manufactures, might rise in the short term faster than Japan's exports to Britain since the latter consist so largely of foodstuffs. But this conjecture is very uncertain, for Japan's costs are probably falling relatively to Britain's in the newer, capital-intensive industries.

In the long run, however, one would expect Britain to derive great advantages from securing unimpeded access to the markets of a country which for a long time to come is likely to enjoy a very high rate of economic growth. Japan, during the next decade or so, will probably attain Western European levels of per capita income and her population in the early 1980s is likely to rise to about 120 millions. Her market will by then have become one of the largest in the world, and free access to it would provide abundant opportunities for the manufacturers of Western countries, especially those who maintain a high standard of invention and technical accomplishment. It is also probable that the Japanese demand for specialities of high quality will increase steeply in the years ahead, and Britain should be able to take advantage of all that this offers to her.

Part III

ASIAN-PACIFIC ARENA
OF CONFLICT

by

Sir Robert Scott

1 THE EAST OF SUEZ DEBATE

East of Suez is, in Britain, an emotive phrase. It evokes the Kiplingesque era of garrisons in India and Burma and symbolises defence debates precipitated by financial pressures. As a discussion of British purposes in Asia, the debate would have been better timed in 1947 than twenty years later. For 1947 was a milestone of far deeper significance in relation to the British position in the Orient than any subsequent year. Defence policy is argued in terms of commitments as if these could be defined and measured, as if they were all distinct and all undertaken in a spirit of altruism at the expense of the hard-pressed British taxpayer, the inference being that Britain is free to make a simple choice between cutting and maintaining commitments. They are neither ends in themselves nor a form of charity. They are means to ends: security, livelihood, the future. If they have ceased to serve these aims they should of course be discarded. As Britain has repeatedly found, though, and most recently in Aden, this is seldom cheap or easy. Hoped for savings which prompt defence economies almost always turn out to be less than expected when set against compensation, commercial repercussions and the cost of redeployment or disbandment. In the long run they can prove to be disastrously false economies. The debate would be more realistic if the word "threats" were substituted for "commitments". Like any other nation Britain can fail to recognise threats or deliberately decide against preparations to meet them. But, unlike obligations, threats cannot be renounced or reduced by act of parliament.

Changing Strategic Circumstances

For over a century India was the core of the British position in Asia. Trading settlements in the Malacca Straits and the acquisition of Hongkong were incidental to the China trade, itself an extension of trade with India and the activities of the East India Company. To counter possible Tsarist Russian threats to India, British troops were stationed on the north-west frontiers and a military presence established in the Persian Gulf. Completion of the Suez Canal in 1869 shortened communications between Britain and India, a development so important that in 1875 the British Government secured control of the canal by purchasing the Egyptian interest. Aden was developed as a coaling station to refuel ships on passage to and from India. After the 1914-1918 war Japan emerged as a major naval power. Although Japan had been an ally in that war, the British Government considered it prudent to construct a naval base at Singapore in order to guard against the risk of a Japanese naval thrust at India and the Indian Ocean.

Policies and attitudes tend to acquire an identity and a momentum of their own long after their original justification has vanished. The transfer of responsibility from United Kingdom hands to India and Pakistan on their independence in 1947 radically altered the basis of the British position in Asia, although it was not immediately apparent that as a result of withdrawal from India the military significance to Britain of the Suez Canal, Aden, the Persian Gulf and Singapore was due for reappraisal. While the maintenance of British forces there had originally stemmed from British responsibilities in India, defence tasks had in the meantime diversified far beyond the primary purpose of defence of India.

A British force in the Persian Gulf, no longer there to guard against Russian ambitions, served to protect the supply of oil for which Britain could pay in sterling and served also to honour pledges to local rulers threatened by their neighbours. At the eastern exit from the Indian Ocean—even though the defence of India was no longer a direct British responsibility and though the threat from Japan had gone with her defeat in war—bases and forces in Malaya and Singapore were needed for their internal security and external defence and, too, as a convenient centre for depots and facilities in the event of British participation in operations elsewhere in the area. With the establishment of a Communist regime in China there was an increased risk of trouble in Hongkong. The availability of British forces in Singapore made reinforcement easier.

Moreover, especially in Australia, Singapore was looked upon as an outpost of Australian defence. Japanese victory in 1942 had had profound effects on Australian thinking. Australia came of age overnight. She was stirred to new awareness of her proximity to Asia, of her vulnerability, of the military weakness of Britain and of her dependence on the United States. Nevertheless, and despite its capture in 1942, Singapore and the maintenance of British forces there came to be regarded as important to Australia and are still so regarded. The consequences for India of the Japanese campaign in Malaya and Singapore were also momentous if very different. The fall of Singapore was a major military disaster for Britain. Yet in a sense—and in a manner never intended or foreseen in Britain—Singapore served its original strategic purpose of preventing a Japanese attack on India. Brief as the campaign itself was, preparations for it, the waging of it and the regrouping afterwards were impediments which imposed a delay and saved India from an immediate Japanese onslaught that would at that time have been exceedingly difficult to repel.

After 1947, when the defence of India ceased to be a British responsibility, freedom of British military passage through the Suez Canal remained important. But no longer was it as vital as when a large proportion of British troops had been stationed in India and it was imperative to make sure they could be quickly reinforced or quickly brought back to Europe. Failure to realise the diminished importance of the canal had grave consequences for the UK in later years when exaggerated notions of its role in British defence planning were still current. The new situation in India had other consequences for Britain in Asia, notably for the army, because Indian Army units which had shared garrison duties outside India ceased to be available in the event of a crisis in Hongkong, Singapore, Malaya, the Persian Gulf or elsewhere.

If the implications of withdrawal from India on the general British position in Asia were not fully realised at the time, there were other factors at work whose combined effect was towards reducing British forces east of Suez. Decolonisation, not only in India but in Ceylon, Burma, South-East Asia, East Africa and recently in southern Arabia, by pruning direct UK political and defence responsibilities, led to the replacement of British forces by those raised by the new nations. Mounting costs of new weapons and new weapon systems, together with recurrent financial strains in Britain, reinforced the general trend towards military contraction.

But the downward trend was marked by erratic and violent swings, sometimes accelerated by balance of payments crises, at other times slowed or reversed by the demands of one political crisis after another. Unforeseen embroilment in Indonesia after World War II prevented rapid demobilisation and withdrawal of British forces. Already, before Indian independence, it was politically necessary to heed Indian warnings that Indian forces which had been fighting the Japanese, a cause defensible as an Indian interest, were not to be used to restore European colonial rule in South-East Asia. This was a further impediment to the withdrawal of British forces. The Communist uprising in Malaya pinned down large contingents of British troops for almost ten years after 1948. Participation in United Nations (UN) action in Korea led to a steep increase in the British defence budget. Riots in Hongkong, trouble in Kenya, crisis in the Persian Gulf, the Indonesian "confrontation" of Malaysia and extrication from Aden: these were some of the interruptions to the trend towards reduction.

Mood of Withdrawal

More than twenty years since it ceased to be a vital British military interest, the Suez Canal has acquired a mystic significance as a slogan in public discussion. Those who regard defence spending as an anti-social diversion of resources from welfare make common cause with those who want to concentrate British forces at home and in Western Europe to proclaim against "East of Suez" as if a line could be drawn on a map as the limit beyond which no British military capacity is or ever will be needed and as though defence factors can be isolated from political and economic elements of policy in the area vaguely described as East of Suez.

The debate is of wider significance than a debate on British military deployment in the Indian and Pacific Ocean areas. Britain is in a process of transition from her old place in the world to a new as yet undefined status. The debate is symptomatic of her uncertainty. Going it alone, merging in a European union, dividing the world into spheres of influence, promoting world government through the UN, acting as broker between East and West, becoming a junior partner of the USA: all these have their advocates.

Uncertainty about her role and purposes has sapped self-confidence and bred undue sensitivity to irresponsible criticism by others. Some in Britain carry this to the point of a guilt complex about the British record, and in their anxiety to make amends disparage their compatriots and indeed the white races generally. Others are disillusioned with the Commonwealth or with the USA or both and want to retreat into Europe. There is indeed an element of escapism in some of the arguments put forward in favour of British membership of the European Communities (EEC), of a desire to turn the back on the rest of the world. There is general preoccupation with domestic social questions, a mood reminiscent of the 1930s when, as of late, there were balance of payments crises and devaluation. The nostrum then was likewise to cut defence and overseas spending; to over-spend at home—to dissipate today what should be saved for tomorrow. The mood is not the product of the welfare state. It led to it. Immense benefits have been brought to the people of Britain by the welfare state in terms of standards of living. But it will last only as long as the foundations of security and economic strength last. There is a danger that the foundations are being weakened in order to add to the super-structure.

The world is not going to be remade on an American, Russian or Chinese pattern, still less on a British one. In terms of impact on the rest of the world, nothing done or left undone at Westminster matters as much as it did. Yet the UK's future depends on general peace and prosperity. As a great trading and seafaring nation, Britain has a permanent interest in international law and order. It matters a great deal to her that she should assess the likelihood of these conditions being met, particularly in the Indo-Pacific theatre, and decide what she can do to help bring them about.

Importance of Indo-Pacific Theatre

Stability in Western Europe is for Britain a vital interest because she is part of the region. But Western Europe is now on the periphery of events. It is neither the centre of world power nor, at present, a source of tensions that could erupt with world-wide consequences. Moreover, there is between the USA and the USSR a kind of military stalemate, which means that on Europe, the principal area of direct Russo-American confrontation, a certain immobility has descended. The front still has to be guarded as Russia's invasion of Czechoslovakia showed in 1968. But threats to Europe's security and welfare, to the world's stability and prosperity, no longer derive from the quarrels of France, Germany and Britain. Instead, they are by-products of pressures in the Middle East or southern Africa or South and East Asia where the super-powers are not directly facing each other in entrenched positions. They are bound up with relations between Russia and America and with world-wide economic problems, such as international monetary reform and aid to less advanced nations often grappling with population pressures.

The purpose of this essay is to sketch trends in the major theatre of conflict, in those parts of Asia which border the Pacific and Indian oceans, and also to discuss the part Britain could play if left free to exercise an individual, if limited, role in the maintenance of order and stability. It is in the Indo-Pacific theatre that the world power balance may be decided. Since the area is not within the clear sphere of influence of either of the super-powers, there is an inclination to seek advantages over one another there that are unattainable in Europe. Britain's 1966 Defence Review accepted the view that Asia was the area in which there was the greatest danger of serious hostilities.[1] Whatever some in Europe may hope, Asia cannot be divorced from the world power situation. The USA has long been a Pacific power, with Washington becoming increasingly pre-occupied with the region's problems, while the USSR has always claimed to be an Asian power and, since Lenin, has accepted the importance of the area for the world's future.

What happens in East Asia, then, will ultimately affect the future of Europe. In that area the biggest factor is China. It is also the least predictable. Only one thing is certain about China: that the process of evolutionary and revolutionary change which began a century ago is not yet finished.

[1]*Statement on Defence Estimates, 1966* (H.M. Stationery Office, London, February, 1966, Cmnd. 2901) Part 2, Ch. II, para. 24, p. 8.

2 CHINESE FACTOR IN GLOBAL STRATEGY

There is an oddly repetitive rhythm in Chinese affairs. Centuries of relative calm are succeeded by a century or two of disorder before the nation settles into a new groove. From time to time academics, civil servants and a college of heralds ran the country with smoothness and efficiency. They tended, however, to become so circumscribed by their own yardsticks of conformity, so certain that they alone knew what was best for the multitude, that there developed a loss of touch with reality. In time the long-suffering and patient Chinese turned against their rulers not only because they became oppressive but because they were aloof. When explosion comes in China it is apt to be bloody and prolonged. Shedding the old order and donning a new one has sometimes taken a couple of centuries, punctuated by intervals to recuperate.

The Taiping Rebellion, just over a century ago, marked the beginning of serious revolt against the Manchu dynasty. A lull in the second half of the nineteenth century was broken by the Boxer Uprising and another pause, a few years later, was shattered by the war-lord era until the Nationalists established unity in 1928. But that was soon disrupted by Japanese invasion which, however, failed to heal the breach between the Nationalists and the Communists. Unity was not restored until the latter achieved power in 1949 and ruled in comparative calm for some fifteen years, when Chairman Mao Tse-tung himself, instituting the Cultural Revolution, interrupted it in a hurry to accomplish too much too quickly.

Like any other new revolutionary government, the Communists' first task was to consolidate their power by crushing opposition and demonstrating strength. The first was not difficult even though there were many areas not under Communist control. The Nationalists had fled to Taiwan and opposition in China was not organised. The second, a show of strength, was effected with callous ruthlessness through a nation-wide campaign of public trials and executions. But their biggest problem was not consolidation of power. Rather it was the application of power to transform Chinese society on a communist pattern. Indispensable to this was the eradication of anti-Communist ideas. In terms of practical politics in China this meant the destruction of American influence.

US prestige stood high in China. Americans had been prominent in commerce and had enjoyed extra-territorial status like most other foreigners. But unlike the British, French, Japanese, Italians, Russians and Germans, the Americans had never had any special territorial concessions of their own in the big seaports and inland cities. There was, moreover, a long record of American support for China over international issues. American money had been subscribed for missions, hospitals and universities in China and for Chinese students to go to the USA on a scale far exceeding that of any other country. Only a short time before the Communist rise to power, the USA—by defeating Japan—had freed vast areas of China from Japanese occupation. By millions throughout China, the USA was looked upon, after World War II, as a benefactor and friend. It was an image that had to be changed if the new rulers hoped to inculcate communism.

Extirpation of American Influence

Making allowance for the magnitude of their problems, the new regime succeeded fairly rapidly in asserting its authority over most of the country. Public relief at the prospect of peace and of currency stabilisation helped. So did public reactions in the USA stemming in part from American frustrations over unsuccessful attempts to persuade the Nationalists and Communists to compose their differences. But only in part. To the Chinese Communist Party the USA represented not only a political and economic philosophy inimical to communism. It was also identified as the principal foreign supporter of the Nationalists and as a country and a people with immense prestige in China. Even before they came to power in Peking, the Communists accordingly contrived incidents which inflamed American opinion. In 1948 and 1949 they harassed the US Consulate in Mukden. American diplomatic and consular staff were withdrawn from China in 1950 after seizure of American property in Peking had roused great indignation in the USA. These developments wrecked any prospects of early negotiations on American recognition of the new Government of China, negotiations which had been widely expected throughout the world including Britain which, like Burma, India, the Soviet Union and others, had recognised the new regime by January, 1950.

British recognition was not welcomed in Peking excepting in so far as it might lead to Anglo-American friction. Recognition by the USA might have carried much greater dangers for the new regime in pursuit of their policy of extirpation of American influence. They took steps to forestall it by anti-American agitation which served the secondary purpose of turning US public opinion away from any thought of recognition as well as the primary purpose of justifying seizure of American enterprises in China.

Within a few months the question of American recognition became academic. War in Korea broke out in the middle of 1950. Chinese intervention in that war later in the year, increasing American support for the Nationalists in Taiwan and later the war in Vietnam cumulatively ruled out any later possibility of recognition. It is an issue that will cease to be dormant only when the Chinese themselves estimate that it is in their interests to establish direct diplomatic relations and contacts with Washington. That is a long way ahead. Whatever assurances the Americans might demand, if recognition were in prospect, it is certain that on their side the Chinese would insist on withdrawal of recognition of and support for a rival regime in Taiwan.

The Cultural Revolution

A government that emerges after revolution is usually composed of men without experience of administration. This was not the case in China where the new leaders had had many years' practical experience governing large areas and controlling strong armies. Even so, much had to be improvised. Power had to be delegated to men and women, often young and inexperienced, whose main qualification was blind faith in communism and blind loyalty to the new governors. In a nation of peasant-farmers, collective farming was an unpopular innovation. Rising taxes, geared to unrealistic production targets, became oppressive. The currency began to slip again. Big mistakes were made in industry and in agriculture from which China slowly began to recover in the late 1950s and early 1960s as the central government adopted a more pragmatic and less doctrinaire approach to practical administrative problems; and made more use of trained managers and technicians instead of leaving too much power in the hands of communist zealots.

Leaving management to managers promoted efficiency but had political side-effects of some consequence. In any case, white hot revolutionary fervour can last only a few years before there must be a respite, whether or not the aims of the reformers have been fully achieved. Post-operational depression begins to set in. The older generation has had enough of austerity and sacrifice. The younger generation takes achievements for granted. Disillusion sets in among party workers; and the more extreme and emotional they were to begin with, the more they are likely to suffer from the frustrations of experience and responsibility. With some exceptions reaction after revolution began to follow the normal pattern. Among the exceptions one was all-important: Mao Tse-tung himself, who over the years has personified China to a degree rare in any country at any time. Stalin came to power only after the Russian Revolution and, anyway, had to share hero-worship with Lenin. Mao led the party to victory in China and has remained in power. His objective has been power, not for its own sake, but to secure the aims he has pursued for over thirty years. There is still a long way to go and he is ageing.

The Cultural Revolution and the Red Guard movement were the latest of several attempts by Mao to revitalise the revolution and to rekindle revolutionary zeal among the young. Their ingredients included nationalism and anti-foreignism, powerful stimuli to instinctive Chinese isolationism. Mao believes that without violence, revolution and suffering man cannot develop his full potential. The Cultural Revolution might have had little more effect than its predecessors but for one factor: Mao's age. Rivalry for the succession became inter-twined with revival of revolutionary momentum. At the end of the nineteenth century, in the twilight years of the Manchu dynasty, another ageing ruler, the Empress Dowager, subverted the original aims of the Boxers to her own political purposes, thereby contributing to the downfall of the dynasty. Now that the wilder excesses of the Red Guards have been curbed there is no indication of the succession issue having been resolved or of crusading revolutionary spirit having been re-created.

There is no obvious successor to Mao, no one of comparable stature commanding general loyalty and support. He has been in charge so long that as he fades from the scene the authority of the central government is affected, a danger aggravated by rifts in the army and in the Communist Party deepened and in some instances caused by the Red Guards.

China is behind Russia in industry, agriculture, living standards, military technology and power. It is comforting to suppose that Russia has mellowed, that she is secure, self-satisfied and middle-class with much to lose and little to gain from stirring up trouble. None of this is true of China. (Nor, incidentally, should it be accepted too complacently as true of the Soviet Union.) China's size and population, the gap between communist targets and achievements, the issue of succession to Mao and the lasting wounds inflicted by the Red Guards on the solidarity of the nation make it unlikely that the country will evolve as Russia has done.

Reassertion of World Status

China's Communist rulers set out to modernise, to consolidate and to colonise: modernise agriculture, industry and weapons; consolidate in distant provinces such as Tibet; and colonise in Chinese Central Asia. Recovery of Outer Mongolia and of Taiwan and the revision of some of the common frontier with Russia are, for China, also in the realm of domestic policy although prudence dictated caution in pressing them. Over the years, since the early 1960s, China has been reasserting a claim as a world power. She has been emerging from a period of humiliation. The rest of mankind had carried on as if China did not exist. To the outside world it is natural that China's external aims should attract more attention than her domestic policy. But the expulsion of Western military influence from East Asia and the assertion of world status as the leader of radicalism and revolution—the main features of Chinese foreign policy—are subordinate to internal affairs.

But a Chinese central government whose authority has been weakening may have to re-examine priorities. It is true that the Chinese have remarkable powers of improvisation and that the 1967 harvest was good. For a time at any rate, whilst the Government tries to compose differences between the army and the Communist Party and between the centre and the provinces, life for the ordinary Chinese will not be greatly affected. The turmoil of 1967 will be reflected more seriously in large-scale economic planning and to a lesser extent in transport, where inefficiency is liable to have consequences both for China and for North Vietnam. If it becomes more difficult to organise direct support for North Vietnam, or to handle Russian supplies in transit by rail across China to Vietnam, this will increase Russian and North Vietnamese dependence on sea transport and on the seaports of North Vietnam. It is not surprising that

Russian sensitivity to interference with their shipping is increasing.

The nuclear programme, however, will be kept going so long as the central government can contrive to do so, despite the cost in scarce materials, the diversion of scientific manpower and the demands on power supplies. Centuries of experience of external attack have shown the Chinese Government the risks of neglecting defence. Today, as they see it, they are alone in a hostile world with the two principal foes—the USA and the Soviet Union—at the gates and apparently on the way to establishing a working arrangement between themselves.

For the purpose of analysing Chinese attitudes to others few of her actions have been more revealing than the attacks on Indian forces in October, 1962. Few have been more widely misinterpreted. During the previous decade there had been a series of incidents on the Sino-Indian frontiers which negotiations had failed to resolve or prevent. Mutual antipathy grew as Chinese brutalities in Tibet shocked Indian opinion and as Indian aid to refugee Tibetans irritated China. Peaceful settlement of conflicting territorial claims became remote. To China the matter was urgent. By 1962 she was building roads, in some cases across disputed territory, which were of considerable importance to the imposition of authority in Tibet and to her policy further west in Chinese Central Asia. Indian assertions of their rights threatened completion of the work. Chinese forces drove the Indians back. The short campaign caused shock and panic in India. But it was not a Chinese attempt to conquer India. No military commander would undertake such a task over Himalayan passes at the beginning of winter.

China Not Militarily Aggressive

Despite Indian and Western charges to the contrary, that campaign was consistent with the view that China was not, militarily, aggressive. The point is important because of its relevance to forecasts of Chinese behaviour. Neither traditionally nor under communism is there a tradition of China launching unprovoked military attacks on foreign powers. Nearly three hundred years ago Chinese forces intervened in Korea. In 1950, under the new Communist regime, they did so again. The purpose of the earlier intervention was to repulse a Japanese force threatening Manchuria. The purpose of the later was to repel UN forces approaching the Manchurian frontier. Though the UN branded the Chinese action as aggression it was in fact a response to what the Chinese regarded as a provocative threat to their security.

By contrast with the violence of their reactions in Korea and on the Indian frontier, and the indifference they have shown to world opinion, they have displayed considerable caution in the Formosan Straits and over Vietnam. Fear of American reprisals is no doubt a factor. Yet this did not deter them in Korea at a time when American military and atomic supremacy was unchallengeable even by Russia. The criterion of Chinese military response has seemed to be the imminence of a direct threat and not calculation of the odds against them.

It has therefore been possible hitherto to assume with some confidence that China was unlikely to take a sudden unprovoked major military initiative, though she was capable of violent reaction to a direct threat and though there was of course the danger, as with all countries, of a bad miscalculation so that she might become involved in fighting without intention. From this assumption it seemed reasonable to deduce that however much the Chinese supported the North Vietnamese and incited them to continue the fight, it was improbable that China would intervene openly and in force unless her own interests were directly endangered.

Developments in China in the later 1960s have weakened confidence in the continued validity of this analysis. One of the main factors in world strategy today is that Chinese policy has once again become unpredictable at a moment in history when China, on her way to becoming a nuclear power, is herself in ferment, when fighting continues in Vietnam and when Korea and the Middle East are simmering with trouble. Armed clashes with Soviet forces reflect the steady deterioration in relations between Russia and China. The death of Ho Chi Minh has given both nations the opportunity and the incentive for intrigues in North Vietnamese politics in rival efforts to assert influence. None of the possible successors to Ho in Hanoi could be said to have his devotion to the cause of world-wide Communist solidarity and unification or his deft skill in maintaining balance in North Vietnam's relations with both Moscow and Peking. Competition between Russia and China to play the role of big brother to North Vietnam will certainly intensify tension between them and may lead to serious discord and a major armed clash.

By fomenting anti-American and anti-Russian hysteria in her people China has succeeded in alienating both the leading powers, an unenviable and unpleasant situation which would be fraught with danger for any country, but especially for China whose nuclear programme is, as yet, a military hostage and not an asset. As the Japanese found more than a quarter of a century ago, China cannot be conquered and occupied and controlled by a foreign power. But she could be devastated and her industrial installations and transport system laid waste. As between the Russians and the Americans, the Chinese leaders probably estimate now that they have more to fear from the former, although they have most of all to fear from co-operation between Moscow and Washington. Such calculations may induce Peking to seek some improvement in relations with the United States, which would be a development likely to be given a cautious welcome on the American side because of the part China could play, if she desired to do so, in extricating them from Vietnam on terms acceptable to the US Administration.

If time permits, Chinese policy may well veer in this direction. There are too many difficulties in the way of such a development, both on the American and on the Chinese side, for it to take place in the near future. The necessary time may therefore not be available. Relations between Russia and China may become strained to the point of rupture. The USA would have to assess very carefully the effects on the Soviet Union of moves towards a *rapprochement* with China. The Chinese Government would have to be very sure of themselves before discarding the anti-American propaganda they have so assiduously disseminated to their people for so many years. Perhaps most disquieting of all, there is now a bigger risk of mistakes being made in China either by elements out of control or through miscalculation, a danger to which the Chinese are in any case exposed because of their self-imposed isolation.

3 THE VIETNAM WAR

To a universal chorus of approval the North Vietnamese agreed in April, 1969, to meet the Americans in Paris to talk about peace talks. Washington had been pressing for negotiations for a long time. To question Hanoi's motives in at last agreeing is to strike a jarring note. Throughout the Vietnam War one of its most baffling features has been and still is the attitude of the North Vietnamese towards negotiations. The war has been dramatised out of all recognition to its origins. Yet it is with the origins that the search for a clue must begin.

Ho Chi Minh had devoted his long life to the cause of communism in what used to be called French Indo-China. A few months after the fall of France in 1940 the French Administration in Indo-China, unable any longer to resist Japanese pressure, accepted their demands to be allowed to station forces in Tongking. In July, 1941, Japanese troops moved into southern Indo-China to set up bases from which they were later able to support their assault on South-East Asia. Japanese entry into Indo-China had a profound affect on the communist movement there and on the fortunes of Ho. In 1941, primarily for espionage purposes, the Chinese Nationalist Government supported the foundation of the Viet Minh as a coalition of diverse, and sometimes rival, nationalist and Communist groups, with Ho Chi Minh as general-secretary. He was later imprisoned for a time and a new grouping created, the Vietnam Revolutionary League of which, however, the only effective component was the Communist element. Ho had to be released. It was to the Viet Minh that American supplies were delivered to enable them to form an anti-Japanese resistance movement. Not that they did much resisting. Much of the supplies were hoarded for later use against the French.

Division of North and South Vietnam

It was agreed at Potsdam in July, 1945, that north of the 16th parallel in Indo-China the Japanese surrender, then imminent, should be taken by the Chinese and south of it by the British. The Viet Minh, of whom by that time Ho Chi Minh was the acknowledged leader, moved into the political vacuum in the North but their status in the South was challenged by sects armed by the Japanese who had respected French sovereignty until March, 1945, when they found that French officials were preparing to support an Allied landing. From the ensuing confusion Ho emerged as the undisputed leader of the anti-French forces though his authority in the South was tenuous. Negotiations and clashes with the French continued until, in December, 1946, the Viet Minh launched a major attack on the French garrisons in Hanoi and, soon afterwards, on all French garrisons in North and Central Vietnam. Guerrilla warfare continued at appalling cost to both sides until, after the Battle of Dien Bien Phu in 1954, cease-fire agreements were signed at Geneva in July of that year.

At the Geneva Conference, Ho agreed to armistices. He failed, however, to secure a political settlement beyond a general un-signed Final Declaration, a statement concurred in by most of the participants, but not by the USA or by South Vietnam. From the outset the Americans had been reluctant to participate in the con-ference and to undertake any obligations arising from it because of their distrust of communist good faith. The South Vietnamese, while in principle favourable to unification, refused to commit themselves to the Final Declaration which outlined a plan for national elections, because they did not believe that genuinely free elections could be held in the North so long as Communists were in control.

Armistice gave Ho Chi Minh a breathing space, a base in the North and part of his political objective. But he failed to get a guarantee of unification and he failed to consult Le Duan, then the movement's leader in the South. When, a few years later, Ho Chi Minh realised that unification of North and South Vietnam on his terms was as far away as ever, he reactivated the movement in the South where in fact operations on a small scale had never completely stopped.

This brief sketch of the background to the Vietnam War is a reminder that from the earliest days of Communist activities in Vietnam their political aim of unification under Communist control was hampered by difficulties in forming a united front of all revo-lutionary factions and that northern control over southern Com-munists has never been complete. The background helps also to explain North Vietnamese mistrust of armistice negotiations.

Disillusion at the political outcome of previous negotiations made for caution before exposure to the same risks again. Moreover, North Vietnam is under very severe pressure on food supplies, industry, transport and public services. Labour has had to be diverted, population dispersed, the educational system disrupted. The North Vietnamese Government had made it abundantly clear for a long time that they ardently desired a respite from the bombing. There could be no doubt as to their sincerity in this. American insistence on a reciprocal concession had, however, been a serious obstacle to them because of the semi-independent status of the Viet Cong in South Vietnam. Though the general direction of operations is in the hands of the northerners and though they make a major contribution to the campaign in the south in terms of men, equipment, and supplies, the roots of the Viet Cong are in the South. Guerrilla warfare could be carried on there without northern support. For the sake of the promotion of Communist solidarity—never fully attained in Vietnam—and in the interests of their aim of unification, it would be hazardous for North Vietnam to agree to reduce support for the Viet Cong in return for cessation of American bombing in the north.

Dividends of Psychological Warfare

Despite the outcome of previous negotiations and despite the delicacy of relations with the Viet Cong, the North Vietnamese Government agreed in March, 1968, to meet American representatives. It would be naive to interpret this as a fortunate coincidence, Washington and Hanoi both happening to come to the conclusion that they had more to gain than to lose by talking, and both coming to this conclusion at the same time and independently. The initiative was solely American. Hanoi was quick to see the opportunities offered by an impulsive American gesture which had sprung not from a considered weighing of the situation in Vietnam, but from political necessities and domestic preoccupations in the USA.

The motive of Hanoi in responding as she did was demonstrably not military necessity. The course of the military campaign had taken a turn for the better for the Communists. The explanation lay elsewhere, in their assessment of the political dividends that might accrue to them from talks however inconclusive and however protracted. Unlike most of the rest of the world, Communists are adepts at psychological warfare. Westerners tend to confuse this with public relations and, particularly in the USA, it is apt to be taken for granted that when fighting is going on military considerations must be paramount. This is not wholly true even in all-out war, a war to victory or death, or in a fight for survival. It is far from true in limited war, where operations are limited in area or restricted in types of weapons and where the objective is not complete destruction and subjugation of the enemy but a tolerable political outcome. Communists perceive far more clearly than the rest of the world the inter-relation of political and military instruments of policy.

It has been open to Hanoi to exploit a bilateral meeting with Washington in three ways. First, they could look to secure further reductions in the scale of American bombing of the North, or even its complete stoppage, without imperilling their relations with the Viet Cong and without jeopardising their long-term goal of unification. Secondly they could count with some confidence on intensifying South Vietnamese anxieties about American intentions and hence impairing morale. Thirdly they could hope to induce in the US public a mood of relaxation, a feeling that the beginning of the end of American involvement in Vietnam is in sight. Given the domestic problems in the USA as the Paris talks began—the presidential election, racial tension and the balance of payments situation —this mood which, once engendered, could weaken the American bargaining position and sap their staying power. It is a trend which, short of a catastrophe involving heavy American battle casualties, is unlikely to prove reversible. Nor will the pressure be confined to the USA. World opinion as well as American opinion will be brought to bear on the American negotiators to go further and faster in the direction of acceptance of North Vietnamese proposals than may be wise.

Of these three purposes the second must seem to Hanoi to outrank the others. For if they can succeed in spreading despondency and doubt amongst Saigon supporters, and perhaps in the armed forces of South Vietnam, they may be able to bring down the Saigon Government. They will then be a long way on the road to achieving their political objectives whether the Americans withdraw or not. If they do not withdraw, the remaining problem will be to alienate the people of South Vietnam from the Americans. In this the Viet Cong have already had some success by tactics of harassing American forces and driving them to acts of indiscriminate destruction.

There must always be doubts about the validity of an appraisal of the motives and outlooks of others. The speculative analysis given above of previous reluctance by Hanoi to negotiate and later willingness to talk is, however, at least compatible with the assumptions that they have had in mind previous experience of negotiations and the semi-autonomous status of the Viet Cong and that they now see a possibility, at little military or political risk to themselves, of bringing about political chaos in the South and of stopping the bombing in the north without prior commitment to a cease-fire and without materially reducing their support for the Viet Cong.

Differing Objections: Slow Progress

The deduction to be drawn from this—or any other—attempt to diagnose Communist motives and aims in the Paris talks is not that negotiations are a mistake. The only alternative to negotiations is indefinite prolongation of the war. The case against this is overwhelming, on humanitarian as well as political, economic and military grounds. Prolongation carries also the double risk either of escalation or of American inability or unwillingness to deal with other crises in other parts of the world. The deduction to be drawn is that no opportunity should be lost to talk to the North Vietnamese and to listen to them, but that general relief that contact is being made should not be allowed to obscure the dangers.

Progress is bound to be slow, not only because of mutual mistrust and not only because of the inherent difficulties and delicacies of the problem, but because the objectives of the two sides are different. There are many in the USA, Britain and elsewhere who believe that the first purpose of negotiations must be a cease-fire and that the terms of a peace settlement can be negotiated later. Some even give the impression that they would welcome peace at any price and that the political outcome in Vietnam is by comparison of little consequence. This is patently not the view of the political leaders in either North or South Vietnam though for the people there, after a quarter of a century of hardship, peace and security must be their dearest wish. If the leaders wanted what the mass of the people on both sides desire, it would not be very difficult to arrange an armistice and to agree to convene a peace conference later. It is out of the question to expect the Communist leaders, either in North Vietnam or of the Viet Cong, to agree to such a solution except on their own terms. The Communist objective, in battle or in conference, is a political settlement on their terms. They see prolongation of the fighting in the South as a way, perhaps the only way, to achieve it.

The only responsible approach to this intractable problem is to recognise that in negotiations progress towards a cease fire, or to reduction in the scale of military operations, must be matched by progress towards a political settlement; and that the Communists may estimate it to be in their interests to continue or even intensify activities in the south during the negotiations. The course of negotiations, it must also be accepted, will be lengthy and erratic.

To that summing-up one reservation must be added. In 1967 Britain determined in effect to leave Aden, if possible with honour but if necessary without. If similarly the US Administration is determined to withdraw from Vietnam, and looks to the conference table for no more than quasi-legal trappings to justify and cover retreat, an armistice could probably be agreed—but on Communist terms and in a way that would enable them to pursue their political aims without outside interference.

History of Disorder in Vietnam

Vietnam has a history of disorder and division and a record of persistent national identity that few other countries can match. That identity was maintained through a thousand years of Chinese rule until, in AD 939, the northern portion secured independence. In the centuries that followed there were periods of division into two main parts, with the northern portion pushing south and the southern expanding into Cambodia from whom it seized Saigon and the Mekong Delta in 1701. In the nineteenth century the French, drawn in to protect Catholic missionaries and converts, recognised regional differences to the extent of dividing the country into colonies and protectorates. But it took the French thirty years to pacify the region and assert control.

Although the majority of the population are Annamese about 10 per cent are made up of minorities of mountain tribes, mainly in the North, and of Chinese and Cambodians in the South. Amongst the Annamese, religious differences—Catholics and Buddhists—are acute and politically significant. In the South, there is deep-rooted suspicion of northerners, including of those who settled in South Vietnam after the 1954 division of the country and who now play a part disproportionate to their numbers in the South Vietnamese Government. Communism is a relatively modern divisive factor.

Given their long history of feuding it is not to be expected that

Vietnam will ever be wholly free from unrest though she might in time achieve a measure of stability on the basis of neutrality, international guarantees and eventual unification. Such an outcome, however, depends on willingness by both North and South Vietnam to modify their present political attitudes. Of this there are at present no indications. If they cannot agree on a compromise settlement that is no reason why the friends of either should desert them. Politically, the aim of others should be to limit external repercussions of Annamese dissension, not to usurp their right to decide for themselves.

Inability to agree on a compromise political settlement was, however, no justification for continuing the war at the intensity it reached in 1968. The USA and the Soviet Union find themselves committed on opposing sides in a war over whose conduct they lack control. At a time of growing crisis in the Middle East, in Eastern and Western Europe and in Africa, when China with its nuclear armoury is not under firm control, it is a world interest that relations between the Soviet Union and the USA should not deteriorate. Though neither has clarified the long-range aims of their policies towards Vietnam, there seems to be a certain parallelism between their immediate objectives—to protect their side from succumbing to attack and to avoid escalation. If this is indeed their attitude it may be possible, concurrently with the Paris talks, for the two superpowers to agree between themselves to lessen the intensity of the war in Vietnam by reductions in the scale of Russian support for the North Vietnamese matched by reductions in the scale of American operations.

Wider Implications of Vietnam
With the two heavy-weights involved in Vietnam an internal struggle in a small country remote from both imperils world peace because it creates friction between them and may tempt the Soviet Union to foment trouble elsewhere as a lever to put pressure on the USA. This is a situation calling for patience, perseverance and restraint, not only on the part of the two powers with major responsibility for world peace, but also on the part of onlookers. Attempts to engage the UN in the Vietnam question are more likely to disrupt the organisation than to contribute to a settlement. It is an occasion for secret, not open, diplomacy. There are those in Britain who believe that by virtue of her status as co-chairman of the

1954 Geneva Conference she has a special interest and a special responsibility in Vietnam. It has even been argued that co-chairmanship carries an obligation of neutrality, though no one has been so irresponsible as to suggest that military equipment supplied by Russia to North Vietnam disqualifies her, as the other co-chairman, from attempts to find a way out.

If the preliminary bilateral Paris talks lead to general agreement between the combatants, including South Vietnam and the Viet Cong, on the broad outlines of a phased political settlement and of a phased reduction in military operations, the time may come when an international conference might serve a useful purpose in spreading responsibility for observance of the terms of the settlement. That time is a long way off and may never come. At present a public international conference could not be expected to resolve the problems and might even exacerbate them.

If it is to last, the outcome in Vietnam must be tolerable to the people of Vietnam and to her neighbours, China and the countries of South-East Asia. China has an understandable interest in freedom of access to Haiphong and in freedom of transit across North Vietnam to and from Yunnan. The countries of South-East Asia fear Communist control over Vietnam because they equate this with a dangerous expansion of Chinese influence. Though the analogy of a house of cards or a row of dominoes is an over-simplification, it is inevitable that the establishment of a Communist regime in a unified Vietnam—even if, as is in that event probable, it became a distinctively Annamese brand of communism—would give rise to profound anxiety throughout South-East Asia and prompt re-alignment of policies or even new groupings of nations determined to maintain their independence against this new threat. A unified communist Vietnam, on cordial terms with China or in alliance with her, would almost certainly lead to expansion of Soviet influence in South-East Asia as a counterbalance. It is not to be expected that, if the USA withdrew from Vietnam disillusioned and frustrated, she would readily undertake new obligations in the area even further away than Vietnam from her areas of direct interest.

Prolongation of the war and a cease-fire in circumstances facilitating Communist take-over are both outcomes that carry grave dangers. The goal to work for is a compromise in which none of the parties gets all he wants, but from which all nevertheless benefit; a compromise which it would therefore be in the interests of all to respect. In practical terms this means gradual reduction in the scale of military operations and gradual fostering of direct contacts between the three Vietnamese groups concerned—the South and North Vietnam Governments and the Viet Cong. These, if they can be achieved at all, demand qualities of patience, perseverance, determination to reach agreement and willingness to take the other point of view into account that are rarely found in Annamese. No wars leave deeper scars than civil wars.

The signs point to a long drawn-out continuation of the fighting in Vietnam, with a reduction in the scale of American activity there, but far short of the complete withdrawal hoped for by some. It is indeed difficult to see how complete extrication could be effected. Cessation of the bombing of North Vietnam in October, 1968, was not matched by the Communists with reductions in the scale of their operations. So far as the Soviet Union is concerned, it seemed perversely to have been taken by them as comforting evidence that their main anxiety, the escalation of the war, was relieved and that they could accordingly relax such efforts as they had been making to find a peaceable solution in Vietnam. A campaign costly to the USA in men and money, but presenting no particular threat to the USSR, can be regarded with equanimity. Besides, the Russians must be circumspect when it comes to preaching moderation to the North Vietnamese lest they lay themselves open to Chinese charges of appeasement of the capitalists.

The goal of the Vietcong and the North Vietnamese Government remains unchanged: complete control of the whole country, to be achieved by bringing about the collapse of the Government of South Vietnam, the destruction of the morale of their forces and the humiliating defeat of the USA.

4 SOUTH AND SOUTH-EAST ASIA

Her friends expected too much of India, cast as the greatest demo-
cratic experiment ever made, a counterpoise in Asia to Communist
China. Indian attitudes of non-violence, friendship and neutrality
were to give the world a moral lead towards peace and international
co-operation. All that had to be done was to prime the pump of
economic development. These were pipe dreams that appealed to
Indian vanity but smoke-screened the reality: how a nation—so
proud, populous and poor, clinging so tenaciously to social and
religious traditions that inhibited social betterment and agricultural
modernisation as well as administrative efficiency, with no history of
unity except under Moslem or British rule—could be expected to
enact a role alien to her.

Vast regions in North and South America, in Southern Africa, in
Australasia and in Siberia were colonised by the Spanish, Portu-
guese, Dutch, French, British and Russians just as the Chinese are
today colonising Central Asia. But other areas, in tropical Asia and
in tropical Africa, were never colonised by Europeans. They were
merely occupied and governed for a century or two. With the
departure of the governors the imprint is fading. Older patterns are
coming to the surface. Indigenous characteristics are better guides
than ephemeral Western influences in forecasting their future.

India: Internal Problems

As India rediscovers herself old instincts and habits reveal themselves; namely, provincial and local jealousies, deep divisions of
caste and language, apathy, reluctance to take decisions and responsibility, intellectual brilliance without the practical qualities needed
to apply it constructively, fondness for endless and inconclusive
dialectic. These are qualities and weaknesses manifest in India from
time immemorial, all aggravated by a steep rise in population.

When the British Raj came to India there were some 60m people
of whom the great majority lived at subsistence level. Britain left
six times as many, still mostly living at subsistence level. Another
200m have since been added. Newspapers overseas headline clashes
with China or fighting with Pakistan or famines. A rising tide of

criticism of the Congress Party and of the central government, and the erosion of their authority, are less dramatic but more significant. So is the threat from orthodox Hinduism to the very foundations of a secular state.

Paradoxically, brusque jars from China were salutary experiences that did more to jolt India into reappraisal than the exhortations of her friends, deeply wounding Indian susceptibilities and shaking her faith in moral and ethical values as a basis for relations between nations. India was recalled to the grim realities of a shaky economy, backward agriculture, weak local government and gaps in her defences. It was the last that attracted most attention. Border incidents with China coupled with refusal to compromise over Kashmir have now led to far too high a proportion of the national income being spent on defence. In grandiose developmental programmes there has been too much emphasis on heavy industry. Devaluation of the currency in 1967 proved to be only a temporary palliative and not a cure for underlying economic ailments.

Attempts to resolve their formidable internal problems will absorb Indian energies for many years to come and preclude her from a responsible international role commensurate with her size and importance. The outlook is bleak. Storm signals are already visible on the horizon over issues of "state rights" and "presidential rule" in some of the states. Yet Indians possess exceptional qualities of intellect and sensitivity. Their cultural achievements are outstanding. They cannot be helped effectively unless they help themselves. If they do, their future as a nation may be brighter than now seems probable. If they do not, the trends point to partition and division on a linguistic basis. But India is slow moving. Dissolution, if it comes, will take time.

Pakistan: Problem of Succession

Until the border clashes with China in 1962, India strove to remain uncommitted. On the other hand, Pakistan—previously committed to the anti-Communist side through membership of the South-East Asia Treaty Organisation and of the Central Treaty Organisation—has been gradually veering towards neutrality and to equal friendship with all (except with India). The 1968 decision to terminate the arrangements for an American electronics centre in West Pakistan was significant evidence of Chinese and Russian standing in Pakistan.

Under President Ayub Khan, Pakistan achieved a relatively high degree of political stability, from which economic benefits have flowed. There was good prospect of self-sufficiency in food being achieved by the 1970s. Despite the energy, skill and enthusiasm displayed in advancing the country's economic development, the outlook is rendered uncertain by the general crisis over financial aid to developing countries and the country is burdened by heavy foreign indebtedness, mounting cost of living problems and a rapidly increasing population.

Economic grievances in East Pakistan have from time to time prompted talk of secession. Like India, Pakistan believes herself compelled to maintain defence forces on a scale she can ill afford, a strain on the nation likely to continue as long as relations between the two remain as tense as they are now. President Ayub was the symbol of national unity and the driving force of policy. With his departure from power neither the political stability nor the efficiency of economic management was certain. It even became doubtful how much longer secessionist pressures in East Pakistan could be held in check.

South-East Asia Needs Common Purpose

Geography and wealth are the blessing and curse of South-East Asia. Left to themselves, given a reasonable measure of stability and good government, the easy-going and friendly peoples of the area could enjoy comfortable living standards without undue effort. They never have been left to themselves. Fertile soil and a prodigal variety of vegetable and mineral resources have for centuries attracted traders, adventurers and immigrants from poorer lands: Indians, Chinese, Arabs, Europeans and Japanese. Geographically between the Indian and Pacific Oceans, between Australasia and Asia, it is an area of strategic importance even in the air and space age. This is the principal cross-roads of the world.

Europeans who began to arrive a few centuries ago when the old empires and feudal systems were in a state of decay were drawn into politics whether the home government wished it or not. Once in, they stayed. As oases of stability and prosperity grew round their defended trading posts their authority spread. Wars in Europe were echoed in disputes between settlements. With the single exception of Thailand, South-East Asia was parcelled up between European powers in a new and arbitrary way, on divergent administrative and legal models and with different European languages in use for official purposes. Commercial ties and educational systems were patterned on the metropolitan country. Getting to know neighbours and getting on with them had been difficult even before Europeans arrived. There had been differences of religion and of race and old vendettas. Colonial rule introduced new barriers between neighbours.

If they are not to go the way of the Balkans, the countries of South-East Asia must foster a sense of common purpose as well as maintain links with outside countries. This state of affairs is still remote. Burma is trying to become a hermit state. Cambodia is at odds with her neighbours. Vietnam is too preoccupied with her own tragedy to take part in community life. Malaysia is grappling with mounting pressures welling up between her two principal communities, Malay and Chinese, each comprising about half the population. In Indonesia national unity is still fragile. The city-state of Singapore is populated largely by Chinese, few of whom have ancestral roots there or in the area extending back more than two or three generations.

Thailand: Two Policy Strands

Alone among the countries of South-East Asia, Thailand—thanks to supple and opportunist diplomacy—succeeded in maintaining independence, although in the early years of this century she was forced by French pressure to cede territory in Laos and Cambodia to the French protectorates there and by British pressure to cede territory in the south to the Federation of Malaya. These were areas that had been in dispute for centuries. In 1940, when Japanese forces were already established in Indo-China, Thailand sought security by a policy of neutrality, signing treaties with both Japan and Britain. But she seized the opportunity of French collapse in Europe to campaign in the Mekong Valley to recover areas in Laos and in Cambodia. As a result of Japanese arbitration she secured about a quarter of her claims.

Coinciding with the attack on the US Navy at Pearl Harbour, Japanese troops invaded Thailand, whose capitulation was quickly followed by the conclusion of an alliance with Japan. The arrangement was greatly to the advantage of Thailand. It enabled her to avoid the full hardships of occupation and control and to maintain her identity. With the help of Japan she acquired territory from both Burma and Malaya. In return she permitted the use of her facilities and resources by Japan. Co-operation with Japan was half-hearted and grudging. By 1944 public dissatisfaction led to the overthrow of the Thai Government and to a new and even less co-operative successor. A free Thai movement under Nai Pridi was formed, in contact with the Western allies. It was illustrative of the anomalies of the situation that although Thailand had declared war on the USA the latter refused to recognise the declaration.

The state of war between the UK and Thailand was terminated soon after the defeat of Japan. Thailand was forced to surrender the territories transferred to her with Japanese assistance during the war and to receive an Ambassador from China, a contact she had always successfully avoided in the past lest he became a rallying point for the important Chinese community in Bangkok. Otherwise, Thailand's international relations soon returned to normal. But the next decade was a period of great anxiety and uncertainty. More than once it seemed possible that Thailand—which had survived Burmese invasion in the sixteenth and eighteenth centuries, centuries of friction and war with Vietnam over control of Cambodia, the pressures of the colonial era when she had found herself squeezed between France and Britain, and alliance on the losing side in major war between 1941 and 1945—might succumb to internal dangers as one domestic crisis followed another. By 1954 Nai Pridi was in China apparently seeking Communist support for insurrection in Thailand. There were 60,000 Vietnamese refugees on the Thai side of the Mekong River, mostly supporters of the Viet Minh fleeing from the French. The Thais had little confidence in the cease-fire arrangements concluded at Geneva in July, 1954, and strongly supported signature of the South-East Asia Collective Defence Treaty at Manila in September of that year. They have taken an active part in the organisation set up under it.

Thailand's problem is not her economy. It is security. She has immense agricultural, forest and mineral resources. Through all vicissitudes two constant strands are discernible in Thai policy: determination to survive as a nation and fear of China. To serve the first, Thailand can draw on the exceptional political skill of her leaders; to meet the second, she counts on alliance with the USA. The main problem, however, remains: internal stability. In the north-east there are still some thousands left of the Vietnamese who fled there 15 or more years ago. In the south, Thai forces have failed to destroy Chinese Communists who have found shelter there from Malaysia. Old feuds with Cambodia are not healed. Spreading confusion in Laos infects the Thai side of the Mekong. An all-pervasive American military presence, though guaranteeing defence against external attack, brings problems of its own in terms of inflation and political instability. Pre-occupation with the political scene in Bangkok and a tendency towards opportunism are weaknesses that have often been manifest in the history of Thailand. Sophisticated and ingenious though the leaders are, the years ahead will be a severe test of Thai statesmanship.

Burma and Cambodia: Two Neutralisms

Burma has opted out, hoping to lead a self-sufficient existence on traditional Burmese lines. Fought over twice between 1942 and 1945, as first the Japanese drove out the British and then were in turn driven out by them, Burma has no desire to be a battlefield again. Neutrality and seclusion seemed likely to help in other connections also, in relations with China, by breaking the stranglehold of Indian money lenders, in freeing the economy from dominance by foreign firms and in preserving the Buddhist religion. Rice, timber, oil, cotton, tobacco and rubber were ample for her needs and to leave a surplus for necessary imports.

The policy has now been implemented so inefficiently that the national economy has collapsed. The most striking illustration is rice, now rationed in a country that used to be the world's leading exporter. Failure to develop her resources may in times of scarcity prove to be a temptation to others to put the pressure on Burma. China and India, largest and hungriest of countries, happen to be her neighbours.

Cambodia for long set an example that other South-East Asian nations may be inclined to imitate: neutrality without isolation, alliances without engagement, leaving options open, being wary of neighbours but playing distant big powers off against each other. It was a policy dictated by weakness and by deep-rooted fears of traditional enemies, the Thais and the Annamese. And it was made possible by the skill and ingenuity of a brilliant politician, Prince Sihanouk, the country's Prime Minister. In the Vietnam War, Cambodia avoided declaring herself irrevocably on one side or the other. Until Prince Sihanouk's fall she showed a bias in favour of the Hanoi regime and the North Vietnamese, not out of sympathy with communism, but because a unified Vietnam under Communist control might endanger the future of Cambodia and it seemed prudent to propitiate them in advance. Confusion in China, together with the demise of President Sukarno in Indonesia, weakened two strands in Cambodian external policy and some re-appraisal was on the cards.

Militarily there was a strong case for intervention by South Vietnamese and American forces in Cambodia in order to block the transit route and to deny the use of Cambodian territory as a sanctuary. The case became compe ling once the decision was taken to reduce the American presence in Vietnam. Strong as the military arguments for intervention were, however, it is doubtful whether the eventual results will justify them. In jungle warfare the enemy, like quicksilver, is exceedingly difficult to trap and destroy. The wider the area of the conflict the more scope there is for mercury to flow elsewhere. A somewhat similar state of affairs has ari en in the Middle East where in her search for security Israel has time and again stretched her boundaries and yet found that security eludes her. An inconclusive and indecisive operation in Cambodia is likely to create a situation like that in Laos, leaving her the field of the battles of others. If in the end Prince Sihanouk is able to regain control some of the options will have been closed because of Cambodian dependence on Chinese and North Viet-namese support.

Singapore: Security Problems

Singapore, without natural resources, where even water has to be imported, has two assets; first, geographical situation and, secondly, the industry and brains of her citizens who, next to the Japanese, have the highest standards of living and education in Asia. Her future depends on providing facilities at competitive costs for inter-national trade and international services such as banking, insurance and shipping for all of which she is the natural centre. It also depends on finding employment for the young men and women pouring out of her schools and universities with skills and training in demand throughout the area. But by race they are Chinese. This in itself is an obstacle to finding employment outside Singapore. It is in Singapore's interests to encourage others to adopt more liberal immigration policies even if to achieve this she has to modify the restrictions she imposes on others. The economic dilemma is that the

British free trade policy of colonial days would handicap development of local industries that could offer employment, whilst protectionist policies in a small state with high labour costs and without natural resources are liable—except in industries relying on high capital investment per worker and a small technologically trained staff—to price Singapore products out of world markets.

In foreign policy the course is clear: good relations with all in order to trade with all. But, racially isolated, Singapore has problems of external defence and internal security which make heavy demands on resources. Resolution of her economic, political and defence problems, and harmonising the solutions, present acute difficulties for Singapore. In default of viability as an independent unit, there is the alternative that Singapore may look to China for support and become, as many in South-East Asia have long feared, an outpost of Peking.

Malaysia: Multi-Racial Community

Since the divorce of Singapore, the Malaysian Federation has consisted of the states of Malaya (rich, prosperous and sophisticated), and two new states, Sarawak (a land of jungle, mountain river and swamp with poor land communications) and Sabah (semi-tropical, forests and uplands and in the early stages of development). In Malaya, as in the two new states (much less populous, although in area each is almost as large as all the states of Malaya put together), there is a plural society with all the problems familiar in other multi-racial communities, including racial riots.

In Britain, where these problems are novel and little understood, immigration policy for non-white immigrants is debated with passion and prejudice as if the issues concerned fundamental ethical principles when in reality it is a practical problem of the pace of assimilation, of the time it takes to graft new communities on to old stock. The larger the new group the longer it takes. If there are pronounced racial, social and cultural differences between the new arrivals and the old stock, grafting may be impossible. As many countries have found, if not yet Britain, legislation and goodwill cannot prevent the friction inherent in a multi-racial community, although they may ameliorate some of the effects.

The Malay states, Sabah and Sarawak are at different stages of development. Central government operates from Kuala Lumpur, 600 miles from Kuching, in Sarawak, and over 1,000 miles from

Jesselton, in Sabah. These last two are both regarded by Malayan administrators as distant outposts where conditions are less congenial than in West Malaysia. While standards of administration have come under criticism, there is no doubt that the central government has shown statesmanship in relation to the problems of the Malay peninsula. Stability has been imposed in the mainland states by the adroit adaptation of feudalism to the facts of a multi-racial community in such a way that maintenance of the present system is identified with retention of political and military power in Malay hands. This, however, is not a formula applicable in Sabah and not easy to apply in Sarawak.

In every country in South-East Asia communities of overseas Chinese are to be found, not homogeneous groups but stemming originally from different areas of south China and retaining to this day traces of their different origins. Prospects of assimilation with other races or, without intermarriage, of identification with the countries where they have made their homes sometimes for many generations vary from country to country. They are easier in Buddhist or Christian lands than in Moslem ones, easier where Chinese children have been taught in the language of the country and more difficult where they have been taught in Chinese. Almost everywhere the overseas Chinese have made valuable contributions to economic development, sometimes so successfully that this has roused the resentment of others. But politically, where their numbers constitute a significant percentage of the total population, their presence is a source of tension. Given patience and restraint this can in time be cured to the lasting benefit of the countries concerned and of their citizens of Chinese stock.

Indonesia: Rehabilitation Critical

In Indonesia the problem is size, how to fuse into one nation almost 100m people of complex ethnic structure (but mostly Moslems), scattered through hundreds of islands spread over three and a half thousand miles and speaking many languages and dialects. Great Hindu and Buddhist empires, centred on Java, dominated much of what is now Indonesia in the fourteenth and fifteenth centuries. These broke up under the impact of Islam into small weak states in which—from the sixteenth century onwards—Portugal, the Netherlands and Britain began to establish trading posts. In the next hundred years the Netherlands emerged as the dominant power and remained in control for nearly three centuries.

Over the years the Dutch established uniform patterns of administration and selected the simplest of the many dialects as the standard vernacular language. Basically the system of government was decentralisation, well suited to the geography and circumstances of the vast archipelago. In some ways Java was and is unique by reason of population and tradition. With a population of 60m, the island contains two-thirds of the people of Indonesia, but it is only one-fortieth of the total size. Java is not viable economically without the foreign exchange surpluses earned by other islands.

On independence Indonesia established a unitary state. Given enough capable and experienced administrators this type of government might have fostered national unity without serious damage to the economy. The few administrators available, however, were inexperienced. Moreover, President Sukarno disdained the commonplace tasks of government in favour of the more glamorous target of political unity. The results in terms of neglect of the economy, depreciated currency and friction with some of the other islands brought hardship to the people and ruin to the country.

Despite some anti-Chinese public sentiment the main plank in Sukarno's external policy was friendship with China. There have been Chinese communities in Indonesia for centuries—tin miners, sugar planters and traders—and from time to time sporadic anti-Chinese rioting, as these industrious people became too powerful and too wealthy. Indeed, in the early years of the twentieth century the first manifestations of nascent Indonesian nationalism took the form not of anti-Dutch but of anti-Chinese demonstrations. Nevertheless, on world issues Sukarno found himself aligned with the attitudes of the Peking Government, even though on occasion he acted repressively against Chinese in Indonesia. In his policy of alignment with China he was strongly supported by the Indonesian Communist Party to the point where they weakened their appeal to their own compatriots.

Indonesia and Japan have influenced events in each other in significant but different ways. Repercussions of Russian defeat by Japan in 1904-05, the first instance for centuries of an Asian power defeating a European one, echoed round Asia and sparked the flames of nationalism in the East Indies—and incidentally also in French Indo-China. In 1941, denial of Japanese access to oil from the Dutch East Indies was decisive in the timing of Japan's entry into World War II. After their conquest of the East Indies the Japanese pursued, not always consistently, a policy of collaboration with Indonesian nationalist leaders and shortly before her defeat Japan staged a ceremony of handing over power to them. It is this, and not the later conclusion of negotiations with the Netherlands, which is celebrated annually as the date of independence. Memories of Japanese occupation, however, are still vivid. Japanese hopes of becoming the dominant foreign influence in the Indonesian economy may not be fulfilled rapidly or easily in spite of the impetus Japan originally gave to Indonesian nationalism and in spite of her identification as the nation that gave independence to Indonesia.

The regime in Djakarta headed by President Suharto has been working its way to international acceptance by a policy of neutrality and by tentative gestures of co-operation with its neighbours in South-East Asia. Confrontation of Malaysia is quiescent. In time, Indonesian territorial ambitions may reassert themselves. Meanwhile social and economic ills must take priority. These are urgent, even critical. There is some resurgence of support for the Communist Party and disappointment over economic rehabilitation and continuing inflation. The government will stand or fall according to the measure of success in raising living standards, restoring transport, stabilising the currency, improving distribution of food and other consumer goods and in the rehabilitation of derelict mines and plantations. This is a tall order calling for imaginative statesmanship and a high degree of managerial efficiency and competent administration, qualities all the more difficult to acquire or apply in a nation still suffering from the aftermath of the attempted Communist *coup* on the night of September 30, 1965.[2]

If Indonesia can resolve her central problems of the economy and of national unity, Java will re-emerge as a centre and focus of political development in South-East Asia as she was five centuries ago. But this will at best take many years. The immensity of the problems rules out early solution. In the meantime there is a risk of relapse into civil war and dissolution into independent component parts in a state of hostility to one another. This is the gravest short-term danger confronting South-East Asia because it would destroy the chances of regional co-operation.

[2]For a graphic account of these little-noticed events see Tarzie Vittachi, *The Fall of Sukarno* (Andre Deutsch, London, 1966).

142

5 BALANCE OF POWER

In scale and variety the problems of China, India and South-East Asia—making up half the world's population—are immense. Among the factors conspiring against economic stability are (a) racial and religious friction and ancient feuds, (b) uneven distribution of population that leaves some areas almost empty whilst others are over-crowded, (c) standards of living that in most of the area are far too low to permit economic development to be financed out of savings, (d) a profusion of natural resources but widespread poverty, (e) undue dependence on exports of primary produce and (f) inefficiencies in administration. These problems are aggravated by political instability, for which three reasons might be advanced. There have been difficulties in adapting to the post-colonial environment; as colonial rulers have withdrawn, the administrations replacing them have not found it easy to exert authority over their peoples. Older tensions have surfaced again in the form, sometimes, of nationalist feeling and territorial disputes with neighbours. And then there has been Communist exploitation of discontent and uncertainty.

Asia: Determinant of Global Balance

There is ambivalence in relations between the USA and the Soviet Union. They are confident that each will behave responsibly towards each other on the great issues of peace and war, but mistrust each other's intentions. They are competing for influence in third countries, but are disposed to view China in the same light. Both are caught in the Vietnam War, but are on opposite sides and unable either to extricate themselves or to assert full control. There is the further coincidence that in external policy outside their immediate neighbourhoods the main area of interest is in both cases Asia. Both seem to be giving Africa south of the Sahara lower priority than a few years ago. There is stalemate between them in Europe. On the other hand Soviet policy, like American policy, is extremely active throughout Asia. Since 1955, Russia has greatly expanded the scope of Asian studies. One of the most striking new developments over the whole Asian scene is the degree of her involvement in the Arab-

Israeli conflict, in South-East Asia, in the Vietnam War, in disputes with China and in her growing contacts with Japan. At the same time the Soviet Union maintains her contacts with India, although she may not find it easy to maintain Indian friendship and simultaneously improve relations with Pakistan, one aspect of her drive to gain influence in the whole Islamic world.

If there is to be a new basis for world political equilibrium it can come about only through better relations between the USA and the Soviet Union in respect of their policies in Asia where at present competition between them is keenest but scope for co-operation greatest.

Under the traditional doctrine of balance of power, maintenance of peace depended on preventing a nation or an alliance from becoming so powerful that it could impose its will on others. It gave the apprehensive two options, either to coalesce in resistance to the leading power or, where there were two rivals for power, to support the weaker. Implicit in the doctrine were the assumptions that man was an aggressive animal and nations expansionist so that, if their power grew unchecked, others would be swallowed.

Britain has never been the leading military power. Time and again survival in peace and war resulted from skilfully balancing power, alliances in Europe being formed and reformed to prevent mastery of the continent by a power stronger than Britain herself. The doctrine is now in disrepute. The main centres of power are no longer in Western Europe. Alliances with Germany against France, as in the Napoleonic era, or with France against Germany, as in this century, are irrelevant. Moreover, the underlying assumptions are repugnant to those who believe that mankind has advanced beyond the atavistic stage of perennial tribal warfare to a phase where, perhaps through the UN, the rest of the world can bring collective pressure to bear on an aggressor. The doctrine savours of unprincipled political machinations.

Neither the lessened status of Western Europe nor idealism should blind Britain to the resurrection of the theory of balance in a new form, world balance instead of European balance, expressed militarily by such phrases as "balance of terror" or "nuclear stalemate" and politically as "spheres of influence" or "containment". What is novel today is not the terminology. Rather it is the fact that nowhere is the debate on world equilibrium and grand strategy livelier than in the USA, the most powerful country of all. In its old form, balance of power was a stratagem discussed and used by the weak to frustrate the strong.

In military strategy the advent of nuclear weapons led to what was called a balance of terror. The assumption was that the USA and Russia were implacably and permanently hostile to one another, although each was deterred from fighting by the nuclear arsenal of the other, which would be employed at once, on a devastating scale, in a war between them. It was a theory that did scant justice to the restraint shown by the Americans in the years when they had a monopoly of the new weapons. In the evolution of military theorising the Russians have usually tended to lag behind the Americans— and the Chinese behind the Russians. In the USA doubts were already being expressed about the concepts of instant massive retaliation to any breach of the peace when the Soviet Union, having developed similar weapons of its own, began to proclaim precisely the same views as the Americans were beginning to discard. Newly acquired Russian capacity to inflict destruction on the USA hastened but did not give the initial impetus to new American thinking.

Weapon Dispersal and Diversification

Now the Russians, some years after the Americans, are reshaping their forces to cover a wide range of operations most strikingly illustrated by their increased attention to sea power. The military balance is assuming a more mature form as both possess a variety of weapons and weapon systems which obviate the need for immediate choice between all and nothing in a crisis. This has important consequences. Diversification of armaments and of systems tends to nullify the military advantages of surprise nuclear attack because, whatever the scale of civilian damage, neither the USA nor the Soviet Union can count on destroying the other's military capacity to retaliate. It does more than lessen the risk of surprise. It gives time to check and confirm whether particular incidents, however grave, herald attack or are accidental. Here again, the USA led the Soviet Union in perceiving the military and political significance of dispersal and diversification of weapons.

But not all the consequences make for greater stability. There are new possibilities of applying military power to political ends, an old doctrine which many—though not Communists for whom it has always been an article of faith—had been inclined to discard because of the devastating potential of nuclear weapons. The argument was that possessors of nuclear weapons would hesitate to intervene in political crises lest intervention led to conventional military operations and these to escalation and the use of nuclear weapons. Wars in which the major military powers might be engaged therefore became less likely though more terrible.

Whether or not this subtle theory was at one time valid, it is so no longer. Nuclear weapons were not used in the Korean War. They have not so far been used in the Vietnam War despite the scale and intensity and are unlikely to be used strategically. It is probable, however, that there would be demands in the USA that nuclear weapons should be used tactically, in the last resort, if this appeared the only way to save American units from destruction. With the stationing of Russian naval units in the Eastern Mediterranean the Soviet Union is openly using military power to gain a foothold in the Mediterranean and in the Levant. Further east there are some signs that Pakistan's flirtation with China is cooling and that her relations with Russia are improving. This would be consistent with Soviet aspirations to paramountcy in Arabia and influence in the Moslem world.

Possibility of Russo-American Restraint

Whilst diversification of forces permits flexible application of military power for military or political purposes it is still true that the broad equivalence of capacity makes the Russo-American military balance more secure, although this would be a precarious foundation for world peace even without the new and unpredictable factor of China as a nuclear power. Military equivalence without political accord spells tension. Despite Vietnam—or perhaps because of it— an informal understanding between America and Russia is not out of the question. Bogged down in Vietnam and in Korea, facing mounting racial strife at home, in difficulties over balance of payments, disillusioned with allies and with the results of aid programmes, it is natural that Americans should debate new definitions of their international purposes. For their part the Russians know that, even if they may have some success in eroding Western influence, they cannot change the world balance by force without risk to the Soviet Union. They are nervous lest they are dragged ever deeper into the jungles of Vietnam. In the south-west, Moscow sees signs of resurgence in Germany; in the south-east, an unfriendly

China arming herself with nuclear weapons and even the nightmare of a Sino-German understanding.[3] A few cracks are beginning to show in the solidarity of the Warsaw Pact countries. Defence spending has had to be increased in spite of the cost of the space programme and in spite of the domestic clamour for more and better consumer goods and higher living standards.

Extension to the political field of the tacit understanding to show restraint in the application of their military power in areas of special sensitivity to the other may therefore have its attractions for both super-powers. Co-operation, even if limited to this degree, would open new possibilities of general equilibrium. The impact would be felt everywhere. But the reception would be mixed. Agreement to exercise care in relation to issues believed by the other to be vltal could be taken in Bonn as meaning agreement on the indefinite partition of Germany. If Russo-American understanding developed far beyond agreement to show restraint on issues important to them, to the point of agreeing to abstain from intervention in disputes between third parties where neither had a major interest at stake, some of the implications would be highly unwelcome to those seeking their help. Almost any sign of co-operation between Russia and America, no matter how tenuous, would be interpreted in China as provocative collusion against her.

Sino-Soviet Dispute

The Chinese, like the Russians, see enemies everywhere. The reasons are rooted not in communism but in history and geography. European Russia, land of suspicion and secrecy, has always had a siege mentality. Long dark winters have made their imprint on the national character. Anti-foreignism in China sprang from a mythology of self-sufficiency and of cultural superiority to the Mongols, Manchus, Japanese and Europeans at whose hands she suffered military humiliation. Today, Chinese anti-foreignism is directed mainly at the USA and Russia, though it may be safer to express it against less powerful nations such as Britain. A strong reaction from China is to be expected in the event of co-operation between the USA and the USSR, countries she regards as her most dangerous enemies though for different reasons. The threat from America is to

[3]See, for instance, Rostovsky, "Bonn-Peking? The Attraction of Opposites", *Literaturnaya Gazeta*, Moscow, April 10 and 17, 1968; discussed in Tibor Szamuely, "An Alliance that Russia Fears", *The Sunday Telegraph*, London, May 5, 1968.

the ideology of communism and the survival of the regime in power. The threat from Russia is to the security of her soil and to the unity of the Chinese Communist Party.

Communism is presented to the outside world as an idealistic philosophy of social justice. Its two main practitioners differ on the best tactics to be followed by Communist parties in order to come to power. The Russians prescribe infiltration into key positions of influence in every field of activity and making common cause with all radical movements. The Chinese, on the other hand, advocate national liberation movements employing far bolder tactics of terrorism and revolution. But if a Communist party does gain control, the doctrine becomes a technique of power, one in which a self-perpetuating oligarchy can remain in control by creating the illusion of a mass movement from the bottom calling on the top to impose rigid uniformity; the technique is for economic and social change through selection of priorities by rulers who believe that they, and they alone, know what is best for the nation and how to secure it.

At the root of the Sino-Soviet dispute there is a power conflict complicated by ideological differences. To some extent these turn on differing attitudes towards America. For while the Soviet Union has world-wide contacts with the USA, China is bent on regional advantages against the American presence. It suits her to disrupt Russo-American relations in order to create further difficulties for the USA and score doctrinal points off the Soviet Union. These aims can be prosecuted by efforts to defeat Russia in the international Communist struggle and to rally support from Afro-Asian nations.

Containment Must be Temporary Policy
But with or without a Communist label it is the pressures now working their way to the surface that matter. These have more in common with the nationalist principles of the French Revolution —liberty, equality and fraternity—than with the internationalist class-struggle precepts of Marxism. In the last three or four centuries the most dynamic political force in the world has been the expansionist urge of the white races to the Americas, Africa, Australasia and Asia, including Eastern Siberia. This is what some sections of the non-white world are reacting against today. These reactions are intensified by population growth, unequal living conditions and better communications. They are obscured by cross currents of national interests and characteristics, by old local and regional causes of friction.

148

Before the Red Guards appeared on the scene it was sometimes argued that China was entitled to her sphere of influence, a phrase reminiscent of the partition of Africa in the nineteenth century. Smaller powers today can no longer be treated as pawns. Even if their wishes were ignored there are larger countries, the Soviet Union, Japan, India and Pakistan, to be considered. Neither the partition of Africa nor a Monroe Doctrine is relevant to East Asia. Threats to the independence of states on the American continent came from outside. In East Asia it is not a distant power that is feared; instead it is China and the Chinese.

In 1808, Lieutenant-General Sir John Moore described talk in London of "enveloping" the French as "a sort of gibberish which men in office use without knowing how far it is susceptible of being carried into practice". He might have made the same criticism of the word in vogue today in relation to China: "containment". This is an imprecise term which sometimes, on the assumption that China is bent on territorial expansion, signifies a military policy of forcible resistance to China and sometimes non-military action outside China to halt the spread of communism. In South-East Asia, where anti-Chinese sentiment persists independently of the political complexion of the government in Peking, containment of China and containment of communism are apt to be confused. Acts of discrimination against Chinese are sometimes justified on the grounds that the purpose is containment of communism even though the great majority of Chinese living overseas are not communists.

Containment is by definition negative. At best it sterilises and freezes a source of infection and at worst bottles up pressures which will sooner or later burst out. With the weakening of central authority in China there is a bigger risk of eruption against which military precautions are prudent. The atmosphere, however, is so charged with emotion and tension that by itself a policy of military containment may heighten the risks it is designed to prevent. It is important to look on this as a temporary policy, to be supplemented as soon as conditions in China permit by political action to try to persuade her that her legitimate objectives, including security from attack, can be attained otherwise than by fomenting instability and encouraging revolution. That is a long-term policy and success is not certain, reservations that attach to all the big questions of the times. Outside China, containment is equally inadequate as a description of policy towards communism. Force must be employed to put down armed rebels and deal with threats to national security. Force, though, does not necessarily cure the causes of the rebellion or of the breach of security and may even aggravate them.

In the long run, policies must be positive, not negative, even if fires must be extinguished before rebuilding can start. But, in rebuilding, as many as possible of the fire hazards must be removed. Security, political and economic stability, improvement in living standards, good government and good intelligence: these are the basic conditions of nationhood to be neglected only at peril to the nation. Yet in practice even the simplest and easiest of these conditions, good intelligence—keeping in touch with the people, knowing what their problems and grievances are, hard as it frequently is to find quick and effective remedies—is too often neglected. In this Prince Sihanouk of Cambodia set an example that his neighbours would do well to emulate.

Rapprochement or no *rapprochement* between America and Russia, the outlook for East Asia is turbulent. But for most of the area, as for most of the world, the hazards which *rapprochement* might intensify are infinitely less than those of a drift to war between them.

6 ECONOMIC IMBALANCE

The USA and Russia have exhibited sober and responsible awareness of the consequences of unleashing their nuclear capacity against
the other. Politically there is a faint but growing prospect of mutual
restraint and suspicious co-operation.

There is no matching trend towards general economic balance
which depends, not on the relative economic resources of the USA
and the USSR, but on narrowing the gap between rich and poor
nations. Relaxed political relations between the two super-powers
would not of itself correct the growing imbalance of wealth. The
consequences of this imbalance spill over from the economic to the
political field and jeopardise, as well, the welfare of industrialised
nations by endangering their markets and sources of supply. Causes
of disparity are not all economic. Social traditions, insecurity,
political uncertainties and inefficiencies in administration contribute
to keeping poor countries poor. Fluctuations in commodity prices,
tariffs and other restrictions on trade, oscillations on the foreign
exchanges and shortages of capital are among factors outside national
control.

Gap Between Rich and Poor

Price fluctuations make a double impact. In the selling country,
when low, they unsettle the economy and handicap long-term
investment and development. Abroad, when high, they induce
customers to look for substitutes, which modern technology is
increasingly able to supply. The combined effect is to intensify
pressures towards economic nationalism and import substitution
under protectionism, tendencies visible also in advanced industrialised countries in difficulties over balance of payments. Yet it is now
widely accepted to be in the interests of all, rich and poor alike, to
liberalise and expand world trade.

In international finance the need for better monetary arrangements is universally agreed, however much proposals to this end may
differ. The dollar and the pound sterling are under the double
strain of acting as reserve currencies and as trading currencies.

Capital for development cannot be found in countries where

standards of living are too low to permit savings unless the people are willing to tolerate a dictatorship which retards improvement in living standards in order to divert resources to its own arbitrarily chosen priorities. Part of the price of the Russian space programme is poor housing conditions and shortages of better quality consumer goods. China is acquiring nuclear weapons despite the poverty of the masses. Economic development is a very slow process in poor countries where the welfare of the individual is not subordinated to the real or fancied interests of the state, and in countries where savings are possible, but for one reason or another—lack of confidence in government, mistrust of others or religious dogma—there is no tradition of private investment in public companies.

The problems are well known. So, too, are the results of attempts to deal with them. Repeated attempts to stabilise commodity prices have been disappointing. Commodity agreements, which have limited scope, are extremely difficult to maintain over a period. A synthetic substitute may be developed and reduce demand. The natural product may be over-produced so that the market is saturated. Or an economic crisis in one of the producing countries may tempt it to evade the terms of the agreement.

Inward-looking Policies

Protectionism and economic nationalism, whether as the policy of a single country to protect home industries and to reduce overseas spending, such as is being urged in the USA, or as a regional policy to encourage integration, such as in the EEC, represent a threat to all that has been achieved in twenty years of tariff disarmament negotiations under the General Agreement of Tariffs and Trade (GATT). It threatens the meagre gains scored for the developing countries in the long drawn out, if in the end relatively successful, Kennedy Round of negotiations. In the context of narrowing the gap between rich and poor, the Common Market countries have favoured "inward-looking" policies, concentrating their effort mainly on the ex-French colonies of Africa.

The "inward-looking" character of the EEC has been a source of disappointment, even disillusion, in Britain and, indeed, the attitude of the Six towards British membership has illustrated this characteristic, although the success of the Kennedy Round has ameliorated the harm that might have been done to British trade by exclusion from the EEC. A resurgence of protectionism in the USA and the Common Market would be hurtful to Britain as a country heavily engaged in international trade and yet without free access to a really large market. The value of preferential access to other Commonwealth markets and to the markets of other member countries of the European Free Trade Association (EFTA) would then be appreciated.

At the time of Britain's first application to join the EEC, from 1961 to 1963, the main benefit of acceding to the Treaty of Rome was said to be access to a larger market. This was stressed less forcefully during 1967 on the second application. For in the interim doubts had been cast on the scope for economies of scale and on the degree of market integration likely to be achieved by EEC countries. Moreover, in the case of more sophisticated products where the advantages of large-scale production are real, technological co-operation and sharing research and development costs can be, and are being, effected without British adherence to the all-embracing political and economic requirements of the Treaty of Rome. In the case of the USA, where there is no question of joining the EEC, American firms are reaping some of the advantages of the EEC market by acquiring control of existing industries or setting up new subsidiaries in Common Market countries.

Restriction on Freedom of Action

There has been growing public awareness in Britain of the price to be paid for abandoning "cheap food" policies and for losing tariff preferences in other Commonwealth countries and in EFTA. Taking into account the combined cost of higher import prices for food and the levy payments under the EEC's common agricultural policy, together with the indirect effect on trade in manufactures through increased food costs, Mr Harold Wilson, as Prime Minister, put the cumulative effect of joining the EEC at the end of five years at minus £500m a year on current account.[4] Since the devaluation of sterling in November, 1967, the cost has risen—in part because EEC agricultural prices are tied to gold.

On the political side of the equation, it is beginning to be realised in Britain that to achieve its aims the EEC must develop a supra-national authority and a wide range of common policies controlling

[4]See *Parliamentary Debates*, Official Report, House of Commons, H.M. Stationery Office, London, May 8, 1967, Vol. 746, No. 195, c. 1081.

the fiscal, monetary and economic planning operations of member governments, and that the determination and administration of common economic policies pre-suppose the existence of a central supra-national decision-taking body. Community is indeed a euphemism for federation. Countries like Canada, Australia and India with experience of federal government can detect in the EEC the embryo of federal union, the declared objective of sponsors of the new Europe. All experience of federations shows that however carefully member states seek initially or later to retain some freedom of action and some independence, in a stable federation power gravitates to the centre. Economic integration sets in motion a process which, unless economic integration itself fails, leads inexorably towards political federation.

Involvement in such a political union must entail for Britain, as eventually for present members of the EEC, a severe restriction on freedom of action, both politically and economically. Foreseeing these developments in the light of their own federal experience countries which have hitherto had close relations with Britain have felt obliged to reassess their own positions. Canada, Australia and New Zealand have been orientating themselves towards the USA and Japan and tentative studies have been made for achieving closer economic co-operation in the Pacific area.[5] Like former French dependencies, African Commonwealth countries could become associated overseas territories of the EEC, as was agreed during Britain's first negotiations for membership of the Common Market. For Asian Commonwealth countries there is no prospect of association with the Community, whilst Britain's political capacity—or even willingness, given her own problems that would have to be resolved —to champion the interests of these nations will be greatly curtailed.

Free Trade Treaty Option and the Third World

Loss of preferential access to the British market would pose severe problems not only for developing countries but also for temperate-zone agricultural economies. Global solutions are proposed as a way of dealing with them. The EEC was ready to co-operate in international agreements to meet Australian, Canadian and New Zealand farmers. But little was achieved on this front

[5]See, for instance, Kiyoshi Kojima (ed.), *Pacific Trade and Development*, Vol. I and II (The Japan Economic Research Centre, Tokyo, 1968 and 1969).

in the Kennedy Round negotiations. Britain has declared herself ready to see Commonwealth tariff preferences subsumed in a generalised scheme of preferences for developing countries on their exports of manufactures and semi-manufactures. But the implementation of such a scheme agreed in principle at the second United Nations Conference on Trade and Development, held in New Delhi in early 1968, was hampered by disagreements among the developed countries and in the end could easily be rendered of little value through protectionist safeguards.

Because the Kennedy Round proved such a difficult operation it is widely accepted that a fresh approach to trade liberalisation needs to be adopted. Interest has been growing in the USA and Canada, and more recently in Britain and Japan, in proposals for a multilateral free trade treaty approach that would not be held back by the unwillingness of a major trading nation, or group of nations, to make reciprocal concessions.[6] In order to maintain the momentum of trade liberalisation, and to counter rising protectionism, the Nixon Administration in the USA has been expected to launch some kinds of major trade initiative. Whether it will take the form of another Kennedy Round-type of negotiation, an industry-by-industry approach to free trade, the free trade treaty option or another form altogether is something that remains to be seen. But the initiative will be largely influenced by political considerations, one of which is the need to meet the challenge from the Third World for a fair deal in international trade.

In what could initially be a North Atlantic free trade association, if a free trade treaty approach were adopted, the US Congress might be readier to accept worthwhile tariff preferences for developing countries if they were launched on a co-operative basis with other industrialised countries. The various proposals which have been made for a multilateral free trade association have all envisaged greater access to industrial markets for developing countries.

If a multilateral free trade treaty were embarked upon, embracing North America and EFTA and open to the EEC, Japan, Australia,

---

[6]The most highly developed proposals appear to have been suggested by the Canadian-American Committee. This was in May, 1966. The committee is jointly sponsored by the National Planning Association in Washington and the Private Planning Association of Canada. See *A New Trade Strategy for Canada and the United States* (Canadian-American Committee, Washington, D.C., and Montreal, May, 1966).

New Zealand and other industrial nations, with provision for the developing countries, a material advance could be made in narrowing the gap between rich and poor. In so doing, the initiative would also contribute to political stability and economic growth in such vital areas as South and East Asia. For the industrial nations the initiative would hold out the prospect of a continuing expansion of world trade and help to resolve financial difficulties that are hampering the provision of capital for development.

Japanese Involvement Necessary

In South-East Asia the success of this or any other co-operative plan to stimulate development and expand trade depends on the participation of Japan who is already playing an increasingly major trading and investment role in the area. With the fastest rate of economic growth of any major industrial country, Japan's spectacular progress has given her the resources and the experienced bankers, economists and industrialists. Symptoms of overstrain provide part of the impetus. Like some others in East Asia, the Japanese economy has benefited from American off-shore purchases for the Vietnam War, a stimulus that cannot be counted on indefinitely. Even if fighting continues in Vietnam, balance of payments difficulties will impel the USA to cut spending in third countries if she can. Meanwhile, in Japan, credit purchases of luxury consumer goods have led to widespread indebtedness whilst her production potential continues to grow faster than markets.

Looking for new markets, new sources of supply and new investment outlets, not yet fully recovered from the traumatic experiences of the past fifty years, Japan has displayed much less vigour politically than in economic policy. With nostalgic yearnings for better relations with China, with anti-militarism still a potent element in public opinion even though expenditure on defence is rising, disillusioned with politics which in the main are left to the older generation, conscious that her standard of living depends on trade with the non-communist world, Japan still gives the observer the impression of a nation lacking self-confidence and unsure of its political role. She has the means, the opportunity, and the incentive to take a leading part in economic development in South-East Asia. The old Japanese dream of a Greater Co-Prosperity Sphere in South-East Asia may be realised, this time not militarily but in economic terms, with far-reaching political implications for the region and for Japan herself. She is now scanning even wider horizons than South-East Asia, and beginning to look on Asia in the context of the Pacific, to the possibility of economic association with the USA, Canada, Australia and New Zealand. The concept of "an Asian-Pacific sphere of co-operation" was being quietly promoted by Mr. Takeo Miki almost as soon as he became Foreign Minister. Various factors enter Japanese calculations: the need to ensure long term supplies of industrial raw materials resources; the need for a broad international base for trade expansion and economic development in Asia, whilst recognising that the uncertainties of the Asian scene make it necessary to develop her markets in other countries on the Pacific periphery; the need to insure against a revival of protectionism in other major industrial markets or a decline in exports to Europe.

The only other country in the proximity of South-East Asia and capable of playing an active part in the liberalisation of trade is Australia. Commercially more and more dependent on Asian markets, her aid and trade promotion programmes have demonstrated Australian awareness of their value to her economy and of the political importance of good relations with Asian countries, even if her military alliance with the USA and participation in the Vietnam War are evidence of fears of Asian threats to her security.

Transformation of the Australian attitude to Japan and growth of trade between them, and the beginning of Japanese investment in Australia, were striking developments of the 1960s. With economies that are in many respects complementary, recession in one would damage the other. They are both keenly interested in Indonesia, to Japan a source of supply, a market, and a field for investment. To Australia, four times as large as Indonesia but with one eighth the population, good relations with her nearest neighbour are essential, all the more so because there are seeds of dissension between them over New Guinea. To both Japan and Australia trade with mainland China is important though in both cases formal diplomatic relations are with Taiwan. Freedom of passage across the Indian Ocean is vital for both. Some 45 per cent of Australian exports and 55 per cent of her imports cross it, whilst Japan is heavily dependent on Persian Gulf oil and therefore on stability there as well as, like Australia, on freedom of transit across the ocean.

The nations of South-East Asia cannot contribute as much as

Japan and Australia to international action. But their stake in the economic welfare of the region is direct and they have shown their recognition of this in many international gatherings summoned to discuss aspects of this complex problem. Since 1966 the Japanese have been playing a leading role in the Indo-Pacific region. Tokyo took much of the initiative in the rescheduling of Indonesia's huge external debts after the fall of President Sukarno. Japan was very active in the setting up of the Asian Development Bank in which Australia is a large subscriber. In 1966 the Japanese brought together eight South-East Asian countries to discuss the development of agricultural production in the region. That year both Japan and Australia were to the fore in the meeting convened by South Korea to launch the Asia and Pacific Council of Regional Co-operation.

All this activity, much of it following on from previous meetings, portends regional economic collaboration even if results to date, relative to the tasks, are meagre. But the fact that such meetings take place so frequently and under so many different auspices is significant. As the Colombo Plan has shown in a limited way, concerted action by groups of countries, through different agencies and on a piecemeal basis, can promote economic development and political stability. Effective action to strengthen the economies of undeveloped countries will take decades. Results will be uneven. Time is the crucial requirement if the drift apart of rich and poor countries is to be arrested: yet there can be no certainty that time will be available in the major theatre of world conflict, East Asia. Political and economic co-operation can be fostered only if there is military stabilisation not only there but generally throughout the world. Of this, except in the special and vital sense of nuclear balance between the USA and the USSR, a balance liable to be shaken as others acquire nuclear weapons, there is no sign. On the contrary, the next century threatens to be the most troubled and the most dangerous in human history, though many countries, including Britain, seem oblivious to the dangers.

7 BRITISH POLICY IN EAST ASIA

Decolonisation led to contraction of British military as well as political responsibilities. The long debate on the British role in Asia, however, did not spring from recognition of the interplay of military and non-military factors in policy, a link that is even now not clearly identified. Some of the loudest advocates of an active independent British policy to bring the Vietnam War to an end find nothing incongruous in simultaneously urging military withdrawal from Asia or even wholesale dismantling of British defence forces.

Whatever the outcome in Vietnam there will be consequential military responsibilities, a share of which will fall on British shoulders. If there is a compromise settlement nothing is more certain than that those who want a voice in the settlement will have to underwrite it militarily. If disillusion and frustration induce the USA to withdraw, the resultant chaos in Vietnam will spread outwards, giving rise to fear and uncertainty and even to serious disorders. The general British interest in stemming the tide of anarchy, the desire to have a say in world affairs, a feeling of obligation to respond to appeals from Commonwealth countries whether there is a formal commitment or not, and specific British responsibility for Hongkong make it inevitable that Britain must be ready to give military assistance if this is required. So long as the Vietnam War continues at the present or a lesser intensity it is possible—though not certain—that Britain will be able to avoid new military tasks arising directly or indirectly out of it. But prolongation of the war is precisely what the protests are directed against.

The arguments for British military withdrawal from East of Suez are based, however, neither on belated realisation that her military responsibilities have declined as a result of decolonisation, nor on calculations of new responsibilities that may have emerged or be about to emerge. They spring from financial difficulties, competing demands on the budget, and a psychological mood of withdrawal. These are important considerations but do not justify neglect to assess what is at stake for Britain. A mood of withdrawal is itself compounded of several elements. Irresponsible criticism of British policy and casual insults hurled at her by others, though now taken as a matter of course, cumulatively produce a mood of indifference conditioning the public towards shunning distant responsibilities and towards concentration on relations with neighbours. Closer association with Western Europe is, moreover, a challenge that appeals to youth as a modern substitute for old-fashioned Empire. These intangibles foster a climate of opinion helpful to advocates of British entry into the Common Market.

Difference Between Britain and Japan

But Britain is to an exceptional degree dependent on world-wide stability, orderly change and prosperity. The closest parallel is perhaps Japan, like Britain heavily dependent on foreign sources of supply and foreign markets. Apart from trade, the circumstances of the two nations differ markedly. Japan plays a major role in world trade and is developing her role in international economic and financial policy in spite of the fact that she exerts only minor influence in world politics. It is not a pattern that Britain could imitate.

Unlike Japanese governments, British governments have views on world issues, are ready to express them and are determined to be heard; and the British public expects this of them. In defence policy, there is no Japanese equivalent to the stationing of British forces in West Germany, whose withdrawal would affect European stability and Russian policy. It is not a coincidence that Japan's military strength matches her overseas political influence. Both, though growing, are still slight. The close correspondence between the two can be noted in many countries. Indian prestige and influence collapsed when Chinese attack exposed military weakness. There is an air of unreality or irresponsibility in many speeches at UN headquarters in New York because the speakers represent countries that lack the strength to carry out the policies they are advocating. Prestige abroad and the aggressive assertion of independent status can, however, be bought too dear, as France has discovered. To help to restore French influence overseas after a series of shattering disasters—German occupation, defeat in Indo-China and withdrawal from Algeria—President Charles de Gaulle embarked upon a vigorous programme of military rearmament and modernisation. External policy, which should be the servant of domestic policy, instead became its master. The price, in terms of autocracy and depressed living standards, proved to be more than the French were willing to pay, as the 1968 disturbances showed.

External and internal policies must be brought into harmony, and to be effective external policy must itself be planned as a whole with the diverse elements—political, economic, defence, aid and cultural activities—all welded together to form a single instrument. But the balance between the elements differs. Japan's dramatic industrial achievements enable her to support a world role that is mainly economic, a state of affairs that accords with the present mood of her people. For Britain the case is different. She is too weak to rely on economic resources as the main support of foreign policy. Nor would she be content with a role that was primarily economic even if her resources permitted. There is the double danger that Britain, who must in her own interests take an active part in international affairs, may fail to realise the crucial importance of East Asia as the principal storm centre of the world and may fail to perceive the importance of the policy contribution she could make there.

Value of British Presence

Despite setbacks British foreign policy has on the whole exhibited qualities of patient perseverance, adaptability and common sense unmatched by any other country. Nowhere are these qualities more needed than in relation to the ferment in East Asia. The legacy of trust and friendship left in the immense regions till recently ruled by Britain is dwindling but still significant. It contrasts with for example Japan's relations with her ex-colony Korea. Reactions in Singapore early in 1968 to newspaper suggestions that the USA might replace Britain there illustrated a political asset too often discounted in Britain, where it is not generally recognised that in many parts of the world there is ambivalence in the attitude towards the USA. American drive and energy backed by enormous power are apt to overwhelm their smaller partners in international undertakings. Moreover, there is a general impression that Americans judge only by tangible results, that they play to win and that if they see no prospect of winning they may abruptly abandon the game. The British, on the other hand, are reputed to be more phlegmatic, slow starters but slow stoppers. British influence with the Americans is usually seen to be a brake on American enthusiasms directed towards stopping them embarking on new policies too hastily as well as towards stopping their sudden abandonment.

British influence in any given situation depends, however, on Britain sharing the responsibility. British withdrawal from South-East Asia will seriously weaken her ability to influence American policy there, to the detriment of the interests of her friends in the area and, indeed, to the detriment of the interests of Britain and the USA also.

The constitutional patterns transplanted from Britain to her colonies seldom stand the test of time. Even the legal system usually needs modifications. The pattern of administration is, though, still in the main derived from British practice, a considerable advantage in facilitating British aid programmes. On mixed international staffs British members are useful because they are better than most at adapting and improvising, at lubricating points of friction, at taking into account political sensitivities. The same traits were shown by British military leaders commanding mixed Malay and British forces in operations against Communists in the jungles of Malaya but working under Malayan political direction. These are traits which could have been extremely valuable in Vietnam, but few American soldiers seem to possess them. British firms have similarly exhibited remarkable powers of adaptation to changed conditions in newly independent countries.

It would be neither difficult nor costly for Britain to transmute these qualities and the goodwill she still enjoys into a practical programme for helping underdeveloped countries by training or seconding administrators, scientists, engineers, fiscal experts, accountants and technicians on a far greater scale than anything yet attempted. It is also open to Britain to make an important contribution to the security and stability of her friends in South-East Asia by helping to train their armed forces and police services through the secondment of British personnel and through training schemes in Britain for overseas personnel. These are not new ideas—but far more can and should be done, and done by Britain who is better qualified than anyone else to do it and whose help in these fields is usually more acceptable because her motives are less subject to suspicion. There is another problem of great importance to many countries, including to Britain, where for the first time for two centuries her army will be largely home-based. This is to identify the interests of the armed services with those of the civilian population by means of service training exercises of direct value to the community and by means of educational and vocational training programmes carried out by army instructors for civilians. The

British Army already has a good deal of experience in this field and is likely to expand the scale of these operations. With British help a great deal could be done on these lines in South-East Asia where the need to improve the public image of the security forces is in some areas acute.

Transcending all other issues in East Asia is the question mark over the future of China. Britain's policy of recognising Peking has had little success so far because China has failed to respond. But it is a world interest that Britain should not allow herself to be diverted by paucity of results from a policy that offers a slender hope of drawing China slowly into the international community and averting a war that would dwarf the Vietnam War in intensity, in suffering and in repercussions. In much of South-East Asia the desire for security is coupled with a wish to stand aside from the quarrels of the three major powers—the USA, Russia and China— and with aversion to being treated as pawns in competition between them. French spokesmen have occasionally suggested neutrality as a desirable state of affairs in some parts of South-East Asia, where there is growing sentiment in support. One of the unfortunate results of friction between Britain and France over entry into the Common Market has been a tendency in Britain to denigrate French views on international affairs. In this instance at least French ideas merit very serious consideration. Neutrality for South-East Asia stands little chance of acceptance, however, without wider international backing than France alone could give. No country outside South-East Asia itself could do more to secure general agreement to the concept of South-East Asia as an area committed neither to one side nor the other than Britain.

New Trade Strategy: Basis for a Global Role

If Britain is to make an effective political contribution to East Asian stability, she must retain—within the limitations of an increasingly inter-dependent world—an independent political status and power for independent political initiative. Neither is compatible with subservience to the USA or with absorption into a European union, however closely British interests may in general parallel theirs. Free of the political implications of the EEC, a multilateral free trade treaty, concerning itself only with increasing commerce between participating countries, could be the instrument to enable Britain to play the kind of global role which best suits her global interests and capacities. With Pacific countries also participating, such a framework would offer the flexibility and scope that are still, as in the past, essential to British overseas policy.

There is a second condition if Britain is to make a full contribution in the Indo-Pacific theatre. In the Malayan campaign of 1948-58, in the Korean War, in Malaysian resistance to Indonesian confrontation and in helping to calm India after the Chinese attack in 1962, it was clear that British ability to influence the course of events depended on her acceptance of the military consequences of her policy. There are no grounds for supposing that it will be otherwise in the future, whether the military consequences are active involvement or the presence of forces or the supply of equipment.

Deployment, whether British forces should be stationed east or west of the Suez Canal or of any other place on the map, is an aspect of military planning which cannot be divorced from other military and technical considerations or from relevant political and economic factors. Old theories of close defence and repelling invasion by defending the beaches of Britain long since gave way to the concept of security through deterrence, of preventing attack by convincing the enemy of the certainty of allied reprisals instead of relying on the ability to repel it. The strategy of deterrence in its original starkness, and even the concept of national security, are now giving way to the notion of international security. One day this may be provided by an international standing force. Today it can be achieved only by national contributions to alliances.

Purposes of Defence Policy

New weapons of immense power which can be wielded from great distances, aircraft of increased performance, new possibilities of mobility, surveillance from orbiting equipment, applications of modern technology to a whole range of weapons and equipment— all these have added new complexities to the problem of how to get the best value for money from a limited defence budget. Yet another complication is the time lag, five to ten years or even more, between planning and introduction into use of some of the key items.

The safest way to chart a course through a plethora of defence considerations is to define the purposes of defence policy as simply as possible. For Britain there are two. The first is security of the homeland. In modern conditions this calls for a military contribution to the stability of Western Europe including, if Britain can afford it without seriously depleting other weapon systems, a contribution to the long-range nuclear deterrent forces of the Atlantic alliance, though this is for Britain not an inescapable military necessity. She adds only marginally to the American nuclear armoury.

The second purpose, the product of Britain's dependence on world trade and sea communications, is to contribute towards general international stability and protection of merchant shipping. If relations between America and Russia improve, and if the problem of German unification becomes less acute, there will be more stability and less tension in Europe. The burden of the primary purpose of British defence policy, home security, will become less onerous. But the second purpose is permanent and its importance relative to the first is likely to increase with the years. The centre of power, as earlier argued, has already moved away from Western Europe and so has the main source of friction. It is Asia, not Europe, that is now the cockpit of the world.

In the early years of nuclear weapons there was a tendency to belittle the need to protect sea communications. On the assumption that nuclear weapons of annihilation and obliteration would be used soon after the outbreak of major war it seemed to follow that prolonged large-scale fighting was unlikely, even impossible: it was difficult to envisage a long war and the need to organise, protect and convoy shipping for its duration. But the variety of weapons now possessed by both the USA and the Soviet Union; the prospect of China and perhaps others (India and Japan, for instance) acquiring nuclear weapons; the acquisition by many countries of powerful non-nuclear armaments including submarines, missile-firing warships, and fast rocket-carrying aircraft; and the increasing frequency with which crisis succeeds crisis: these are developments and auguries that cannot be ignored. They point up once again the vulnerability of merchant shipping and the importance of protecting it.

For Britain, compelled to limit spending on defence, the two tasks pose a dilemma because they call for different organisation, training, equipment, degree of mobility and logistic and telecommunications support. She has no option but to rely on the help of others and, in order to ensure that she gets that help and that defence deficiencies will be made good by others in an emergency, to demonstrate to them that she can effectively contribute to common purposes. This, not drawing a line on a map and disclaiming any military task beyond it, is the way to keep defence spending under control without gravely endangering national security and national interest.

Size and Shape of Military Forces

Britain has a valuable and distinctive political role to play in East Asia provided that she accepts its military implications. The issue for defence policy is not whether to remain or to quit: it is the minimum size and shape of the forces needed to support policy. It is doubtful whether the scale of these forces would justify a major base such as Singapore even if Britain could afford the expense. Moreover, the Singapore base is already a political anomaly of doubtful military utility in war when access by sea or by air might be interrupted. From the British point of view the problem of phasing out the base is not primarily a military problem. The defence requirements of Malaysia and of Singapore could be met, if they so wish, by assistance to them to build up their own forces and by sale or loan of the ships, aircraft, weapons and equipment that they need—without the presence of a major British base. The problem of the base is to ensure the continued stability and viability of Singapore despite the loss of the foreign exchange earnings and the impact on employment that would follow British departure from the base.

What Britain needs is not a string of distant bases, but armed forces which are mobile, equipped and trained to support policy. By abdicating a role in world affairs outside Western Europe she could correspondingly disband forces never to be called upon to play a military role outside Western Europe. So long as she aspires to a world political role, even on a modest scale, it is irresponsible to ignore the possible military consequences. Because Britain patently has an interest in what goes on elsewhere and wants to make her voice heard, it follows that whatever the scale of the forces she decides to maintain they must have the capability of effective employment wherever needed. For this purpose they need training, and perhaps depots, in an area to which access is secure, where their presence is not likely to give rise to political complications, where they can take part in joint training exercises with allies and not as far away from the Indo-Pacific theatre as the UK. The security of Australia and New Zealand is and will remain a permanent British interest as is the security of Britain to them. If Canberra sets store on Britain retaining a military capacity in the area of the Pacific and Indian oceans, this is the time for new arrangements to be concluded between Australia and Britain whereby British forces can use facilities in Australia.

The purpose of attempts to stabilise the seething region of South and East Asia, politically and militarily, is not to freeze that mythical state of affairs, the *status quo*. There have been immense changes in the last quarter of a century and there are more to come. The purpose is to create conditions in which changes can be effected peacefully. But change is not an end in itself. It is the social and economic consequences of change that are the criteria and that finally justify, or fail to justify, the policies that produced the change. To Britain, the direct and immediate motives of a policy of promoting stability are primarily economic.

Of the importance of the area to the British economy there can be no doubt. No other West European nation has a stake in it comparable to that of Britain. But that stake is probably more vulnerable than is commonly realised. The ramifications of Britain's involvement range from private enterprise to governmental aid programmes, from manufacturing to plantations and mines, from import and export trade to retail distribution, from banking, insurance, shipping and aviation to employment for technicians and teachers.

Global Trade Network

Britain is the centre of a global network of trade and commerce. Essential raw materials and low-cost food supplies, accounting for four-fifths of her imports, come from distant sources. Four-fifths of her sales are made outside the Common Market. With a population three or four times as large as could be supported, at lower standards, from native resources, her economic problem is imports—where to get them and how to pay for them. However much she struggles to increase exports there is bound to be a gap to be closed otherwise than by exports which, indeed, put extra strain on her balance of payments because of their requirements for imported materials and machinery. That gap can be closed only by invisible earnings, from tourism, investments, services overseas and so on. Increasing concentration on the more industrialised markets of Western Europe and America has been a factor in the decline of such earnings from shipping, insurance and banking, whilst the lowering of trade barriers and tariffs with industrialised nations has stimulated British purchases of finished manufactures.

Her economic health depends on mass markets, on a general expansion of world trade with developing, as well as with developed, countries and on increasing investment earnings from overseas. These are aims that demand co-operation with others on a far wider basis than would be possible in the strait-jacket of the EEC. British support under the GATT for tariff cuts on a range of products exported by developing countries is evidence of awareness of the importance of developing outlets for these countries. The economic impact of British entry into EEC on some of her traditional suppliers and markets seems, however, to be overlooked, as is the penalty in terms of higher cost of living at home along with the price already being paid for ineffectual attempts to gain entry and for uncertainty in the country's boardrooms.

Britain has an opportunity to set her sights on far more ambitious targets than a merger with highly industrialised neighbours. The nature of her economy and the pattern of her trade dictate where her interests lie—in co-operation with others to expand and liberalise world trade as a whole. Problems and conditions in East Asia are so diverse that there is room for a multiplicity of international groupings and agencies. Vigorous British economic policy in that distant and turbulent area should not be regarded as altruism or even as far-sighted realisation of the dangers for the rest of the world inherent there. The justification is that trade, stability and development are major British interests and that her own resources are too limited to achieve significant results alone. She must co-operate with others whose interests are similar. In East Asia there is scope for all industrialised nations to play a part. But in the case of Britain, her contribution is not to be judged solely in terms of economic resources she can make available to the common effort. She has a distinctive and important political and administrative contribution to make.

Conclusion

Provided that she retains independent political status and accepts a share of the burden of military stabilisation, by skilful use of her relatively strong political influence British policy can be more effective. The three major components of external policy are for Britain inseparable. She cannot strengthen her economy except in conditions that permit world trade to expand. She cannot help to bring about these conditions except by an active political role which she cannot play without accepting its military consequences. Yet she cannot maintain the necessary military support without a healthy economy.

The word "role" is a misnomer. It suggests optional leisure activity, strutting and posturing abroad, a status symbol. What in fact it is all about is a job that will earn Britain a livelihood and ensure her future in a disorderly and feverish world where she can no longer count as of right on a seat at the Board of Directors. She has to prove that she has skills and experience of value to others which entitle her to the wages she wants to maintain the way of life she likes.

Obsession with Europe is not enough even though a stable home environment is essential. Britain is too vulnerable to the impact of distant crises. If her external policy is to serve long-range national interests it must be directed towards world stability and prosperity and Britain must make use of every skill and instrument at her disposal, political, economic, and military. This she could do in a multilateral free trade association.

Part IV

PIONEERS OF AN
OPEN WORLD

by

Leonard Beaton

1 COMMONWEALTH BEFORE WORLD WAR II

The British national debate about trade strategy has rightly extended itself into broad political considerations. The unity of commercial and political policy has been understood. One school of opinion favours a protected European trading area in the context of a developing European political unity; another favours intimate imperial links and argues for a Commonwealth trading system; a third would make no significant links—certainly no permanent links—with others and would favour a tough and self-sufficient economy supporting an independent role in the world.

In examining the proposal for a general free trade area strategy in co-operation with the United States and other advanced Western countries, it is equally important to see the whole political and commercial context. A free trade commitment would be logically attached to a political policy which extended and made more permanent Britain's loyalty to the American-led North Atlantic Treaty Organisation (NATO), the Organisation of Economic Co-operation and Development (OECD) and the system under the General Agreement on Tariffs and Trade (GATT). It would look, as NATO looks, to the continued unity of the English-speaking world as the basis for a larger unity in the countries of the West. This will obviously have important effects on many elements in British policy—on the European Communities (EEC), on the European Free Trade Association (EFTA) countries, on relations with the Middle East and so on. A basic development in policy of this kind demands a thorough reassessment of what exists and the direction in which policy as a whole ought to move.

Need for Reassessment

Studies have appeared on a great variety of the economic and political implications of British support for a free trade treaty approach, under article 24 of the GATT, to the further liberalisation of world trade.[1] This study concerns just one aspect of the problem:

[1]This proposal, which has stimulated wide interest, was put forward in *A New Trade Strategy for Canada and the United States* (Canadian-American Committee, Montreal and Washington D.C., May, 1966).

the Commonwealth. In considering the issues which the Commonwealth raises, it seemed necessary to look in a general way at the objective and purpose of the Commonwealth itself and at the kind of future it might have. The association has played a major part in shaping British trade policy and political commitments over the years and this policy has recently fallen into widespread disfavour. Indeed, to a great extent it has been reversed in recent times. Nevertheless, even if the policy of retrenchment is maintained and extended it will take many years to achieve its full effect. At present, however, there are signs of a revival of interest in the world-wide Commonwealth links and the future is by no means certain. This essay therefore seeks to explore the nature and importance of the association for British policy. Only then will it be possible to assess the implications of a free trade treaty strategy in co-operation with the Americans, Europeans, Canadians and other designed to open the greatest markets to all those willing to accept reciprocity.

Inter-regional Association

The Commonwealth of Nations stands outside the states system of our time. The world is accustomed to sovereign entities; to alliances; to satellites or colonies; to international organisations. It comprehends the region, the continent, the treaty linkage of the weak to the strong. But there is no obvious category for this loose, ill-organised association whose basis is a common experience of the British Empire. Observing essentially the same facts, some people think it is a mythical entity with no effective life and others see it as a flexible and successful instrument of international life. Although the Commonwealth lacks political life (but for a secretariat founded in 1965), it has played a large part in bringing Canada, Australia, New Zealand and South Africa into the great wars of the twentieth century in close association with Britain and it has brought Britain, Australia and New Zealand to the defence of Malaysia. It has sustained and developed one of the most ambitious sectors of international trade and played an important part in the initiation of aid programmes by the industrial and developed to the poor and undeveloped.

In the post-1945 period, the Commonwealth was one of the recognised groupings of states in the rough ordering of United Nations institutions. Britain and France as permanent members of the Security Council were broadly defined as representing the

Commonwealth and Western Europe; and it was the general practice to have another Commonwealth country among the non-permanent members. This practice has largely fallen into disuse. Recognition of the Commonwealth as an organising element in the confusion of an order containing over 130 sovereign entities has declined in favour of continental and regional groupings: the Latin Americans, Africans, Arabs, Europeans, sometimes Afro-Asians. The countries formerly of the French Community, the *pays franco-phones*, have remained a much more recognisable grouping in international society.

Not surprisingly, the Commonwealth in Britain has always meant the countries of the Empire as well as those which have become independent. Thus, for example, immigration from the West Indies has always been treated as Commonwealth immigration, even when all of it (in earlier years) or some of it (in later years) was from dependent territories. Strictly speaking, however, the Commonwealth of which Rosebery wrote was a Commonwealth of Nations: a relationship of those once united who wish in independence to retain and develop their common life. It is this Commonwealth which is the subject of the present paper. Any development towards multilateral free trade would affect the Commonwealth in its internal economic life and would presumably divide it between those who joined and those who did not. Students of the broader implications of various trade strategies must therefore be concerned with the association and its life. They might also choose to learn from some of its methods.

Commonwealth and Nazi Germany

The shape and character of the Commonwealth for its older members, including Britain, was given in the period between 1900 and 1945. All the countries which had been given independence, or were being given independence, had shared to a greater or lesser extent in the imperial enthusiasms of the late nineteenth century. All (with the possible exceptions of Newfoundland and New Zealand) had also reacted to these: there were substantial populations which had resented this mood with its overtones which many thought to be unattractively moralistic, patronising, xenophobic or even racist. Among the seven countries of the Commonwealth in the 1920s (Britain, Canada, Australia, New Zealand, South Africa, Ireland, Newfoundland), the least enthusiasm was to be found in Ireland and

South Africa—the Irish view being shown in neutrality in World War II and the South African in widespread hostility to the war which was declared on a parliamentary majority of only one.

Large and important sectors of opinion in Britain, Canada and Australia disliked what was seen as an essentially Tory creation. But when it came to a decision about the conquest of Europe by Nazi Germany, Britain and the Commonwealth countries (except for the only other one in Europe, namely Ireland) decided to declare war at the same time as France and to dedicate their men and wealth to a common cause. When it is noticed how many countries which were directly threatened chose to remain out of it—the Soviet Union, the Scandinavian countries, Switzerland, Italy, Yugoslavia —and the attitude of all other independent countries of the Western Hemisphere, the near-unity of the Commonwealth becomes an extraordinary event. British attitudes to this have varied, though on the whole there was an assumption that these were British countries and so naturally joined together in the time of peril. The notion that Britain stood alone after the fall of France has seldom been questioned. It is perhaps best expressed by the theme of the second volume of Churchill's war memoirs: "How the British people held the fort alone till those who hitherto had been half blind were half ready." It is a broad definition of "the British people".

Smoot-Hawley Tariff and British Preference

The pre-war Commonwealth also had a capacity to act together in trade matters. Faced with the disastrous consequences of the American Smoot-Hawley tariff, the association fought back with its preferential system, which has survived for more than 35 years through remarkably changing circumstances. A zone of relatively free trade was preserved against a disastrous return to high tariffs led by the USA. For some reason, the Americans themselves have always deeply resented the Commonwealth's internal arrangements and have tried, without success, to have Commonwealth countries raise their tariffs against each other in the context of a general lowering of trade barriers under the GATT. The Commonwealth countries have consistently resisted this and agreed merely that their preference margins could be eroded away by a general lowering of trade barriers. As the lowering of tariffs has proceeded through the various stages of the GATT's history, the preferences for one Commonwealth country in another have become less significant, just as the preferences of one American state over foreigners in another American state have become less significant. It has been customary, however, to discount the importance and permanence of these preferences, partly in order not to offend American opinion and partly because of the old dislike of the works of Tory imperialists by liberals and radicals of all kinds.

These achievements of the pre-war Commonwealth undoubtedly owed an important part to the notion that Britain was a major power. The psychological importance of the Royal Navy, in particular, to distant and lonely countries like South Africa, Australia and New Zealand should not be under-rated. With them, if not with Canada, there was a real sense of a security contract in which they supported the empire and the empire would support them. Canada, lacking the American mythology about Europe, was more specifically and consciously aware that she had a part in European security and that the North Atlantic was rapidly becoming a narrow sea. The grasping of this simple truth by the USA has been perhaps the determining fact of World War II and the system of European power which followed it.

For all countries of the Commonwealth, including Canada, as for other similar countries like Argentina, Britain was an important trading partner. Her wealth and industrial strength made her a significant market and a major source of capital and manufactures. Her cheap food policy did much to develop the great food producing areas of the new worlds. The British islands could exercise a powerful magnetic force because of their traditions of sea-power and open trading. Many other things are needed to explain the early pheno-menon of the Commonwealth, not least the general admiration among civilised men everywhere of the institutions of law and government which the British people had evolved and worked with success. But the lower and harder facts of power (or imagined power) and markets played a significant part in the ordering of imperial affairs. As C. S. Lewis assures us, the highest cannot stand without the lowest.

2 POST-WAR CHANGES IN THE COMMONWEALTH

Many things changed during and after World War II. The most important of these was clearly the decision by Britain that she must leave India in 1948 followed by the mounting tide of decolonisation which over 20 years carried the Commonwealth's numbers up to 28 (and would have added still more had Ireland and South Africa not dropped out and Burma, the Maldive Islands and the protectorates and mandated territories not excluded themselves). At the same time, the entry of the USA into the great range of problems which had preoccupied the Commonwealth gave the association itself a secondary character, the appearance of having few unique functions. Secure at last in their power, the Americans went into Europe late but decisively. Their armies secured distant parts of the world by permanent garrisons in West Germany, Okinawa and South Korea. Their guarantees, by treaty and evident commitment, became the most important element in the security of the older independent countries, and most notably of Britain and Australia. In security, in trade, in capital markets and (finally) in aid, the modest Commonwealth efforts were suddenly swept up into a vast system on a scale which had previously been unthinkable. In achievement, this outdid the Commonwealth's highest hopes; but it obscured the function of the association itself. To have been right about Hitler, about tariffs, about mutual security, about aid (in the great Colombo Plan initiative) was perhaps of historical interest; but when the same things were being done on a global plane with the support of far greater powers, the Commonwealth had difficulty in discovering what specific function it might be expected to fulfil.

The post-war Commonwealth was undoubtedly launched on its new size and character by the personal convictions of Jawaharlal Nehru. In absorbing the new independent India (and also Pakistan) the Commonwealth balance shifted. India brought not just her vast population and problems but also her view of the world. The decision that a republic could be a member was a matter of form, even if it was delicate and even painful for those who had for so long rejoiced in a splendid and shared monarchy. But the Indian determination to stay out of the great European conflict between what became the NATO powers and the Soviet Union and her allies created a central difference of style and objective. The doctrine of non-alignment which spread steadily through the post-colonial world of Asia, Africa and the Caribbean put many Commonwealth countries outside the security order which the British, Americans and others were trying to build. Commonwealth countries with serious security problems—Pakistan, Malaysia, Singapore—were less enthusiastic about non-alignment than those who had been so busy achieving independence that they had had no time to notice what a dangerous world they lived in.[2] But they were in a minority. The majority, following the lead of India, threw themselves enthusiastically into the international institutions which had been constructed under Anglo-American leadership with the general support of Western Europe and Latin America. Where, as with the UN, the institutions also enjoyed the support of the Soviet bloc, there was most enthusiasm: but generally the Western structure, based on principles of non-discrimination, proved acceptable and was looked to for aid, markets, capital and occasionally security. In education, books, broadcasting, civil service organisation, military training and many other things, the new Commonwealth countries showed a fairly consistent preference for British methods and institutions. There were exceptions, notably the long Pakistani involvement with the USA and the briefer Ghanaian experience with Soviet co-operation. But Commonwealth methods, particularly British, were widely preferred where they were available.

Influence of Continentalism

In most countries there has been a conscious tension between the imperial past and the prevailing continentalism of the mid-twentieth century, a movement to which the US, contemplating its own union, has given almost unfailing support.[3] The notion of a great African union has been deeply felt throughout Commonwealth African countries; India, Pakistan, Ceylon, Malaysia and Singapore have a strong sense of being Asian and have felt a need to

[2]This is not a purely ex-colonial phenomenon. The illusion that all dangers come from bad men and that the last of the bad men is about to go, ushering in a dawn of security, is a deep-seated part of the British political inheritance which the Commonwealth has in common.

[3]The notable exception has been Asia where a continental solution has more appeal to China than to the United States.

show Afro-Asian respectability by playing down continuing dependence on the old links; Canada has shown a growing sense of her place in the Western Hemisphere; and so on. Others, like Australia, New Zealand and some of the independent countries of the West Indies, have been conscious of the need to preserve wider links to avoid regional absorption.

The European debate in Britain has rather surprisingly taken this shape. If there is a prospect of a European union, the obvious alternatives are union or independence. As independence will undoubtedly prove to be even more attractive to the British than it has to the French, the unionists have preferred to conduct the debate with Europe and the Commonwealth as two apparent alternatives. In the early stages, the debate was heavily weighted to the European side: Europe, it was argued, was rich and would convey this to Britain while the Commonwealth was poor and would drain Britain; Europe was secure while the Commonwealth offered an infinite commitment to defend others with no prospect of reciprocity; Europe had a great cultural unity and historic character which would refresh a Britain weary with too much exertion while the Commonwealth at best reflected back only the same images which had become stale at home.

As time has passed, however, the argument has shifted and has become more evenly balanced. First, America has ceased to stand as automatically as she herself thought on the European side of the argument. While urging Britain to join in the movement to unite the western half of the continent, she has encouraged successive British Governments (which needed no encouragement) to become embroiled in the anti-French campaign inside NATO and outside; she has urged Britain (which needed no encouragement) to help her in the development of an anti-proliferation system for nuclear weapons which, while it might exclude India, should certainly include West Germany; and she has discovered the Commonwealth-based British security involvement in the great Indian Ocean arc running from Australia through South-East Asia and India and Pakistan to the Persian Gulf, the Arabian Peninsula and East Africa. Faced with the prospect of being the only Western power in the Asian world, the US has recoiled from the Eurocentric destiny which once seemed so obvious for Britain.

Another shift in the argument has been caused by closer examination of the European movement. The economic troubles of France have suggested that the formation of a Common Market does not automatically bring prosperity. A period of a nominally European priority in policy made Anglo-French and Anglo-German relations in the mid-1960s worse than they had been for a long time. Renewed Soviet aggression in Europe has caused hesitations among those who thought it obvious that the Americans should bring to a gradual conclusion their unnatural involvement in the defence of Western Europe. In addition, the notion of an open-ended free trade association with the Americans has come into public debate as an ideal objective inside or outside the Common Market. The result of all this is somewhat paradoxical. The decision of Mr. Harold Macmillan, when Prime Minister, that influence could only be maintained in Washington in the years to come from a secure European base has become more and more questionable. The secure European base has receded, with entry into the European Communities disturbingly costly and the importance of these Communities themselves increasingly open to doubt. On the other hand, Britain's special acceptability in Commonwealth countries becomes more interesting as these countries are forced, for various reasons, on to the world stage. These trends have not reversed the Commonwealth/European argument: but it seems fair to say that they have introduced a balance into the debate which might combine with widespread continuing public attachment to the Commonwealth to produce a new balance of forces. All Tory politicians are aware of the power of imperial causes in the party and among its voters. Much radical opinion is also actively concerned with Commonwealth issues. There are few families in Britain without links in Canada, Australia, New Zealand or some other part of the Commonwealth.

Level of British Effort

The Commonwealth cause has suffered more than the European cause in the British national debate from a sense that Britain is over-committed to the outside world in general. There are three reasons for this, all working together. The first is the sense of economic failure which derives from comparative statistics with other developed countries and the growing sense that everything else must be abandoned to put these right; the second is the growing realisation that those who prosper in doing little or nothing for the international order are respected and admired; the third is the decline in the belief that there is a monolithic Communist menace directed from Moscow which must be defeated wherever it shows itself. Decolonisation has also removed the obvious grounds for British concern with the political character of parts of the world in which Britain previously had direct responsibilities.

In this context, it is worth thinking back on the level of British efforts. The material and manpower losses of World War I are only just being forgotten. An immense and passionate involvement in Europe in the inter-war period had its expression in the League of Nations and the resulting resolution in the determination, reached in the autumn of 1939, to bring about the defeat of Germany at almost any cost. The economy was mobilised for war to a far greater extent than any other in Western Europe (including Germany). After the war, a large and so far permanent commitment to the direct defence of West Berlin and West Germany was entered into and large forces were permanently stationed on the continent for this purpose. With the Americans, NATO was constructed, Britain taking second place in direction and also in the expenditure of resources. An arms base for European war, including nuclear weapons, was maintained and developed at great expense. Britain wanted and got the influence of a great power. She played a prominent part in the development of the post-war European order and in bringing the power of the USA effectively to bear on European security. The costs of this have been high. The rewards have undoubtedly been immense: but the achievement of a secure order tends to go unnoticed except by those with memories of insecurity.

While Britain was thus deeply involved in Europe, always the first priority, major challenges to her authority in various overseas territories emerged in the form of terrorist organisations. Lengthy and expensive anti-terrorist operations were conducted in Palestine, Kenya, Malaya and Cyprus.[4] These were a consequence of ruling these territories; and since British rule has now given way to independence this is of only historical interest. But the anti-terrorist operations form part of a general period in which Britain gradually became convinced that she was over-extended and doing too much.

In addition, however, British troops became involved in the

[4]For an account of British tactics in the Malayan Emergency, and a discussion of their application in similar situations elsewhere, see Robert Thompson, *Defeating Communist Insurgency* (Institute for Strategic Studies, Chatto and Windus, London, 1966).

defence of independent states: twice for Commonwealth countries and once for what was essentially an American protectorate. The Commonwealth countries were Malaysia and Cyprus. In Malaysia, a small original commitment steadily grew under threats from Indonesia until 21 battalions and massive air and naval forces were committed to the defence of a 1,000-mile frontier in Borneo.[5] This was brought to a successful conclusion by a combination of jungle domination and political pressure. In Cyprus, British troops on her sovereign bases brought a minimum of order in 1964 to a disintegrating communal situation between Greeks and Turks, and then induced the UN to take over the problem using British as well as other UN troops. In Korea, Britain joined with other countries under American leadership in a hard two-year war to protect South Korea from invasion.

All this, combined with many smaller efforts, makes an impressive total. Much British talent and wealth was absorbed in meeting these demands. Finances which were formerly collected from the countries being protected, whether colonies or occupied Germany, gradually reduced or dried up. The sense of urgency passed out of the problems of the international order in general and the overseas Commonwealth in particular. This tendency was greatly exaggerated by the emergence of a comparable group of countries which did little or nothing for world security and whose economic statistics were the admiration of the communications world, which must inevitably rely heavily on the measurable. West Germany, Japan and Italy, stripped of their colonies and limited in their military efforts, devoted themselves with remarkable success to generating wealth. France poured resources into her small Africa and Caribbean ex-colonies but refrained from other commitments. Canada showed willing in the UN and NATO but on a carefully limited scale. It is not surprising that Britain gradually began to dream of emulating her equals rather than providing a substantial additional contribution to the international efforts of the USA. Thinking which began along these lines led inevitably away from the Commonwealth.

The sense of over-commitment may not make sense in terms of total British resources, which are now greater than ever. But with the loss of the Indian Army and the central responsibilities which gave point and purpose to overseas efforts, the feeling is hardly surprising.

[5]The conduct of this operation is described in General Sir Walter Walker, "How Borneo was Won", *The Round Table*, London, January, 1969.

In trade matters, however, the experience has been somewhat more *bizarre*. Those who have not watched the situation develop by steady stages may find it more difficult to believe.

Traditional British policy permitted free entry into the mother country for the goods of colonies. As the British tariff gradually rose in the long retreat from general free trade, colonies and then independent Commonwealth countries were, generally speaking, able to avoid it. In the same way as between all metropolitan countries and overseas territories, Britain's Commonwealth trade grew to substantial levels. It gradually became enmeshed into the complex series of arrangements which went with the sterling area. Countries in this area attached their currencies to the pound sterling, held much of their reserves in London and co-operated in common financial defence of the group. For many years all sterling area countries imposed physical import restrictions on non-sterling goods: and this had the predictable effect of carrying British exports to these countries up to astonishingly high levels.[6] Although Britain did not enjoy the free entry into most Commonwealth countries that she granted in return (many did not even give preferences), to be the only industrial country whose goods did not require import licences into many countries was a massive advantage. Britain's share of Australian imports, for example, grew to over 50 per cent.

Misunderstanding of EEC Membership

The dismantling of the sterling area's physical import restrictions in the late 1950s made British exports vulnerable to attack from the Americans and also from the growing industrial strength of Western Europe and Japan. The British proportion of Commonwealth imports declined, as did the Commonwealth proportion of British exports. At the same time, many Commonwealth countries were suffering from the reduction in food and raw material prices and a resulting need to restrict all imports. In spite of these factors, the growth of markets was enough to keep the volume of British exports to the Commonwealth growing. In normal circumstances, this large sector of national export trade, with its great growth potential (as the Japanese well understood), would have been cherished and

[6] Of total British exports, 32 per cent went to the Commonwealth in 1938, 40 per cent in the high days of sterling area import restrictions in 1952, and 30 per cent when these had been dismantled in 1965.

developed. Instead it became the object of what might almost be called official hostility.

The difficulty arose through the misunderstanding of the problem of entry into the EEC. When Mr. Macmillan took the decision in 1961 to seek entry, a decision he stated as one to see what terms would be available in the event that the Government and Parliament were to decide to seek entry, he was aware that there was serious French opposition. Nevertheless, he believed that France would not choose to veto British entry, a position that was perfectly arguable. What was curious, however, was that he committed himself and his Government not to enter the EEC unless reasonable arrangements were made for the rest of the Commonwealth, the other countries in EFTA and British agriculture. This seemed to offer the French a perfectly simple way of keeping Britain out without resorting to publicly unreasonable conduct in the eyes of their EEC partners. By standing on the word of the treaty and allowing effectively no additional arrangements to incorporate the special shape of Britain, they could apparently rely on the British Government itself to break off the negotiation. Such arrangements would have been in sharp conflict with the Rome Treaty practice of erecting no new barriers to existing trade. Nevertheless, the existing treaty wording, rather than the premises on which the negotiations among the Six themselves had been based, were adhered to; and this wording was applied to one sector after another of British trade with the Commonwealth.

Faced with the failure of its negotiating hopes, the Macmillan Government had to go backward or forward and it decided that it must go forward. The fact that in the end the French Government decided that it must express open unwillingness to contemplate British entry does not here concern us. The point is that Britain was forced to agree to the virtual complete dismantling of Commonwealth trade arrangements for artificial and mistaken negotiating reasons. Had the EEC been designed to include Britain, or were it to expand willingly for the purpose, Commonwealth trade would be dealt with rationally and constructively. It became, however, a vehicle for an irrelevant French objective: namely a British decision to stay out. The strange thing is that the attitudes generated in the course of this negotiation have become to a large extent permanently established. Commonwealth trade has been seen as a British liability rather than an asset; most Commonwealth countries have been persuaded that British membership in the EEC must be hostile to their interests; and Britain has become obsessed with the alternatives of Commonwealth or Common Market, discussed earlier.

Support of Public Opinion

All these experiences, taken as a whole, have produced a strong sense of weariness with the Commonwealth in Britain. Other factors have, of course, played a part. The arrival of cheap travel and the high British standard of living started a movement of Commonwealth workers into Britain which has generated a strong public reaction. The use of the word Commonwealth as a euphemism for skin colour has deprived the Commonwealth notion of its proud national origins in the minds of British people. Where the pre-war Commonwealth was the pride of the Tories, the arrival of a number of states ruled by those whose political formation had been in anti-imperialism shifted the focus of Commonwealth sympathy to the left.

In opposition, Mr. Harold Wilson used to praise the Commonwealth for not being a rich man's club, an adequate clue to why he so rapidly abandoned it once in power. But there was also the feeling that a Labour Government would be loved by the new Commonwealth or at least supported in its efforts to build a better world. No such flow of affection was detected. When a small white minority took over Rhodesia, a territory which Britain claimed as part of her sovereign realms, most of the Commonwealth showed no sympathy with the British Government's decision to dismiss any possibility of using force. The old imperial sympathy and respect found too little symbolism and comprehension to keep it strong. In the best international circles, Americans ridiculed the Commonwealth, even if politely, and Europeans expressed sympathy and occasionally curiosity. A caricature of what the Commonwealth had been—something for which Britain provided all markets, aid and capital, which Britain defended, which came to Britain's support in all circumstances—was summoned up to show how impossible it was.

Among the articulate public, its support seems to have retreated into the ranks of traditionalists with international instincts, a relatively small group. Among the public as a whole, however, Commonwealth sentiments appear to be remarkably resilient. In January, 1969, Opinion Research Centre (on behalf of the Gemini News Service) asked a quota sample of 946 electors if they agreed with the statement that "the Commonwealth is valuable and should not be allowed to break up". In all, 67 per cent agreed, 20 per cent disagreed and 13 per cent did not know. To the statement "the Commonwealth has outlived its usefulness and should be wound up", 21 per cent agreed, 66 per cent disagreed and 13 per cent did not know. Seventy-six per cent thought it would be a good thing if the Commonwealth worked more closely together on trade and political matters. On the same day, *The Sunday Telegraph* published a Gallup Poll in which electors were asked whether Europe, the Commonwealth or America was most important to Britain. The percentages were: Commonwealth 34, Europe 26, America 25, Don't Know 15. Seventy-eight per cent thought it was important for Britain to have a close relationship with the Commonwealth countries.[7]

Such was the situation as the decade of the 1960s moved towards its confused close. The Commonwealth apparently survives in the hearts of the people but not in articulate sentiment and not in the calculations of men in power. Who is right?

[7]See *The Sunday Telegraph*, London, January 26, 1969. For the results of the Opinion Research Centre's poll see *The Sunday Times*, London, January 26, 1969.

3 SECURITY, PROSPERITY AND THE CHARACTER OF THE WORLD

It is not customary in Britain to draw up schemes of basic national objectives in the American manner. No doubt this is just as well. The American efforts in this direction generally suggest that it is only their rooted pragmatism which saves them from expending their resources on irrelevant objectives. Nevertheless, any discussion of the Commonwealth is inevitably so broad that it must be related to a general view of the world as a whole. Overall, there would seem to be three main national objectives in external policy: (a) the security of Britain, broadly interpreted and extended into the indefinite future; (b) the prosperity of the country and those for whose welfare it is concerned; (c) and the achievement of the most acceptable character in the world as a whole.

A. SECURITY

Britain is not one of those countries which can find its security objectives in its geography. The Soviet Union dwells on images of German-led NATO hordes pouring east or American missiles dropping out of the sky; West Germany can see the same thing looking the other way; Israel can plan for the promised Arab invasion; and so on. Threats, nuclear and conventional, to the British Isles can be conceived; but they have not had a high priority in defence planning which has been devoted to deterring more distant but more likely situations whose consequences would be serious. In this decade, for example, Britain risked war with the Soviet Union (in company with the USA, France and West Germany) to maintain the present status of West Berlin; and she committed herself heavily to the protection of Malaysian territory on the island of Borneo against Indonesia. Both of these were responses to the actions of others. It is possible to argue that Britain had no more need to act in these situations than Japan: or that she should have acted in one and not the other: or that while she had an interest it bore no relationship to the risks that were run and the costs that were undertaken.

These issues involve so many uncertainties that it is very difficult to reach an agreed security policy and stick to it over a period of years. The priority for armed forces able to engage in European continental warfare—German or Russian-type land-mobile forces with heavy equipment and vast fire-power—emerged from World War II and continued for many years. Associated with this, the nuclear forces were given strong government backing. After the Suez expedition of 1956, however, there was a strong shift towards light mobile forces able to operate a long way from home. These were designed to meet the certain requirements for forces able to act quickly throughout the world. As the 1960s closed there was a shift back to a continental strategy under the leadership of Mr. Wilson and Mr. Denis Healey, as Britain's Secretary of State for Defence, with promised withdrawals from overseas bases in the early 1970s. Mr. Wilson once said that Britain's front line was on the Himalayas. He later seemed to come to the conclusion that it was on the Elbe. Others might argue, and he himself might come to argue, that it is on the Channel. The occasional hints that in the absence of better behaviour by the West German Government (suggestions which emanated from both Mr. Macmillan's and Mr. Wilson's administration) suggest that there are times when British governments are capable of persuading themselves of this. The theory that the best defence is home defence (preferably with an American guarantee) is one on which Japan, West Germany and Italy have prospered.

Disintegration of International Order

In all security calculations, the uncertainties have never been greater. It is seriously argued that there has never been a Soviet threat to Western Europe and that Russian behaviour is entirely explicable as a response to anticipated threats from the NATO powers. It is also argued that in the presence of the nuclear forces that now exist a major war of any kind is impossible. Alternatively, it is held by leading students of modern strategic problems that nuclear weapons have for all practical purposes become confined in their function to the deterrence of each other and that conventional superiority is usable and effective. While Soviet intentions are uncertain, where China is concerned both the power and the intentions are uncertain. The disintegration of an international order guaranteed by the great powers and for most purposes enforced by the USA and Britain is probably going on and there is no knowing where this will stop. The lifting of international pressure has been most evident in the conduct of the Arabs and Israelis, where local freedom of action has grown steadily. It has also shown itself in Nigeria and Rhodesia, where the views of outsiders have been shown to mean little. This could lead gradually to a pattern of conflict among the many weak countries with a possible growth through conquest of new larger national or imperial units; or conceivably a range of protectorates. This last possibility may already be coming about on the South African borders and could be one result of the military superiority of Israel over neighbours she is unwilling to absorb. In addition, the major new industrial powers will presumably at some time try to convert their economic power into military and political power. One way or another, this will have to be absorbed into the world order. Japan is the most obvious example at present. In Europe there is an obvious group of unforeseeable security implications in the efforts to create a new political unity: the effect on the Soviet Union, the effect on the USA, the problems of finding a balance between central and local power and the risk of European civil war to prevent the discontented from reasserting sovereignty. As these developments take place nuclear explosives and other forms of mass destruction weapon will probably become available to a considerable number of countries should they choose to adopt them.

Such uncertainties make it dangerous to produce simple solutions. What is needed is a structure which can act, if necessary, to meet a direct challenge and which can also work steadily to handle the worst dangers before they emerge. Since 1940 the first premise of British policy has been to secure and maintain the American alliance. The strength, the like-mindedness and the readiness to become involved in the difficulties of others which the Americans have shown in the last quarter century leave little doubt that this premise is sound. The European security order has been built on an American commitment of both nuclear and conventional forces: it is difficult to conceive of any other reliable solution.

Dangers of Isolationism

An effective order over a wider area will also depend on the readiness of powers able to act to become involved in the security problems of others. There is a strong resistance to this by everyone concerned. The weak find it an insult to their sovereign independence and the strong fear the unknown consequences of involvement. The experiences of the Americans in Vietnam and the contemplation of what might have happened to the British in Borneo if there had been a major war with Indonesia have led these two powers to hesitate before making any new commitments. In Britain's case, at least, old commitments are being cast away and the Americans may not be far behind.

Britain's withdrawal into Europe is based on an implied premise that where a British vacuum is created the Americans will be required to fill it. This could be a serious error. At a time when bitterness with the Vietnam experience dominates American policy there is no disposition to become involved in new parts of the world. The sense that none of her allies, and particularly her European allies, is taking any significant part in maintaining the world order could help to extend the new isolationist mood in the USA. That American instinct of withdrawal could ultimately extend itself to Europe as well as to Asia. Europe's importance and the striking success of the NATO system naturally discourage such a tendency. But it has long been an American doctrine that more of European security should be in the hands of Europeans and a British withdrawal into Europe will exacerbate this tendency. The difficulty of the doctrine is that the security of Western Europe almost certainly depends on the overwhelming strength of the USA, a strength which is mainly represented by its nuclear armoury but which also includes its depth and inaccessibility to conquering Soviet armies. Europe cannot replace the nuclear weapons in the foreseeable future and it can never achieve the depth.

Vietnam teaches another lesson. Where the security problem is tied up with the survival and health of the state itself, an outside power which is to be effective must have political as well as military strength to offer. It may be doubted whether this is possible except where there is much in common in the political traditions of the two countries. In Vietnam, France might have been able to inject the needed political strength if she had had the will and the power. The USA could not. Her vast military efforts were lost in the quagmire of a weak and disintegrating state apparatus. Britain was able to achieve what she did in the Malaysian Emergency because she was operating at the political-military level.

A further point must be made. The danger of nuclear proliferation (and possibly other weapons of mass destruction) will only be contained if the countries concerned have a real sense of security. They will judge this in many cases from what others appear to be ready to do for them and also by what happens elsewhere when threats arise. The strength and character of the international order will be judged by how it responds to challenges. Its growing impotence has been amply demonstrated in the successful Rhodesian rebellion and the vain effort of the great powers and the UN to prevent and then to deal with the results of the recent Arab-Israeli war.

British Security and World Order

These considerations, taken together, suggest that it is in the interest of European security (through the American alliance), the world order, and the construction of a reasonable barrier against the spread of means of mass destruction that Britain should remain able and willing to act in the defence of those with whom she has a close political understanding. These are overwhelmingly Commonwealth countries. She cannot, of course, give unqualified security undertakings except in the most unusual circumstances. But she should be ready to act over a wide range of challenges in many parts of the world. British security depends on the general character of the world order: and the Western powers, led by the Americans, are in a position to secure reasonable standards of international conduct. Britain's part is where she is specially trusted and able to apply her political-military skills with discretion. The Americans alone cannot do it; nor can the Americans and British alone. Others must be brought in where they can be effective, as the Australians have proved effective in South-East Asia and the Canadians (increasingly) in the West Indies. It is no accident that these relationships have been mainly Commonwealth relationships.

The notion that British security is European security and that Britain's overseas efforts have been a kind of extended aid programme is a simple but dangerous error. British security will be found in a healthy international order, as will American security. In neither case is there an obvious threat to the national homeland (apart from thermo-nuclear weapons, now in the hands of five countries). Both could survive, as the Russians have survived, sealed up behind powerful forces in a fortress home. But they would look out, as the Russians look out, on a bleak and hostile world in which the methods and ideologies of others would predominate. It might not be as amiable an environment as the world outside the Soviet Union has been since the fall of Hitler.

B. PROSPERITY

All Commonwealth countries are committed to large and growing levels of world trade. The British Empire was intensely trade conscious and was proud of the high levels of trade which developed within it. Britain became dependent on the markets which colonies and Commonwealth countries provided for her manufactures; and most of the other Commonwealth countries came to rely on the British market for their exports.

The search for markets goes on now as before. This is a political as well as a commercial enterprise and the Commonwealth has been actively concerned about its own trade and that of the wider world. It naturally welcomed the prospect of liberalised world trade through the formation of the GATT: and thoughout its life there has been general support from Commonwealth countries for successive rounds of tariff reductions.

Objectives of British Trade Policy

The Commonwealth itself has sustained a liberal trading system among countries of very different wealth and development for many years.[8] It provides an example of what can be done through enlightened co-operation. Not only have trade levels been high and sustained, but the sterling area group has maintained an efficient system of reserves and payments, combining this with the world's most advanced banking, insurance and shipping facilities. The result is that levels of trade within the group are at unusually high levels; and as a result the best growth prospects for many Commonwealth members, as world trade liberalisation progresses, probably lie outside the Commonwealth. This predictable fact is often cited as some kind of evidence of the unimportance of Commonwealth trade. A firm which is well established in one market and opening another will naturally have higher growth rates in the second. It will also be very foolish if it allows its position in the first market to disintegrate. This is the proper attitude of Commonwealth countries to Commonwealth trade.

[8]No thorough assessment has been made of the impact of the Commonwealth preference system on member countries, but the subject is discussed in Harry G. Johnson, "The Commonwealth Preferences", *The Round Table*, October, 1966. Also see R. W. Green, "Commonwealth Preference: Tariff Duties and Preferences on United Kingdom Exports to the Preference Area", *Board of Trade Journal*, Board of Trade, London, June 11, 1965; and Green, "Commonwealth Preference: United Kingdom Customs Duties and Tariff Preferences on Imports from the Preference Area", *Board of Trade Journal*, December 31, 1965.

Two obvious objectives present themselves to Britain, in particular, in approaching the question of markets. The first is to achieve the most favourable possible access into the largest possible potential markets with, where possible, a good fall-back position in the event of a return to protection; and the second is to play a part in opening up the markets of the developed countries to poor countries so as to increase their earnings of foreign exchange.

The search for free entry into large industrial markets has been given a strong impetus by the formation of the EEC. In a period of twelve years, three substantial industrial powers and the Low Countries have dismantled virtually all barriers to trade among themselves and embarked on a customs union. Membership in such a union would certainly be attractive to a country in Britain's position; and three major political efforts have been made to open the market to British exports as well. Success in achieving membership would, however, have had certain disadvantages. It would have resulted in new barriers to trade with Commonwealth countries, with unpredictable but no doubt negative results. It would have removed future trade policy from specifically British hands and might have inhibited the search for still larger markets, particularly in the USA, had the union proved unwilling to abandon its internal preferences. The European market is a prize worthy of sacrifice: but entry into a customs union implies that it is the only or at any rate the main prize.

The important thing about British membership, however, is that it appeared and still appears to many to be an objective that can be achieved. That is no doubt the reason for the strong support for it both in industry and government in Britain.[9] While the two attempts to gain membership have been gaining the strong support of much British opinion, a wider free trade strategy has grown up *ad hoc* in British policy. A free trade area was suddenly proposed to Canada without preparation and never followed up. With more consistency one has been built with eight other European countries (EFTA) and, separately, with the Republic of Ireland. Free trade between developed Commonwealth countries, a condition which Canadian secondary industry is approaching and Australian may not be far behind, is no doubt a possibility. It is made more difficult to achieve

[9]It is also held that while its economic advantages may not be striking there are real political advantages in the unity of Europe. This is a broad and fundamental question beyond the scope of this paper.

194

however, by the one-sided fact that Britain offers virtually complete, free entry to Canadian or Australian products while Canada's and Australia's preferential tariff impose substantial charges on imported British goods. They are lower than those charged on other countries, but they are far from free trade. An advance towards bilateral free trade would only seem possible if Britain first committed the negative and illiberal act of erecting (or threatening to erect) a tariff against Canadian or Australian goods so as to give these countries some incentive to enter into free trade. Such arrangements may yet come.

It remains true that the scope for expansion of British exports in the Commonwealth is substantial, but not equal to other parts of the world. In many markets, the primary objective would seem to be to protect the existing position. Canada and Australia offer some of the finest export opportunities in the world, as the Americans, Japanese and Germans, among others, have been demonstrating. But taken as a whole the Commonwealth is not in an ideal phase for industrial exporters. Its many poor countries are having difficulty in attracting investment, suffering from the decline of aid programmes (and the high cost of tied aid), suffering from low prices for their exports and rising prices for imports, and having to make substantial repayments on aid received in past years. It is a gloomy picture and one which the Commonwealth itself can do little to improve. The rich among the 30 members are few and far between: and the situation is not helped by the conviction of Britain, the most important Commonwealth power, that she has been going through an economic crisis of historic proportions.

In economic terms, therefore, the Commonwealth must look to a holding operation. The free entry which Commonwealth countries have enjoyed into the British market is a model for all the developed countries. Its benefits are very great. The currency they earn has no ties and carries no debts. Britain gets goods more cheaply than her population could get them in any other way. Industries are developed which can go on to conquer markets in other industrial countries because they are by definition efficient. There are few better and more simple applications of the self-evident truths of liberal economic theory.

The trouble is that there is no significant and obvious element of reciprocity. It survives, as so much in Commonwealth life survives, on reason and goodwill and on the remarkable instincts which dictated Britain's attitudes to Commonwealth affairs until recently.

In trade, then, the Commonwealth does not in itself constitute a policy: it must be regarded as an exceptionally enlightened sector of British policy which may in certain respects be costly, but which corresponds to the realities of international life. A continental trade strategy will naturally cut across this, although (as argued above) the particular arrangements for Britain's Commonwealth trade negotiated in the 1961-63 British application to join the EEC were dictated by special bargaining conditions. Since these have not yet been put into effect, Britain's relations with the Commonwealth remain open and directed towards the objective of free trade. They form part of a broad free trade strategy and make most sense in a liberal world economy. Commonwealth trading arrangements are a partial sector of the free-trading world economy which all secular forces say should come but which the folly of the continentalists, —American, European, African and other—may yet block.

C. CHARACTER OF THE WORLD

Of 126 members of the UN, 28 are in the Commonwealth (Tonga and Fiji not being members of the UN). Many, of course, are small, but so are many other members of the UN. And some members of the Commonwealth are large: India, Pakistan, Nigeria, Britain in population; Canada, Australia and India in area. What happens in these countries will be important to the balance and shape of the world as a whole. It will not determine them; but no particular group or area can do that.

All members of the Commonwealth—and others, not in the Commonwealth, like the USA, Burma, Ireland, South Africa, Israel, Jordan, the Maldives—are to a greater or lesser extent heirs of the British political tradition. In some cases, as, for example, Trinidad and Tobago or Jamaica, this is very strong and conscious. In others, as for example Cyprus, it is not. The situation varies with the length of British rule, the predominance of the English language, the existence of other and stronger political and cultural traditions and many other factors. For most members of the Commonwealth, however, the British political and legal tradition is in most respects the national tradition. The law, the armed forces, the press, radio and television are conducted according to the general methods which have been evolved in Britain. This is partly because British rule brought them inevitably in its train. But it is also to an important extent because of the assent which Britain's institutions commanded in the hearts and minds of many people. This certainly explains the decision of the great majority of modern colonies to join the Commonwealth on reaching independence. In a considerable number of cases, eight of the 26 countries of the new Commonwealth,[10] there has even been a break with the republican tradition begun by the Indians and a decision to retain the monarchy, at least temporarily.

No Society of Angels

It was hoped, in vain, that respect for the British tradition would ensure the survival of parliamentary democracy and the rule of law throughout the Commonwealth. Liberal democrats established what they conceived to be the principles on which the organisation was founded: and they were deeply depressed when in one country after another these were abandoned. There was then a tendency for advocates of the Commonwealth to argue that multi-racialism was the principle to which it all owed its existence: and for her defiance of this South Africa was put in a position where she chose to fall out. This approach to a political entity—the notion of principles—is a curious one. A political society normally exists simply because it exists or because of some community of sentiment, geography or experience. If this includes certain principles, it is usually the business of those in the society to do their best to see that the principles are given proper respect and effective life. In the case of South Africa, however, the idealists of the Commonwealth were not content to accept its existence and to work for the ultimate success of its best principles. A kind of unspoken bill of rights was applied and South Africa was found wanting. Unfortunately, South Africa soon showed her importance by salvaging the white minority regime in Rhodesia which the Commonwealth collectively had tried to bring back under British rule.

The important point is not that this is a society of angels conducting themselves according to righteous principles. It is that in this society the best of the common tradition is generally respected as an ideal. Over the next half century many men are going to influence the development of these diverse countries according to what they conceive to be the best lines. These men are seeking and will be

[10]Barbados, Ceylon, Jamaica, Malta, Mauritius, Sierra Leone, Trinidad and Tobago and Fiji.

seeking the best examples so that they may observe what others have achieved and see how much is relevant to their own experience. Britain's political development was influenced profoundly by the fact that the men who were responsible for it in its great periods were steeped in the experience of Greece and Rome. Her cultural development was owed to the tradition of the grand tour and the close links with France and Italy. Little or nothing was copied precisely. But the best models were observed and, where relevant, adapted to the British tradition.

This is an endless and imperfect process. To be the object of such activity is attractive to those who believe that their own way of doing things is valuable and important for the world. One evident reason for the decline of British interest in the Commonwealth is the mood of depression about the national inheritance and the feeling that someone else—the model is seldom identified—does things better. This feeling is not so evident in other Commonwealth countries where students going abroad, for example, overwhelmingly prefer to go to Britain.

The case for the Commonwealth as a central concern of British policy is that this process will itself make for a better and more agreeable world, and that such influence (which does not imply domination) is good for the countries concerned. If Britain has anything to offer, she will be listened to with greatest attention in the countries of the Commonwealth. That the same is not true of Western Europe can be seen already from the disappointment of British hopes of persuading the EEC countries that in trade with less developed countries or in farm policy they could look with advantage to the British system.

The kind of world in which Commonwealth and other new countries find themselves will of course have a profound effect on their character. If the Western group of powers provides them with markets, and also with capital and aid, the West will be a powerful magnet. If, on the other hand, the international economic order proves inaccessible to those without strong bargaining weapons, they will inevitably look elsewhere. Unless the trading pattern which the Commonwealth has begun can be protected and expanded, the less developed countries will have to seek their salvation with others. There may be no alternative: the Russians and Chinese may have nothing more to offer. In that case, great areas of the world are likely to remain backward and chaotic. This is in itself an undesirable prospect without raising the threats—which may or may not exist—of Communist menace or nuclear proliferation into angry hands.

Domination by the Military

The kind of security order will also have important results, with implications for economic development. Most Commonwealth countries have spent their conscious history in the safety, or apparent safety, of the British Empire. They share with the British themselves the insular belief that heavy military expenditure is not part of the natural order of things. There can be little doubt that the modest standing armies of Britain herself and also of the USA have had a great deal to do with the success of civilian institutions and the spectacular growth of commerce and industry. Permanent and heavy military commitments change the character of states. They bring a high proportion of the ablest men into the armed forces; and in a relatively undeveloped country the army more or less inevitably becomes the predominant force in the state. Armies are not the ideal vehicles for the evolution of modern, enlightened and prosperous societies.

This problem will depend to an important extent on the kind of protection small and weak states can expect from the world order as a whole. It is one of the weaknesses in the American approach to small states that they have consistently seen local armies as bulwarks against Communism. They have also displayed a misplaced puritanism with the notion that people should defend themselves and that it is weak and unsatisfactory to rely on others. They have conveniently forgotten their own reliance on the Royal Navy, before independence and long after. Their great economic development was made possible by their position in a security system, however unrecognised, which made very modest demands on their economy and manpower. This should be an ideal in relation to the many small and weak nations in the world today. If these nations, observing the fate of others, decide one by one to divert their resources to security, their prosperity will be damaged and their political development distorted.

Of the traditional three circles of British foreign policy—America, Europe and the Commonwealth—the USA is undoubtedly the most important. Indeed, neither of the other circles is easy to sustain in the absence of a close relationship with the Americans. Alone with Western Europe, Britain will be too particular and too weak to protect her interests effectively: and Western Europe itself would enter into an entirely different relationship with the massive unified power of the Soviet Union if the power of the USA was withdrawn. Similarly, the great developments of Commonwealth security and prosperity depend on steadily increasing American commitment, carrying with it more enlightened policies in West Germany, Japan, Canada, Australia and elsewhere. The disproportion of poor to rich and weak to strong (especially if Britain's overseas military strength is dismantled) will be too great. The Commonwealth never was and never will be a closed system operating as a bloc. But it can still attack a great many problems in its own life. It can develop its links in education, science, the professions, journalism, parliaments. It can be involved. It can take the notion that there is no such thing as a far-away country from oratory into policy. Above all, it can sustain the achievement which laid the foundations of the British Empire on admiration and respect. According to "a Conservative" (widely believed to be Mr. Enoch Powell) writing in *The Times*, the Commonwealth is "the ghost of the British Empire sitting crowned upon the grave thereof". The metaphor is that of Thomas Hobbes, writing in 1651 of the Papacy and the Church of Rome:

"And if a man consider the original of this great ecclesiastical dominion, he will easily perceive that the Papacy is no other than the ghost of the deceased Roman empire, sitting crowned upon the grave thereof."[11]

It is an impressive metaphor which has enjoyed the fame of repeated quotation. Three centuries have passed since it was written. The Roman Empire is an even more distant memory. Yet its so-called ghost continues to impress the minds of men and to play a great part in shaping the world around it: and especially the people whose civilisation and ways were shaped by Rome. The comparison is a profound, if unintended, comment on the surviving ghost of the British Empire.

Commonwealth and an Open World Economy

A Commonwealth with the character of the present association can, of course, be adapted to any development. In the 1950s, British and Canadian commitment to NATO as the central element in their policy and the decision by others—Pakistan, Australia, New

[11]*Leviathan*, Part 4, Ch. 47.

Zealand—to align themselves with the USA in formal security treaties created strong differences between the Western and the non-aligned in the Commonwealth: but it did not particularly affect the Commonwealth itself. Indeed, the association was quickly seen as an appropriate vehicle for achieving understanding between the aligned and the non-aligned. Where British trade policy is concerned, the Commonwealth countries accepted the loss of preference implied in British accession to EFTA; and after expressing deep concern in 1962 over the consequences of facing the EEC tariff at British ports Commonwealth governments adapted to what they regarded as a British decision which ought to be respected.

This said, it is obvious that British entry into a European customs union would end the special tariff relationship which has been such a prominent feature of Commonwealth life in recent years. On the precedents of the Treaty of Rome (as was argued above), it would be reasonable to continue Commonwealth free entry into Britain in the same way as free entry for Moroccan or Tunisian goods was maintained into France. In the special circumstances of 1961-3, however, it was agreed that the amount and volume of such goods was so great as to exclude such an arrangement. Most discussion of British accession to the European Communities since that time has taken this as an obvious starting point. Many of the effects of this policy on Britain's relations with the Commonwealth have been felt even without British entry into the European Communities. Valuable markets have turned their eyes elsewhere: and Japan, in particular, has been quick to exploit the bargaining position which this produced.

In so far as Commonwealth trade relations are preferential, they have inevitably and properly been eroded away by all the moves towards liberalised trading relations. To maintain a preference margin it is necessary to keep up tariffs against others. The formation of the GATT and its successive rounds of tariff cuts have left the tariffs within the Commonwealth unchanged but they have reduced the preference margins. To take the GATT to its ultimate conclusion for a group of nations would clearly eliminate all preference margins for Commonwealth goods as compared to those from members of the free trade area. This is already true of the EFTA countries where, for example, Canadian preferences over Scandinavia on the British market have disappeared.

It is most unlikely that anyone in the Commonwealth will be

jealous of the loss of preferences provided they face no new tariffs. They would naturally resent what the British negotiators with the EEC used to call "reverse preferences". Most if not all Commonwealth countries would undoubtedly set out to achieve membership in the proposed multilateral free trade association over a shorter or longer period. The less developed majority would be greatly helped if the first stage of such an arrangement brought them preferential access to the markets of member countries, and especially those of the USA. Although there is no necessary link between such an arrangement and free trade among the developed countries, those who have generated the growing drive towards Atlantic free trade have generally favoured an early and substantial reduction in protection against the goods of the less developed countries. The Commonwealth would naturally welcome such a development, containing as it does an overwhelming proportion of developing countries and a Britain which is already the leader among the developed countries in welcoming the goods of the poor.

It is therefore reasonable to argue that a move toward broader free trade would serve the fundamental objectives of Britain's Commonwealth policies and would serve the association itself. In constructing an open world economy it would clearly make the open Commonwealth economy, to the extent that it exists, less unique and in itself less important. But this would be proof of success and not of failure.

The future and achievements of the Commonwealth would not themselves be affected fundamentally by Atlantic or worldwide free trade. But the two together form part of a similar pattern of an open world society for those who choose to participate, stimulating the flow of goods, ideas, methods and people. It is not surprising that both have attracted hostility among nationalists, continentalists, racists and those who consciously or unconsciously depend on the closed society.

BIBLIOGRAPHY

BIBLIOGRAPHY

This volume deals with politico-strategic factors in the Asian-Pacific region which will have to be taken into account in the formulation of any new trade strategy for the 1970s that might be designed to promote the further liberalisation of international trade and investment. The particular trade strategy which appeals to the authors is the free trade treaty option. Since it was first mooted in its contemporary form in May, 1966, a considerable literature on the subject has developed. The bibliography below compiles for the benefit of the general reader as well as the specialist the main contributions to the discussion of the proposal for a multilateral free trade association among developed countries. It also covers associated policy issues and includes a selected list on related subjects.

SYSTEM AND CONDITIONS OF WORLD TRADE

GERARD CURZON, *Multilateral Commercial Diplomacy* (London: Michael Joseph, 1965).

RICHARD N. GARDNER, *Sterling-Dollar Diplomacy*, revised (New York: McGraw-Hill, 1969).

KARIN KOCK, *International Trade Policy and the GATT: 1947–1967* (Stockholm: Almqvist and Wiksell, 1969).

GARDNER PATTERSON, *Discrimination in International Trade: Policy Issues 1945-65* (Princeton: Princeton University Press, 1966).

ERNEST H. PREEG, *Traders and Diplomats* (Washington D.C.: Brookings Institution, 1970).

ALFRED MAIZELS, *Industrial Growth and World Trade* (Cambridge: Cambridge University Press, 1963).

DAVID W. SLATER, *World Trade and Economic Growth* (Toronto: University of Toronto Press, for the Private Planning Association of Canada, 1968).

CURRENT ISSUES IN WORLD TRADE POLICY

A Foreign Economic Policy for the 1970s, Vols. I–IV (Washington D.C.: US Government Printing Office, for the Joint Economic Committee, Congress of the United States, 1970).

BELA BALASSA, *Trade Liberalisation among Industrial Countries: Objectives and Alternatives* (New York: McGraw-Hill, for the Council on Foreign Relations, 1967).

BELA BALASSA et al., *Studies in Trade Liberalisation: Problems and Prospects for the Industrial Countries* (Baltimore: Johns Hopkins Press, 1967).

BELA BALASSA and MORDECHAI KREININ, "Trade Liberalisation under the Kennedy Round: the Statistical Effects", *Review of Economics and Statistics*, Department of Economics, Harvard University, Cambridge, Mass., May, 1967.

BYRON BERNSTON, O. H. GOOLSBY and C. O. NOHRE, *The European Community's Common Agricultural Policy: Implications for US Trade* (Washington D.C.: US Department of Agriculture, 1969).

RICHARD N. COOPER, *Economics of Interdependence: Economic Policy in the Atlantic Community* (New York: McGraw-Hill, for the Council on Foreign Relations, 1968).

JOHN O. COPPOCK, *Atlantic Agricultural Unity: Is it Possible?* (New York: McGraw-Hill, for the Council on Foreign Relations, 1966).

GÉRARD and VICTORIA CURZON, *After the Kennedy Round* (London: The Atlantic Trade Study, Trade Policy Research Centre, 1968).

WILLIAM DIEBOLD Jnr., "New Horizons in Foreign Trade", *Foreign Affairs*, Council on Foreign Relations, New York, January, 1967.

H. EDWARD ENGLISH, "Nixon's Economic Opportunities", *International Journal*, Canadian Institute of International Affairs, Toronto, Spring, 1969.

JOHN W. EVANS, *US Trade Policy: New Legislation for the Next Round* (New York: Harper and Row, for the Council on Foreign Relations, 1967).

BRIAN FERNON, *Issues in World Farm Trade* (London: The Atlantic Trade Study, Trade Policy Research Centre, 1970).

Future of US Foreign Trade Policy, Vols. I and II (Washington D.C.: US Government Printing Office, for the Joint Economic Committee, Congress of the United States, 1967).

J. PRICE GITTINGER, *North American Agriculture in a New World* (Washington D.C. and Montreal: Canadian-American Committee, 1970).

Issues and Objectives of US Foreign Trade Policy (Washington D.C.: US Government Printing Office, for the Joint Economic Committee, Congress of the United States, 1967).

HARRY G. JOHNSON, *World Economy at the Crossroads* (Oxford: Clarendon Press, 1965).

206

HARRY G. JOHNSON, "Trade Preferences in Developing Countries", *Lloyds Bank Review*, London, April, 1966.

HARRY G. JOHNSON, *Economic Policies Towards Less Developed Countries* (Washington D.C.: Brookings Institution, 1967).

HARRY G. JOHNSON, "The Kennedy Round", *The World Today*, Royal Institute of International Affairs, London, August, 1967.

HARRY G. JOHNSON, "World Trade Policy in the Post-Kennedy Round Era", *The Economic Record*, Economic Society of Australia and New Zealand, Melbourne, June, 1968.

HARRY G. JOHNSON, "Trade Challenges Confronting Commonwealth Countries", *International Journal*, Canadian Institute of International Affairs, Toronto, Winter, 1969–70.

CHARLES P. KINDLEBERGER, *American Business Abroad* (New Haven: Yale University Press, 1969).

MORDECHAI KREININ, *Alternative Commercial Policies: Their Effect on the American Economy* (Ann Arbor: Institute for International Business and Economic Development Studies, Michigan State University, 1967).

MORDECHAI KREININ, *Trade Arrangements among Industrial Countries: Effects on the United States* (Baltimore: Johns Hopkins Press, 1967).

THORKIL KRISTENSEN, "The Economist and Farm People in a Rapidly Changing World", *International Journal of Agrarian Affairs*, Institute of Agrarian Affairs, Oxford, May, 1967.

CHRISTOPHER LAYTON, *Trans-Atlantic Investments* (Paris: Atlantic Institute, 1966).

HARALD B. MALMGREN and DAVID L. SCHLECHTY, "Technology and Neo-Mercantilism in International Agricultural Trade", *American Journal of Agricultural Economics*, American Agricultural Economics Association, New York, December, 1969.

HARALD B. MALMGREN, "Trade Policy and Negotiations in the 1970s", in *A Foreign Economic Policy for the 1970s*, Vol. II (Washington D.C.: US Government Printing Office, for the Joint Economic Committee, Congress of the United States, 1970).

RAYMOND F. MIKESELL, "Changing World Trade Patterns and America's Leading Role", *The Annals*, American Academy of Political and Social Science, Philadelphia, July, 1969.

JOHN M. MUNRO, *Trade Liberalisation and Transportation in International Trade* (Toronto: University of Toronto Press, for the Private Planning Association of Canada, 1969).

ALFRED C. NEAL, "Economic Necessities for the Atlantic Communities", *Foreign Affairs*, Council on Foreign Relations, New York, July, 1967.

Non-Tariff Distortions of Trade (New York: Committee for Economic Development, 1969).

BERTIL OHLIN, "Aspects of Policies for Freer Trade", in RICHARD CAVES, HARRY G. JOHNSON and PETER B. KENEN (eds.), *Trade, Growth and the Balance of Payments*, Essays in Honour of Gottfried Haberler (Amsterdam: North-Holland, 1965).

BERTIL OHLIN, *Interregional and International Trade*, revised (Cambridge, Mass.: Harvard University Press, 1967).

JOHN PINCUS, *Trade, Aid and Development* (New York: McGraw-Hill, for the Council on Foreign Relations, 1967).

HENRY S. REUSS and ROBERT ELLSWORTH, *Off Dead Centre: Some Proposals to Strengthen Free World Economic Co-operation* (Washington D.C.: US Government Printing Office, for the Joint Economic Committee, Congress of the United States, 1965).

SIDNEY E. ROLFE and WALTER DAMM (eds.), *The Multinational Corporation in the World Economy* (New York: Praeger, 1970).

WILLIAM ROTH, "The President's Trade Policy Study", *The Atlantic Community Quarterly*, Atlantic Council of the United States, Washington D.C., 1968).

JEAN ROYER, *The Liberalisation of International Trade during the Next Decade* (Paris: International Chamber of Commerce, 1969).

JEAN-JACQUES SERVAN-SCHREIBER, *The American Challenge*, English edition (London: Hamish Hamilton, 1968).

SPECIAL REPRESENTATIVE FOR TRADE NEGOTIATIONS, *Future United States Foreign Trade Policy*, Roth Report (Washington D.C.: US Government Printing Office, 1969).

Towards a New Trade Policy for Development (New York: United Nations, 1964).

GERALD TRANT, DAVID L. MACFARLANE and LEWIS W. FISCHER, *Trade Liberalisation and Canadian Agriculture* (Toronto: University of Toronto Press, for the Private Planning Association of Canada, 1968).

SIDNEY WELLS, *Trade Policies for Britain* (London: Oxford University Press, for the Royal Institute of International Affairs, 1966).

P. A. WESTERMAN, "Changes in the World Wheat Situation and the 1967 International Grains Arrangement", *Quarterly Review of Agricultural Economics*, Bureau of Agricultural Economics, Canberra, January, 1969.

THE FREE TRADE TREATY
OPTION

A New Trade Strategy for Canada and the United States (Washington D.C. and Montreal: Canadian-American Committee, 1966).

"A Report on NAFTA", *Columbia Journal of World Business*, Graduate School of Business, Columbia University, New York, September-October, 1968.

FRED BERGSTEN, "Towards a Dollar Zone", *Interplay*, New York, March, 1969.

HUGH CORBET, "The Multilateral Free Trade Area Proposal", *The Bankers Magazine*, London, August, 1968.

HUGH CORBET, "Une nouvelle stratégie des échanges commerciaux", *Le Monde Diplomatique*, Paris, June, 1969.

HUGH CORBET, "Strategy for an Open World Economy", *Intereconomics*, Hamburg Institute for International Economics, Hamburg, March, 1970.

WILLIAM DIEBOLD Jnr., "Doubts About Atlantic Free Trade", *The Round Table*, London, October, 1967.

H. EDWARD ENGLISH, "Atlantic Trade Policy: The Need for a New Initiative", *Moorgate and Wall Street*, London, Autumn, 1965.

H. EDWARD ENGLISH, *Transatlantic Economic Community* (Toronto: University of Toronto Press, for the Private Planning Association of Canada, 1968).

THOMAS M. FRANCK and EDWARD WEISBAND (eds.), *A Free Trade Association* (New York: New York University Press, 1968).

THEODORE GEIGER and SPERRY LEA, "The Free Trade Area Concept as Applied to the United States", in *Issues and Objectives of US Foreign Trade Policy* (Washington D.C.: US Government Printing Office, for the Joint Economic Committee, Congress of the United States, 1967).

Sir ROY HARROD, *Dollar-Sterling Collaboration* (London: The Atlantic Trade Study, Trade Policy Research Centre, March, 1968).

Sir ROY HARROD, "Atlantic Free Trade Area", *The Three Banks Review*, Manchester, December, 1968.

HARRY G. JOHNSON (ed.), *New Trade Strategy for the World Economy* (London: George Allen and Unwin, 1969; and Toronto: University of Toronto Press, 1969).

HARRY G. JOHNSON, "Some Aspects of the Multilateral Free Trade Association Proposal", *Manchester School*, Manchester Statistical Society, Manchester, September, 1969.

HARRY G. JOHNSON, "The Case for a Multilateral Free Trade Association: the Asian Interest", *The Philippine Economic Journal*, Manila, Vol. IX, No. 1, 1970.

HARRY G. JOHNSON, PAUL WONNACOTT and HIROFUMI SHIBATA, *Harmonisation of National Economic Policies Under Free Trade* (Toronto: University of Toronto Press, for the Private Planning Association of Canada, 1968).

HARRY G. JOHNSON and HUGH CORBET, "Pacific Trade and an Open World", *The Pacific Community*, Tokyo, April, 1970.

MORDECHAI KREININ, "Effects of an Atlantic Free Trade Area on the American Economy", *Southern Economic Journal*, University of North Carolina and the Southern Economic Association, Athens, Georgia, July, 1966.

SPERRY LEA, "Americans for Free Trade", *The Round Table*, London, January, 1967.

SPERRY LEA, "Will Nixon Adopt Free Trade?", *The Round Table*, London, July, 1969.

HANS LIESNER, *Atlantic Harmonisation* (London: The Atlantic Trade Study, Trade Policy Research Centre, 1968).

ROY A. MATTHEWS, "Canadians for Free Trade", *The Round Table*, London, April, 1967.

JAMES MEADE, *UK, Commonwealth and Common Market: A Reappraisal* (London: Institute of Economic Affairs, 1962).

JUDD POLK, *United Kingdom, Canada, United States: a Family Affair?* (New York, United States Council, International Chamber of Commerce, 1968).

DAVID ROBERTSON, *Scope for New Trade Strategy* (London: The Atlantic Trade Study, Trade Policy Research Centre, 1968).

DAVID ROBERTSON, "EFTA and the NAFTA Proposal: An Economic Appraisal", *The World Today*, Royal Institute of International Affairs, London, April, 1969.

DAVID ROBERTSON, "Proposals for a North Atlantic Free Trade Area", *The Year Book of World Affairs*, Institute of World Affairs, University of London, 1969.

MAXWELL STAMP ASSOCIATES, *The Free Trade Area Option* (London: The Atlantic Trade Study, Trade Policy Research Centre, 1967).

M. D. STEUER, *American Capital and Free Trade* (London: The Atlantic Trade Study, Trade Policy Research Centre, 1969).

RALPH I. STRAUS, "A Proposal for New Initiatives in US Foreign Trade Policy", *Orbis*, Foreign Policy Research Institute, University of Pennsylvania, Philadelphia, Spring, 1967.

MERLYN TRUED, "Flexible Exchange Rates and a New Free Trade Initiative", *The Times*, London, October 14, 1968.

DAVID WALL, *The Third World Challenge* (London: The Atlantic Trade Study, Trade Policy Research Centre, 1968).

DAVID WALL, "How NAFTA would Benefit South Asia", *Asian Review*, London, June, 1968.

DAVID WALL, "Markets for the Under-Developed", *The Round Table*, London, October, 1968.

INGO WALTER, "Non-Tariff Barriers and the Free Trade Area Option", *Banca Nazionale del Laboro Quarterly Review*, Rome, March, 1969.

WORLD POLITICS AND THE FREE
TRADE TREATY PROPOSAL

LIONEL GELBER, *World Politics and Free Trade* (London: The Atlantic Trade Study, Trade Policy Research Centre, 1968).

ROY A. MATTHEWS, "Canada Between Europe and the United States", *Agenor*, Bruges, No. 3, 1967.

Sir ROBERT MENZIES, *The English-Speaking Peoples in a Changing World* (Oxford: Ditchley Foundation, 1967).

NILS ORBIK, "NATO, NAFTA and the Smaller Allies", *Orbis*, Foreign Policy Research Institute, University of Pennsylvania, Philadelphia, Summer, 1968.

ARTHUR SCHLESINGER Jnr., "America's Need for Allies", *The Round Table*, London, July, 1968.

ARTHUR SCHLESINGER Jnr., "Britain's Atlantic Option", *Interplay*, New York, January, 1969.

GEOFFREY WILLIAMS, *Natural Alliance for the West* (London: The Atlantic Trade Study, Trade Policy Research Centre, 1969).

ATLANTIC COMMUNITY

H. C. ALLEN, *The Anglo-American Predicament* (London: George Allen and Unwin, 1960).

HENRY G. AUBREY, *Atlantic Economic Co-operation: The Case of the OECD* (New York: Praeger, for the Council on Foreign Relations, 1967).

ALASTAIR BUCHAN, *Crisis Management: The New Diplomacy* (Paris: Atlantic Institute, 1966).

HAROLD VAN B. CLEVELAND, *The Atlantic Idea and its European Rivals* (New York: McGraw-Hill, for the Council on Foreign Relations, 1966).

W. T. R. and ANNETTE B. Fox, *NATO and the Range of American Choice* (New York: Columbia University Press, 1967).

THEODORE GEIGER, "End of an Era in Atlantic Policy", *The Atlantic Community Quarterly*, Atlantic Council of the United States, Washington D.C., Spring, 1967.

THEODORE GEIGER, *The Conflicted Relationship: The West and the Transformation of Asia, Africa and Latin America* (New York: Praeger, for the Council on Foreign Relations, 1967).

LIONEL GELBER, *America in Britain's Place* (New York: Praeger, 1961; and London: George Allen and Unwin, 1961).

LIONEL GELBER, *The Alliance of Necessity* (New York: Stein and Day, 1966; and London: Robert Hale, 1967).

LIONEL GELBER, "The American Role and World Order", *The Yale Review*, Yale University, New Haven, Summer, 1967.

JOHN HOLMES, "Dilemmas of Consultation and Co-ordination in the North Atlantic Treaty Organisation", *International Organisation*, World Peace Foundation, Boston, Winter, 1968.

HENRY A. KISSINGER, *The Troubled Partnership: A Re-Appraisal of the Atlantic Alliance* (New York: McGraw-Hill, for the Council on Foreign Relations, 1966).

RONALD STEEL, *Pax Americana* (New York: Viking Press, 1967).

EUROPEAN INTEGRATION

JAMES JAY ALLEN, *The European Common Market and the GATT* (Washington D.C.: University Press of Washington, for the Institute for International and Foreign Law, Georgetown University, 1967).

MAX BELOFF, *The United States and the Unity of Europe* (Washington D.C.: Brookings Institution, 1963).

BELA BALASSA, "Trade Creation and Trade Diversion in the European Common Market", *Economic Journal*, Royal Economic Society, Cambridge, March, 1967.

MIRIAM CAMPS, *Britain and the European Community 1955-1963* (London: Oxford University Press, for the Royal Institute of International Affairs, 1964).

MIRIAM CAMPS, *European Unification in the Sixties* (New York: McGraw-Hill, for the Council on Foreign Relations, 1966).

HAROLD VAN B. CLEVELAND, "The Common Market After de Gaulle", *Foreign Affairs*, Council on Foreign Relations, New York, July, 1969.

G. R. DENTON (ed.), *Economic Integration in Europe* (London: Weidenfeld and Nicolson, 1969).

WILLIAM DIEBOLD Jnr., *The Schuman Plan: A Study in Economic Co-operation 1950-59* (London: Oxford University Press, 1959).

LUDWIG ERHARD, "Prospects for European Integration", *Lloyds Bank Review*, London, January, 1969.

ISAIAH FRANK, *The European Common Market: An Analysis of Commercial Policy* (New York: Praeger, 1961).

RANDALL HINSHAW, *The European Community and American Trade* (New York: Praeger, for the Council on Foreign Relations, 1964).

LAWRENCE B. KRAUSE, *European Economic Integration and the United States* (Washington D.C.: Brookings Institution, 1968).

ROBERT L. PFALTZGRAFF Jnr., "Britain and the European Community 1963-1967", *Orbis*, Foreign Policy Research Institute, University of Pennsylvania, Philadelphia, Spring, 1968.

JAMES E. MEADE, HANS LIESNER and SIDNEY WELLS, *Case Studies in European Economic Union: The Mechanics of Integration* (London: Oxford University Press, 1962).

TIBOR SCITOVSKY, *Economic Theory and Western European Integration*, revised (London: George Allen and Unwin, 1962).

CARL S. SHOUP (ed.), *Fiscal Harmonisation in Common Markets* (New York and London: Columbia University Press, 1967).

EUROPEAN FREE TRADE
ASSOCIATION

Building EFTA: A Free Trade Area in Europe (Geneva: EFTA Secretariat, 1968).

HUGH CORBET and DAVID ROBERTSON (eds.), *Europe's Free Trade Area Experiment: EFTA and Economic Integration* (Oxford: Pergamon, 1970).

VICTORIA CURZON *et al.*, *The European Free Trade Association and the Crisis of European Integration* (London: Michael Joseph, 1968).

The Effects of EFTA on the Economies of Member States (Geneva: EFTA Secretariat, 1969).

S. A. GREEN and K. W. B. GABRIEL, *The Rules of Origin* (Geneva: EFTA Secretariat, 1965).

JOHN S. LAMBRINIDIS, *The Structure, Function and Law of a Free Trade Area: the European Free Trade Association* (London: Stevens, 1965).

"Legal Problems of the EEC and EFTA", *International and Comparative Law Quarterly*, British Institute of International and Comparative Law, London, Supplementary Publication No. 1, 1961.

S. J. WELLS, "EFTA: The End of Transition", *Lloyds Bank Review*, London, October, 1966.

ECONOMIC INTEGRATION ELSEWHERE

H. W. ARNDT, "PAFTA: An Australian Assessment", *Intereconomics*, Hamburg Institute for International Economics, Hamburg, January, 1968.

SIDNEY DELL, *Trade Blocs and Common Markets* (London: Constable, 1963).

H. EDWARD ENGLISH, "Japan's Developing Trade Strategy", *The Round Table*, London, April, 1968.

KIYOSHI KOJIMA, "A Pacific Economic Community and Asian Developing Countries", *Hitotsubashi Journal of Economics*, Hitotsubashi University, Tokyo, June, 1966.

KIYOSHI KOJIMA (ed.), *Pacific Trade and Development*, Vols. I and II (Tokyo: Japan Economic Research Centre, 1968 and 1969).

KIYOSHI KOJIMA, "Pacific Free Trade Area", *Intereconomics*, Hamburg Institute for International Economics, Hamburg, March, 1968.

SPERRY LEA, *A Canada-US Free Trade Arrangement: A Survey of Possible Characteristics* (Washington D.C. and Montreal: Canadian-American Committee, 1963).

ROY A. MATTHEWS, "Free Trade with the United States: a Possibility for Canada?", *Weltwirtschaftliches Archiv*, Vol. 97, No. 2, 1966.

SABURO OKITA, "Japan's New Global Outlook", *The Round Table*, London, October, 1968.

F. W. HOLMES, *Freer Trade with Australia?* (Wellington: New Zealand Institute of Economic Research, 1966).

A. D. ROBINSON, *Towards a Tasman Community?* (Wellington: New Zealand Institute of Economic Research, 1965).

PETER ROBSON, *Economic Integration in Africa* (London: George Allen and Unwin, 1968).

ARTHUR SMITH, SPERRY LEA and THEODORE GEIGER, *A Possible Plan for a Canada-US Free Trade Area* (Washington D.C. and Montreal: Canadian-American Committee, 1965).

PAUL and RONALD WONNACOTT, *Free Trade Between Canada and the United States: The Potential Economic Effects* (Cambridge, Mass.: Harvard University Press, 1967).

AUTHOR INDEX

H

GENERAL INDEX

67, 71, 78; non-tariff barriers, 4, 16, 18-19, 26, 72; import tariffs, 9, 15-18, 66-7, 151, 157, 176, 184, 195; indirect export subsidies, 18, 21, 65, 66, 68; import licences, 65; voluntary export restrictions, 68, 71-2, 78; *see also* preferential tariffs
Trinidad and Tobago, 196, 197*n*
Tunisia, 24, 201
Turkey, 24

Union of Socialist Soviet Republics (USSR), balance of power, 32, 113, 129, 143-7, 151, 158; and Europe, 32, 113, 143, 181, 188; and Middle East, 32; and Africa, 32, 143; and China, 32-3, 116, 118-22, 131, 143, 144, 145, 147-8; in Asian-Pacific region, 32; in South-East Asia, 33 144, 163; naval power, 33-4; and Japan, 50-1, 54, 141, 144; and Asia, 114, 143-4; merchant navy, 120; North Vietnam and, 121, 129-31, 144, 146; Britain and, 109, 188; Pakistan and, 133, 144, 146; and India, 144; Arab-Israeli conflict, 144; standard of living, 145, 147; and the Mediterranean, 146; in the Levant, 146; and weapon dispersal, 145-6; and Germany, 146, 147, 165; and nuclear weapons, 145-6, 151, 158; *see also* Warsaw Pact
United Nations, 76, 112, 120-1, 129, 144, 174-5, 179, 183, 192, 196
United Nations Conference on Trade and Development (UNCTAD), 23, 24, 25, 88, 155
United Nations Economic Commission for Asia and the Far East, 76
United States of America, isolationism, 8, 303; agriculture, 19-21, 22; in South-East Asia, 30, 33, 163; in Asian-Pacific theatre, 32, 39; China

and, 32, 59, 116-17, 120-2, 147-8; in European defence, 37-9, 182, 188, 191; and nuclear weapons, 38, 121, 145-6, 151, 158; and trade with Japan, 45, 47, 50-2, 54, 55*n*, 57-60, 61, 77-8, 80, 99, 100, 103-4, 156; and Japanese foreign policy, 60; in Far East, 60, 82; and Canada, 63, 154; and Pacific trade, 79, 82, 154, 157; and Australia, 90, 154, 157, 201; and New Zealand, 90, 154, 201; and the Pacific, 114; in World War II, 116, 123; and Vietnam War, 123-9, 131, 143, 146, 159, 191; and Thailand, 136; and Cambodia, 138; and Asia, 143-4; and Africa, 143; and weapon dispersal and diversification, 145-6; and Korea, 146; and policy of deterrence, 173; and Pakistan, 179, 201; *see also* Britain; EEC; multilateral free trade area; NATO; PAFTA; USSR

Viet Cong, 125, 126, 127, 131
Viet Minh, 123-4, 136
Vietnam, *see* Indo-China, North Vietnam; South Vietnam; Vietnam War
Vietnam War, and Japanese trade, 58, 61, 156; China and, 117, 121, 123-4, 128, 130; Britain and, 127, 159; Cambodia and, 137-8; and Australia, 157; *see also* Indo-China; USA; USSR

Warsaw Pact, 147
West Germany, and Britain, 160, 181, 189; economic expansion of, 183; and NATO, 182; and USA, 178, 180, 200; and EEC, 181; and USSR, 188; *see also* Germany

Yaoundé Convention, 24
Yugoslavia, 176

For Product Safety Concerns and Information please contact our EU
representative GPSR@taylorandfrancis.com Taylor & Francis Verlag GmbH,
Kaufingerstraße 24, 80331 München, Germany

Printed and bound by CPI Group (UK) Ltd, Croydon, CR0 4YY

08/05/2025
01864362-0007